THE COMPLETE
ENCYCLOPEDIA OF
HERBS

THE COMPLETE
ENCYCLOPEDIA OF
HERBS

Magnificent photographs and detailed
descriptions of hundreds of different species

NICO VERMEULEN

REBO
PUBLISHERS

© 1998 Rebo International b.v., Lisse, The Netherlands

This 2nd edition reprinted in 2004

Text and photography: Nico Vermeulen
Translation: Stephen Challacombe
Cover design: Minkowsky Graphics, Enkhuizen, The Netherlands
Editing and production: TextCase, The Netherlands
Typesetting: Hof&Land Typografie, The Netherlands

ISBN 90 366 1502 X

Contents

Introduction **7**

    Explanation of the symbols 7

    Explanation of botanical and other terms used 10

    Natural chemical and biological weapons 11

    Toxicity within herbs? 14

    Herbs and spices 15

    Picking herbs? 16

    The herb garden 17

Herbs from A–Z **19**

    A   *Acanthus hungaricus – Avena sativa* 19

    B   *Ballota nigra ssp foetida – Buxus sempervirens* 62

    C   *Calamintha nepeta – Cytisis scoparius* 70

    D   *Dactylopius coccus – Dryopteris filix-mas* 103

    E   *Ecballium elaterium – Euphrasia stricta* 114

    F   *Fagopurum esculentum – Fumaria officinalis* 124

    G   *Galega officinalis – Grindelia squarrosa* 129

    H   *Hamamelis virginiana – Hyssopous officinalis* 142

    I   *Ilex aquifolium – Isatis tinctoria* 156

    J, K   *Jasminum sambac – Knautia arvensis* 161

    L   *Lamiastrum galeobdolon – Lythrum salicaria* 163

    M   *Maclaeya cordata – Myrtus communis* 179

    N   *Narcissus 'Thalia' – Nymphaea alba* 198

    O   *Ocimum basilicum – Osmunda regalis* 205

    P, Q   *Paeonia lactiflora – Quercus robur* 217

    R   *Raphanus sativus – Ruta graveolens* 244

    S   *Salix alba – Syzygium aromaticum* 256

    T   *Tagetes patula – Tropaeolum majus* 282

    U, V, W   *Urtica dioica – Zinnia elegans* 296

Index **312**

Acknowledgements **320**

6

Introduction

All the plants in this encyclopedia have one thing in common: humans can benefit from them in some way. The useful plants that are dealt with in this book do not include those used by humans solely as vegetables. The potential uses of these herbs is very wide: colouring of food, tanning of leather, plant protection, to make poison arrows, for drugging fish for primitive means of catching them, as narcotics, aromatic substances, flavouring or seasoning, to produce gums and resins, or as a medicine.

The Latin name of yellow-flowering Inula dysenterica syn. Pulicaria dysenterica, *or common fleabane, is derived from its use to treat dysentery.*

This broad range of economic uses of plants is central to this encyclopedia, resulting in more herbs being included than in many other books about herbs which tend to restrict themselves to the medicinal and culinary benefits. Such books often only consider soft-stemmed herbaceous plants, ignoring woody trees and shrubs such as the laurel or bay tree which features in so many recipes. Some other books only deal with plants that are hardy in the northern European latitudes but this overlooks many of the spices from the tropics, such as pepper, nutmeg, and clove. All these plants can be found in The Encyclopedia of Herbs, regardless of whether they are woody plants or from tropical climes. The emphasis is of course on herbs that can be grown in our climate since this is above all a plant book with hints on cultivation.

Recipes for use of these herbs as self remedies have not been included for safety reasons. Many of the

Left: The strands of wool are dried after each soaking.

herbs have substances that used in the correct dosage can be medicinal but dangerous in excess. The correct dosage differs from one person to another. Some of these substances can also cause allergic reactions or be dangerous when combined with other substances. For this reason we urge that you seek expert advice, particularly in the use of the medicinal and potentially poisonous plants. This book is not intended as a guide to herbal remedies and the author and publisher accept no responsibility for the use of any of the herbs described in this book.

Explanation of the symbols

☤ *Medicinal herbs*

Of all the uses of herbs, the most important since time began has been their medicinal properties. Now that many medicines are chemically synthesised, the culinary uses compete with the pharmaceutical. In the past the only treatments available were based on the use of herbs. Operations were not performed until the Renaissance and before this time if herbal remedies did not cure, the result was death. Herbs were consequently vitally important. Apothecaries were highly regarded people but most herbal remedies were created and dispensed by women. With the development of medical science these women were largely replaced by doctors but some were also persecuted as witches. Yet the Renaissance doctors also developed the use of herbal medicines. Herb gardens were planted at

The Hortus Botanicus of Leiden in The Netherlands reconstructs the herb garden laid out by Clusius 400 years ago.

the major universities in the sixteenth and seventeenth centuries to research the medicinal properties of herbs. Many were indeed found to have the medicinal effects that had been attributed to them for centuries. Once the chemical constituents could be synthesised, the herbs themselves slowly receded into the background.

Today once more, many healers have turned back to herbs. This is not just because of the inherent properties of the herbs but because of unease at customary medical practice which generally fails to take a holistic view of a person. Doctors have become so specialized that, frequently they are unable to treat other than a specific part of the body. The holistic view of the body is denied by this process. In contrast, homeopaths and herbal healers do take a holistic approach. This beneficial process is overshadowed by the many "quacks" who engage in "fringe" or alternative medicine who in the most favourable cases treat their patients with inoperative remedies. Meanwhile the patient is not receiving the appropriate course of treatment. Fortunately there are signs that practitioners with the required medical knowledge are turning to herbal medicine.

Plants which contain medicinal substances are indicated in the encyclopedia with the ♃ sign.

/ Herbal dyestuffs

Colour played a role to escape the grey existence in the oldest known cultures.

The leather, wool, and cloth from which shoes and clothing were made was coloured with dyestuffs, while tribes which wore no clothes painted their skin. The colours were often of symbolic significance, denoting the tribe or clan to which they belonged as still seen today with the different tartans of Scottish clans. Non Scots also wear the tartan because the colours bring a bloom to life.

Genista tinctoria, *dyer's greenweed.*

The natural colours of vegetable dyes on wool.

Wool can be dyed many colours using vegetable dyes.

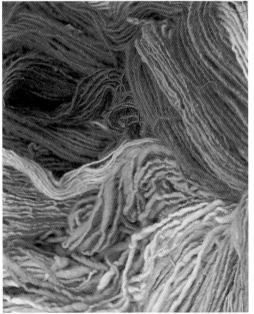

Chemical dyes and pigments were virtually unheard of before well into the nineteenth century so that natural pigments and vegetable dyes were used for colouring things. The dyeing process was refined across many centuries and produced superb results.

Hence it was not dissatisfaction with the colours produced by these natural dyes but price and colour fastness that won the day for chemical dyes. These could be produced far more cheaply on an industrial scale and they were more resistant to repeated washing. Vegetable dyes are virtually only used by enthusiasts, and with wonderful results. It is often not possible to say precisely which colour a plant will produce. This is not just dependant on the choice of plant but also on the part of the plant used, the cloth itself, and any other treatment it receives: pre-soaking, dyeing, over-dyeing, and the time allowed for dyes to be absorbed before washing. Plants which can be used to dye leather, fabrics, and wool are indicated in the A–Z listing with the ✐ sign.

⚱ *Aromatic herbs*

Many herbs give off scent, most of which we find pleasant or delightful. The aromatic properties of herbs must have been the first to be discovered by humans and they eagerly made use of them from ancient times. In the wild they mostly spread their scent when they were brushed against, encouraging those on foot to take another stride. Sprigs or leaves were picked to be taken home to spread on the floor where, when walked upon, wonderful fragrances were released in the home. This led to the practice of sprinkling herbs throughout houses.

The use of aromatic herbs became increasingly more sophisticated: they were planted in Medieval gardens along paths so that the skirts of the ladies would brush them. Dried herbs were sewn into small pillows to use as herbal cushions or mixtures

The scent of wild marjoram fills the mountains of southern Europe. Perfumes are among the things made from it.

of scented herbs were placed in an open bowl as a pot-pourri.

It was discovered that the scent could be concentrated by soaking the appropriate parts of the plants in oil. Thus arose the perfumed oil lamps which have once more come into vogue. The herbs were also distilled to concentrate their scent and to use them in perfumes and other cosmetics. Such uses are indicated in the A–Z entries with the ⚱ sign.

♨ *Culinary herbs*

When we think of herbs, our first thoughts tend to be of those used to give flavour and aroma to food. Good cooks know how to use them with great subtlety, so that their flavour does not dominate but instead enriches the flavour and aroma of the other ingredients. The quality of the herbs (above all their freshness), correct amount, stage in cooking in which they are introduced, and choice of the appropriate herb to complement a dish determine the result. Fresh herbs are generally best, followed by frozen herbs, then by recently dried ones. Pre-packed ground or chopped herbs quickly lose their aroma and cannot therefore be kept for ever. The over use of herbs is the most common fault but the moment of their introduction is also very important. Bay leaves are cooked with the dish but many other herbs lose their aroma and must be introduced at the end of cooking. The question of

Lovers of fine food grow herbs near the kitchen door.

Basil is perhaps the king of culinary herbs.

Explanation of botanical and other terms used

Decoction: A method of extracting substances from harder plant material, such as bark, roots, stalks, seeds, and berries. For best results, the plant material is broken, chopped, or ground fine and then placed in cold water which is brought to the boil. Once the water boils, the covered pan is placed on a low heat to simmer for between ten minutes and an hour. Once removed from the heat, the decoction is strained and is then ready for use.
A fairly common measure for herbs that can be used in unlimited quantities is 100 to 150 grams ($3^1/_2$ to $5^1/_4$ ounces) fresh herbs to $1^1/_2$ litres (approx. 3 pints) of water. Use about half the quantity of dried herbs. This makes about 1 litre (approx. 2 pints) of decoction which can be used in the same was as an infusion or extract (herbal tea).

which foods are enhanced by which herbs is a question of personal taste with potential surprises in store. In the A–Z listings, this book restricts itself to the most generally accepted uses. Herbs with culinary uses are indicated with a sign.

Cosmetic herbs

Pictures and names of herbs often adorn the packaging of cosmetics. These soften the skin, prevent dandruff, or have some other benefit for the skin or hair. Herbs which are used in soaps, skin lotions, shampoo, bath oils, and similar products are indicated in the A–Z listings with the sign.

✳ Other herbs

Some plants are poisonous and are used to kill insects or are smeared on the tips of arrows to kill warm-blooded creatures. Crushed herbs are also used to throw into water to drug fish so that they float to the surface where they can be caught. Others are used by people as narcotics to drug themselves, in order to forget their troubles or to cause hallucinations. Sometimes the herb is just used for its enjoyment, such as tobacco. All the uses of herbs which are not medicinal, culinary, cosmetic, or as dyestuffs are indicated by the ✳ sign.

Infusion: The herb is placed in hot water in the same way that tea is made. The term tea is sometimes used in this book where infusion would also be correct. Water that has just boiled is poured on the herbs and left to infuse for five to ten minutes. The liquid is then poured out using a tea strainer. Herbal tea can also be drunk cold.
Flowers, upper stems, and young leaves are the most suitable for making herbal tea. With herbs that may be used in unlimited quantities, taste determines the quantity of fresh or dried herbs to use. This is often 100 to 150 grams ($3^1/_2$ to $5^1/_4$ ounces) fresh herbs to 1 litre (approx. 2 pints) of water. Use half the quantity of dried herbs.
With herbs that must not exceed a set dose, the total dosage of the infused herbs must be calculated. Herbal tea is made freshly each day and one cup, three times per is often drunk.

Lavender is often incorporated in soap or added to bath water.

Ointment: An ointment is a greasy substance based on oil and water or fat and water. The addition of herbs provides either a medicinal or cosmetic ointment. Unlike salves, ointments are absorbed into the skin.

Homeopathy: A method of healing in which very minute amounts of substances are used to treat ailments that in a healthy person would produce symptoms of the disease.

Compress: A method of treatment in which herbs or their extracts are held in contact with the skin. With a wet compress, a piece of lint or gauze is placed in the decoction, infusion, or tincture, then wrung out, and placed against the skin. With a dry compress, the herbs themselves are held against the skin. The herbs are freshly crushed or briefly boiled before being held in place with a lint or gauze bandage.

Herbal vinegar: When herbs are placed in vinegar, their aroma and taste is imparted to the vinegar. When the vinegar is then used to make a dressing or is used to dress a salad, the flavour is in turn added to the food. Herbs retain their shape and sometimes their colour too when immersed in acidic vinegar so that a bottle of herbal vinegar can decorate a kitchen.

Syrup: A solution of decoction, infusion, or tincture in water with sugar or honey added is a syrup. This increases the effective life of the medicine and makes it more palatable, which can help to get children to take their medicine. Normally about 500 grams to 1 kilogram of cane sugar, brown sugar, or honey are dissolved in 1 litre of the decoction or infusion. To create a syrup for a tincture, 500 millilitres of boiling water is used with 1 kilogram of cane sugar, brown sugar, or honey. The syrup is dissolved by stirring over a gentle heat and removed from the heat once it has boiled. To use, one part of tincture is added to three parts of syrup.

Tea: See infusion.

Tincture: Liquid extract created by soaking the herbs in alcohol or ether. Normally a mixture of alcohol and water is used. Depending on the purpose for which the tincture is to be used, the herbs are steeped in 20 to 90 per cent proof alcohol. After about two weeks, during which time the mixture is shaken or spun regularly, the liquid is

Tobacco is both a pleasure-giving substance and an extremely poisonous insecticide.

poured off. The solid matter is then pressed and the liquid that is thereby derived is the tincture.

Salve: A greasy substance based on wax, fat, petroleum jelly, or vegetable oil into which herbs can be added. In contrast with an ointment, salves are barely or not absorbed into the skin, so that the salve seals the skin.

Natural chemical and biological weapons

The substances we derive from plants are almost always intended to protect the plant. The way in which this happens is sometimes clear as with damage to the bark of a spruce which causes resin to seal the wound in order to protect it from infection by viruses and fungi. Normally the protection is far more complex than this and it is not out of place to talk of chemical weapons against the organisms that menace the plant: animals, fungi, viruses, and bacteria.

Bottles of herbal vinegar with wild marjoram, lemon thyme, marigold, and nasturtium.

Elder flowers (with slices of lemon) make a delicious syrup if left to steep in sugar water for a few days.

All these organisms do their best to survive: these attackers use the plant as food but the plant has to do its best to prevent tissue being lost through infection or through being eaten. Consider insects which eat the plant: these can kill young plants and weaken older ones: this is why many plants form substances to deter them. This can be a simple substance which is poisonous for certain insects. The plant will survive for a time as a result but insects reproduce rapidly and new generations are formed. Each new generation may have slightly different characteristics to the parents and sooner or later there will be insects that are more resistant to the plant's poison. These insects sometimes direct their full attention to this type of plant because as specialists they have no competition from other insects for whom the plant is still poisonous.

The plant will also react to being eaten. The seeds from this plant will include some that differ slightly from the parent plant and it may be that they contain a further substance which is poisonous for the poison-resistant insects. The insects will therefore leave these plants alone and eat the others that have not adapted leaving the adapted plants to grow large and to set their seed. The insects have created room for the seeds to grow by eating the other plants.

Of course the insects also adapt once again and so it goes on. It has been happening for millions of years. It is therefore no wonder that plants have developed such a complex range of chemicals. They contain all manner of chemicals that were developed once upon a time as deterrents. Sometimes these are still operative but often the purpose has long passed because the insects have adapted. In other cases these individual substances are no longer harmful to animals on their own but they combine with other chemicals to create a cocktail of poisons. Plants with a broad range of deterrent chemical appear to have the advantage because they are less sought after by voracious insects and harmful fungi and bacteria. Nature is more complex than this though: plants need copious nutrients plus ample sunlight and water to grow. Plants also have to compete with other plants, making sure that they do not grow taller and take away their light. The production of chemical deterrents takes energy from the plant, which cannot be used for growth. Plants therefore have to be economical with the production of chemical deterrents. It is a question of the right strategy: some plants grow so rapidly that they quickly grow tall, even if they are nibbled at. These plants make virtually no deterrent substances. Others protect themselves slightly against initial attack, while others still place the emphasis on protective armoury but pay the price with slower growth. Finally, there are the opportunists. These leave the production of protective chemicals to circumstances. Ragwort *(Senecio jacobaea)* is a good example of this. If the plant is in the full sun, where it can grow in ideal conditions, then a great deal of protective chemical is made but if sited in a shaded spot the plant makes far less because it needs its energy for growth.

Evolution does not run smoothly. Rapid developments are followed by periods of calm. During such periods it seems as though either the plant or attacking animal has the winning hand. Consider the ragwort, which protects itself against being eaten with seven different alkaloids. Most grazing animals are deterred but not the caterpillars of the cinnabar moth *(Tyria jacobaeae)* which extensively eats ragwort without any affect to them. Indeed the caterpillar uses this to its advantage. They consume so much poison that they are inedible for birds and other enemies. The caterpillars exhibit their poisonous nature with their yellow and black striped bodies which they stretch out on the plant in the sun. Ragwort survives the caterpillars but does not flower in years when caterpillars are abundant. When they reach plague proportions, there are too few plants and most caterpillars do not get enough food to develop into moths. The following year there are therefore few moths and the ragwort is able to flower once more. In the intervening year the plant survives as a root ball.

The examples above may seem complex but are relatively simple examples of the chemical warfare plants wage against their attackers. The knives are constantly being sharpened and ingenious new plans unfolded such as the detection and alarm substances that prove that plants are far less passive (vegetative) than is often thought. If the leaves of an apple tree are infected by spider mites, the chemical composition in the leaves changes and special scent is given off. The smell attracts warrior mites that eat the spider mites. In fact the tree is crying for help from the warrior mites.

The apple tree can help itself sometimes. Certain species of apple appear to be resistant against the fungal infection that causes scab. The trees are not immune to the fungus but ensure they do not get a hold on them. Trials have shown that the leaves of these species wilt as soon as any trace of the fungus is detected. Apparently the fungus exudes a substance that is recognized by the leaf. The tree reacts by sacrificing the affected leaves, allowing

Rue (Ruta graveolens) *will cause skin irritations.*

them to wilt. This prevents the fungus having a source of nutrients and from infecting the rest of the tree.

In this power struggle between plants, fungi, viruses, bacteria, insects, and other animals, the plants make complex mixtures of substances, which we value for their aroma, refined taste, as medicine, or dyestuff, or the many other uses that man has found for the substances from plants.

Once you grasp the complexity of the chemistry within plants you will wonder at the knowledge of the herbalists of old. They did not possess any sophisticated equipment to analyse the composition of herbs yet in spite of this, they attained a phenomenal level of practical knowledge which still serves us to this day. Occasionally modern science calls the working of herbs for a particular ailment into question but far more frequently research has proven what our elders knew all along: many ancient herbal remedies are indeed effective.

Toxicity within herbs

Herbs contain substances which can heal us or make us ill. This depends on the complaint, the dose taken, and the sensitivity for the substance – which differs from person to person. Many people imagine that natural substances are less harmful than chemical ones but this is misguided. Some plants contain such powerful toxins that ingesting a small amount can be lethal. In spite of this, fatal poisoning and serious illness resulting from ingesting herbs is almost unheard of. A far greater danger is taking an overdose of medicine derived from herbs. These are preparations in which the amount of active ingredients have been artificially increased. Poisoning through the use of medicines is by far the most common form of poisoning.

Children and poisonous plants

Parents and others responsible for the care and education of children often worry about the toxicity of house and garden plants, imagining that children might be poisoned by them. Consequently children are often told frightening tales about plants. This understandable reaction ensures that the children will have a distorted view of plants when they are adults themselves. Such imprinting is not easily set aside.

The facts are that of all the cases of poisoning recorded, very few result from plants and toadstools. Most children between one and three years old will eat plants because they explore the world with their mouths but this rarely has any serious consequences because the children eat too little of the plant. Treatment is available for the small number of cases that do occur and these do not have a fatal outcome. Poisonous plants are indeed less dangerous for children than a bag of marbles.

There are certainly recorded cases of children suffocating through swallowing marbles.

Having reduced the "bogey" of poisonous plants to sensible levels, parents and others caring for children need to be aware of two potential threats from toxic plants.

1. Toddlers who put things in their mouths to investigate them. Do not leave children under four years old alone with poisonous plants.

2. Research has shown that teenagers experiment with drugs, some of which can be found in plants. Since establishing the correct dose from such sources is difficult, this can have harmful consequences.

Make children aware from the age of four of the existence of poisonous plants, especially of the most harmful ones: plants that cause skin irritations such as hogweed and rue; and those appetising-looking berries and seeds of toxic plants such as the rare herb-paris *(Paris quadrifolia)*, and more common lily-of-the-valley. Make children aware from the age of twelve that the active substances in plants can vary considerably in their potency.

Teach children about poisonous plants, such as the foxglove.

Herb-paris produces just one toxic berry.

Herbs and spices

Spices are parts of plants that are added to food in order to impart their taste or aroma but this is equally true of herbs. Spices are generally regarded as the more piquant or pungent flavourings. Nutmeg, clove, and pepper are clearly regarded as spices by everyone.

Spices almost always originate in far distant lands and from exotic and secretive plants. Cloves were extremely important in ancient China and were sought out there by Europeans. Cloves are the dried flower buds of an evergreen tree that grows wild on the Moluccas in Indonesia. These dried cloves were traded long before the birth of Christ. Their appearance in the tombs of the Egyptian pharaohs is evidence of a lively trade between the lands surrounding the Indian Ocean. Chinese writings about the clove have been found from

Finished blooms of the clove tree.

Drying of cloves.

Dried cloves.

The oldest clove tree on the island of Ternate. It was planted illicitly in the time that this was punishable by death.

this era. Noblemen were required to perfume their breath with cloves before addressing the Emperor. For a long time, the trade in cloves was in the hands of Arab sailors, who took advantage of the changeable monsoon winds to sail their vessels to and fro between Africa and South-East Asia. They were gradually repressed in the seventeenth and eighteenth centuries by European traders. The Dutch took over the trade of the East Indies archipelago and consequently had a monopoly on cloves. The clove plantations on the neighbouring island of Ternate were rigorously felled and the owner of any land on which cloves were subsequently planted faced the death penalty.

Resistance was punished by grotesque means. The population of the Banda islands were decimated by the "sea hero" Piet Hein because their ruler had refused to accept the enforcement of the Dutch.

The Dutch enforced their monopoly on cloves in order to demand astronomical prices for them. At one time, a pound of cloves was just as expensive as a pound of gold. Fortune seekers understandably attempted to break the monopoly and eventually they succeeded in smuggling a specimen from Ambon so that cloves were cultivated on Madagascar and Zanzibar. And where did most of the cloves harvested on these islands end up? They were shipped to the East Indies because the highest consumption in the world was centred there. They were not only used for spicing oriental cooking but were important for giving tobacco a distinctive taste and aroma. Today, virtually all

Weighing cloves.

Cigarettes with the aroma of cloves.

Aromatic cigarette smoker on Sulawesi, Indonesia.

Indonesians who smoke buy cigarettes perfumed with oil of cloves, which also spread the aroma of the spice.

Collecting herbs

The old herbals suggest that certain herbs should be gathered as particular "magical" moments, such as when the moon shines on St. John's night. Although this may sound absurd to our modern ears, there are good and bad times to gather herbs. The amount of the active substances vary from day to day and even from hour to hour. Research has shown that the amount of opium produced by a poppy varies widely. Although there are many plants with their own optimum moment of harvest, there are some general guiding rules. Most herbs contain the maximum active substances just before flowering. When this is not contained within the roots, the tops of the plants usually have the greatest concentration. Generally the best time to gather them is in the morning just after the dew has gone.

Drying herbs

Professional herb gatherers have ingenious drying cabinets in which the herbs can be dried rapidly so that little of their active substances is lost. Although the drying method varies for different types of herb, the general rules that follow apply to most.
Dry the herbs as quickly as possible but not in the full heat of the sun.
Herbs with volatile oils will lose these with artificial heat through evaporation. Hang herbs up in as airy a position as possible to prevent fungal growth. The herbs will be dried after about one week and are then ready for further treatment. Herbs generally remain useable for about one year. After this they lose their freshness, aroma, and efficacy.

Herbs are hung up to dry in a shaded airy place.

The herb garden

Once herbs were collected from the wild and taken home but people soon discovered they could take the entire plant home with them to grow close at hand to have a constant supply of fresh herbs. This is possibly how gardening began. It appears that the first gardens were herb gardens.

Undoubtedly those early herb gardeners also enjoyed the beauty of the herbs because most have great decorative value, as can be seen from the illustrations in this encyclopedia. It is not really surprising that the useful was combined with the delightful in decorative herb gardens. Today we make stylish use of attractive herbs, sometimes featuring their greyish foliage or highlighting the delightful flowers for others. Depending on the personal taste of the gardener, herbs such as sage can be trimmed to create a formal hedge or allowed to grow freely to form a natural-looking garden.

Sage fronds flowering in a natural-style garden.

Sage (Salvia officinalis) *trimmed to create a formal hedge.*

Herb garden.

Acanthus hungaricus

Acanthus hungaricus

Acanthus hungaricus syn. A. balcanicus, A. longifolius

The flowers of *Acanthus hungaricus* strongly resemble those of the better known *Acanthus mollis* which has its flowers distributed evenly along the flowering stem whereas *A. hungaricus* has four

Malva sylvestris *(common mallow)* between marguerites

clearly defined rows one above the other. The natural habitat in the wild is rocky highlands from the Balkans through to northern Greece, where they are mainly found in partial shade. The main flowering is in July but the flower stems which have bloomed remain attractive until the autumn. In their natural habitat they can resist severe cold winter weather but not when combined with damp soil. For this reason, plant them in a raised bed or in well drained soil. For use see *Acanthus mollis.*

℞

Acanthus mollis.

Acanthus mollis

The leaves of *Acanthus mollis* probably decorated the Corinthian columns of ancient Rome and Greece. Stylised leaves can be seen carved in stone, on the capitals at the top of the columns, which bear a close resemblance to the plant and are therefore referred to as "Acanthus motifs."
For cultivation, see *A. hungaricus.* Specimens from the 'Latifolius' group are mainly planted in gardens because the broader leaves are better able to stand cold wet conditions.
The various species of the *Acanthus* genus are difficult to differentiate because of the many varieties and hybrids. For this reason it is not possible to suggest with any certainty which species is intended in old herbals. The medicinal properties are

generally related to *A. mollis* but that is not to say that other species do not share them. Modern research into *Acanthus mollis* has shown that in particular it contains a great deal of tannin, with the greatest proportions being found in *A. mollis* 'Latifolius'.

The leaf is used in compresses to bring down swellings. The roots readily ooze a slime and can be used in a compress for burns, dislocation, and gout. *Acanthus* is also prescribed for internal use as a remedy for diarrhoea.

℞

Acanthus spinosus.

Acanthus spinosus

The flowers of *Acanthus spinosus* closely resemble those of *A. mollis*. The difference can be seen with the foliage. The narrow pointed leaves are often cut to the midribs, with spiny margins. This species originates from the countries to the east of the Mediterranean.

℞

Achillea millefolium, *yarrow.*

Achillea millefolium

YARROW, MILFOIL, SOLDIER'S WOUNDWORT

The Trojan hero Achilles of Greek mythology is supposed to have tended the wounds of his fellow combatants with the plant bearing his name. Nowadays *Achillea* is used for more innocent cuts. Held against a cut, it stems the bleeding and disinfects the wound.

The leaves of wild yarrow are finely branched to form many leaflets. The flower bears flowerheads in high summer that are flat corymbs of white to pale pink. They are mainly found on verges and poor grassland. These plants do best on well-drained soil where they spread their roots and can be invasive.

Yarrow contains many different active constituents. The bitterness can be used as a replacement for hops in beer brewing. According to the botanist Linnaeus you would get drunk more quickly with beer brewed this way.

The volatile oils which give yarrow its distinctive aroma, even when growing, are used as scent such as herbal bath products.

Yarrow is picked at the full flush of flowering for its dyestuff which can be used to dye wool yellow, orange, and brown.

Achillea millefolium, *yarrow.*

Achillea ptarmica, *sneezewort.*

Prolonged used of yarrow can make the skin more sensitive to sunlight and contact with the sap can make the skin photo sensitive, causing inflammation through exposure to ultra-violet rays.

Yarrow has a wide range of medicinal uses: infusion of the flowers and leaves with other herbs makes a bitter herb tea that purifies the blood, guards against colds, fever, stomach, and intestinal ailments. The tea heightens the appetite for food. Once people used to chew yarrow leaves for toothache. Mainstream medical science recognizes the efficacy of yarrow for menstrual spasms in women but the treatment should only be prescribed by a doctor and not at all by pregnant women.

Allergic reactions can occur to treatment with yarrow administered both internally and externally. Some people are so sensitive that they suffer rashes if they lay in a field with yarrow.

The tender young leaves can provide a fresh but bitter accent to both salads and soups. Yarrow aids the digestion and breaks down fat.

Achillea ptarmica

SNEEZEWORT

Sneezewort grows as a wild plant in abundance alongside rivers and damp places, especially on clay soils, fenland, or heavier loams. The plant flowers in July with white flowerheads, which are larger than those of yarrow but with fewer blooms to each corymb. Depending on the nutrient and moisture, the plant can grow 100–150cm (39–5ft)

Achillea ptarmica, *sneezewort.*

high. The roots used to be ground and chewed, with the bitter sap driving away toothache. Its name comes from the use of the powdered plant being used as snuff.

Achillea ptarmica 'Perry's White'.

Aconitum napellus, *monkshood.*

Aconitum napellus, *monkshood.*

Achillea ptarmica 'Perry's White'

This is one of the double flowerhead cultivated forms of *A. ptarmica.* grown in flower gardens. It is not known if they contain the same active constituents as the wild sneezewort. Other double flowerhead forms of *A. ptarmica* include 'Boule de Neige' (syn. with *A. ptarmica* 'Schneeball') and 'The Pearl'.

Aconitum napellus

MONKSHOOD, ACONITE, WOLF'S BANE

This aconite is regarded as one of the most toxic plants in Europe. The sap was probably used long ago as arrow poison, similar to the more recent use of other aconites for this purpose in India and Japan. The plant contains a cocktail of toxic constituents including the alkaloid aconitine which appears to be very effective in helping the plant to survive on mountain pasture where, especially in damp places, it is one of the few tall plants. If the plant was not poisonous, it would certainly be grazed by the cattle. The plant grows to about 100cm (39in) high and flowers from May to August. The lethal dose of aconitine for an adult is 3–6mg. Paralysis is followed by death through heart failure or suffocation. Fortunately the plant tastes extremely bitter. Cultivated garden varieties are said by some to be less poisonous but take great care, even with touching the plant, because the poison can penetrate the skin. The skin initially looses its sense of feel and then swells up.

Aconitine is used medically as a pain killer and is also used in a skin salve to deaden rheumatic pain. Other uses include treatment of the pain of gout, sciatica, and for coughs pr pains following colds. In homeopathy, aconitine is used for shock, colds, fever, influenza, hyperventilation, anxiety attacks, flushes, and pain. Its use in regulated in some countries. When flowering is finished, the plant can be used to dye clothing and wool green.

⚕ /

widely in central Europe but is also found more rarely in north-west Europe.

The plant flowers between June and August and grows between 50–100cm (20in–39in) high with many side shoots so that it is more unkempt in appearance than the erect monkshood.

✳

Acorus calamus, *sweet flag*.

Aconitum lycoctonum *ssp.* vulparia.

Aconitum lycoctonum ssp. *vulparia*

WOLF'S BANE

The botanical name of the yellow wolf's bane refers like the common name to the poisoning of wolves and foxes. *Vulpes* is Latin for fox and *lycoctonum* originates from Greek for "wolf killing". The plant is just as poisonous as the blue monkshood, but this yellow species has a much wider distribution in the wild. It grows in lower-lying areas, particularly beside streams and rivers and on moist, fertile but alkaline soil. It is found most

Acorus calamus

SWEET FLAG, CALAMUS, MYRTLE FLAG

This plant is a successful colonist. Calamus roots were imported from South-East Asia in the Middle Ages for use, among other purposes, to protect against the plague. By the middle of the sixteenth century, the plant itself arrived in western Europe where it now grows wild along the banks of ditches and streams. Although the plant cannot self-seed itself in Europe, it has spread by fragments of its roots being carried by water to other sites.

Oil of calamus is used medicinally, albeit not without risk. There are four distinctly different populations of *Acorus calamus*. Oil of calamus from the European and, to an even greater extent, eastern

Actaea rubra *syn.* A. erythrocarpa.

Asian populations contain the carcinogenic asarone. Only the forms found in the United States and Siberia are free of asarone, making them suitable for medical use.

Oil of calamus is used for coughs, influenza, and tuberculosis but other uses have overtaken these: the strong scent is used in bath oils and perfumes.

Sweet flag is sometimes used in toothpaste and also occasionally as a culinary herb. When dissolved in spirits such as genever and liqueurs, the bitter taste of oil of calamus increases the appetite.

Sweet flag used to be shredded and scattered on the floor so that when walked upon a wonderful scent was released.

In India they have discovered that the vapour of oil of calamus makes certain types of insect infertile, preventing them from reproducing.

♆ 🍶 ⚕ ☕ ✳

Actaea rubra syn. *A. erythrocarpa*

RED BANEBERRY

This plant is the American equivalent of the European Herb Christopher *(Actaea spicata)*. Some regard the plant from the western parts of the United States and Canada merely as a variety of *A. spi-*

Actaea rubra, *red baneberry*.

cata but there is a clear difference. The ripe berries are shiny red rather than the black of Herb Christopher. The entire plant is extremely toxic but people use the roots in America for menstrual problems.

Actaea spicata syn. *A. nigra*

HERB CHRISTOPHER

Herb Christopher is used for evil purposes. William the Conqueror is reputed to have smeared the sap of the black berries on the saddles of those knights he did not like, resulting in skin irritations and itching blisters. This does not sound like St. Christopher, the patron saint of travellers but the name stems from another role of St. Christopher, as the patron saint of gravediggers. The herb was considered to ward off the spirits which guarded treasures.

Herb Christopher is an extremely poisonous plant of wooded slopes in Europe but there are no known fatal accidents. The preparation of this plant as medicine is work for skilled experts who can determine the correct dose. The herb is used to induce vomiting, externally for toothache, and for

Adonis aestivalis.

St. Vitus dance. Present days medical uses of the root include treatment of rheumatism in the hands and feet.

Adonis aestivalis

Adonis aestivalis is an annual plant with herbaceous growth which grows to about 40cm (16in) and flowers from May to August with dark red blooms with dark centres and has linear thread-like leaflets. The entire plant contains adonin, a toxic glycoside. Even though *Adonis aestivalis* has lower concentrations of these substances than the false hellebore *(Adonis vernalis)*, it remains a poisonous plant and should only be used medicinally under medical supervision.

Infusions of *Adonis aestivalis* are used as diuretic, sleeping draught, and cough medicine.

Species of *Adonis*, especially *A. vernalis* (false hellebore) are used to create medicines for stimulating heart function. The substance used is similar to those of *Digitalis* (foxglove) and are often prescribed in its place, to avoid the long-term effects of *Digitalis*-derived drugs.

Aegopodium podagraria

GROUND ELDER, GOUTWEED

Ground elder is one of the most invasive of weeds in a garden. The roots continually creep further and further and form yet another plant. Ground elder is especially invasive in open, humus-rich soil. The plant is originally a European woodland species but has been taken to other continents. The plant is popular as a ground cover plant in the

Aegopodium podagraria *'Variegatum', variegated ground elder.*

Aegopodium podagraria, *ground elder.*

Aesculus hippocastanum, *horse chestnut.*

Aesculus hippocastanum, *horse chestnut.*

United States. The variegated form *A. podagraria* 'Variegatum' is less invasive and is often planted in gardens.

Ground elder has been used since Medieval times as a medicine against gout and is known as "St Gerald's herb" in some countries because St. Gerard is the patron saint of gout sufferers. It is also taken internally for sciatica and externally as a compress for gout. The herb contains a natural fungicide.

Tender young leaves can be added to salads and also cooked in the same way as spinach. The plant is not poisonous but can easily be mistaken for other cluster flowering herbs that are toxic.

The entire plant can be used to dye wool and fabrics. The colour is greenish-yellow to burnt orange depending on the pre-treatment and can also be used to make brown with further treatment.

Aesculus hippocastanum

HORSE CHESTNUT

The horse chestnut originates from the Balkans and was brought to other parts of Europe in 1576. The route taken to Europe was via Constantinople, where the Turks used it medicinally. In Europe, the tree was used for ordinary and quartan fevers. It was later discovered that these were malaria and that quinine derived from the bark of a South American tree of the *Cinchona* genus was more effective.

Present day medicinal usage is for ailments such as enteritis, diarrhoea, and gout.

In herbal medicine horse chestnut is prescribed for improving the circulation of the blood, strengthening arteries, and treatment of haemorrhoids, and varicose veins. The leaves and fresh shells contain useful dyestuffs for woollens and fabric, giving good colourfast yellow, orange, and above all brown.

Agastache foeniculum syn. *A. anethiodora*

ANISE HYSSOP, BLUE GIANT HYSSOP, FENNEL GIANT HYSSOP

Even honey made from the anise hyssop tastes of aniseed. In America, beekeepers sowed entire fields with the plant to create this unusual honey. The plant is a native of North America and is mainly cultivated in Europe as an ornamental plant but we can make tea with it, just as the native Americans did, and enjoy its aniseed flavour. The herb is beneficial for those with a cold, opening the pores and encouraging a cleansing perspiration and also soothing sore and blocked up airways. The entire plant has an aroma akin to liquorice but tastes of aniseed. The leaves are delicious and refreshing in a salad.

Agastache foeniculum grows to about 100cm (39in) tall in a border and flowers in July and August with ears full of pinkish blue flowers. Provided it is not planted in heavy, wet soil, it will survive frosts to minus 20°C (minus 4°F). It closely resembles *Agastache rugosa*.

Agastache foeniculum, *anise hyssop.*

Agastache foeniculum, *anise hyssop.*

Agastache rugosa, *Korean mint.*

Agastache rugosa syn. *Lopanthus rugosus, Cedronella japonica*

KOREAN MINT, WRINKLED GIANT HYSSOP

Korean mint originates from China, Korea, and Japan, clearly at the opposite end of the world to the anise hyssop and yet they so closely resemble each other that some plant specialists do not recognize them as different species. This may seem strange given the distance between them but it is not. There are other species which are found in the Far East and on the West coast of America. The two continents were once joined.

The Asian species has been used for centuries in Korea in precisely the same way the native Americans utilized the plant. The aniseed-flavoured tea relieves the first symptoms of colds, reduces queasiness, and stimulates the appetite. The plant cleanses through perspiration, and aids digestion. This makes them an excellent choice for salads.

Agastache urticifolia

The sepals of this species are clearly longer than the other two examples of this genus listed here, otherwise there is little difference between them with flower spikes of similar length (15cm/6in) and pink to blue colouring. This species originates from the western parts of the United States and can be used in the same way as the other two species.

Agastache urticifolia.

Agave americana syn. *A. altissima*

CENTURY PLANT

Agave americana forms an enormous rosette of leaves that can be several meters wide. After some ten to twenty years of steady growth it suddenly produces a flowering stem from the centre of the rosette some 10m (30ft) long in a matter of weeks, after which the entire rosette of leaves dies back with the flower. The name century plant is a bit exaggerated since the plant flowers sooner than this. Agaves can only be grown as container plants in northern Europe because they are not at all hardy. *Agave americana* originates from Central America where the plant is used as both medicine and source of pleasure. When the young flower stem is cut off an abundance of liquid flows from the plant. In Mexico this liquid is drawn off and made, with yeast, into the drink known as *pulque* and

Agave americana, *century plant.*

vino mescal. The plant also delivers a substance used as an insect repellent.

The medical uses include treatment of scurvy, rheumatism, venereal disease, and as a diuretic. This plant is still used in the treatment of syphilis and gonorrhoea, plus for liver complaints, jaundice, and to cleanse the intestines.

℞ ✳

Agave americana 'Striata'

CENTURY PLANT

Variegated forms of *Agave americana* are more common in cultivation than the original species type. The best known is *A. americana* 'Marginata' which has broad yellow leaf margins. With A. a. 'Variegata', the leaf margins are cream and with *A. a.* 'Medio Picta' there is a broad white marking through the centre of the leaves. The foliage of A. a. 'Striata' is striped with yellow to pale yellow. The variegated leaf forms grow more as less as well as the original form and can be used in the same way.

℞ ✳

Agave americana 'Striata'.

Agrimonia eupatoria, *agrimony.*

Courtesy The Kruidhof, Buitenpost

Agrimonia eupatoria

AGRIMONY, STICKLEWORT, COCKLEBUR

Orators and singers sound melodious when they first gargle with an infusion of agrimony. This was just one of the many uses for which agrimony was recommended. The ancient Greeks wrote that the herb (which was offered up to the goddess Athena) was a cure all for such diverse ailments as warts, snake bites, rabid dogs, and jaundice. Today the uses of agrimony are somewhat more narrowly defined. The herb helps in cases of diarrhoea, stomach and intestinal ailments, and gall stones. Gargling with an infusion of bitter agrimony not only creates a supple larynx, it also appears to heal gum infections.

Agrimony flowers from mid summer with stems that can be 100cm (39in) long, although they are usually much shorter. Clusters of mellow yellow flowers are born on the stems. This plant prefers alkaline-rich soil that is not too moist in partial shade.

℞

Agrostemma githago, *corn cockle.*

Agrostemma githago, *corn cockle.*

Agrostemma githago

CORN COCKLE

Farmers were not happy to see the delightful pink flowers of corn cockle in their corn because bread baked with grain containing it had a toxic effect on those who ate it, resulting in irritation and sometimes inflammation of the stomach and gut. Consequently the corn cockle disappeared from our fields.

Corn cockle is an annual plant that grows to about 100cm (39in) high and its slender habit could be seen at its finest in arable fields with the support of other plants. Sow this in the autumn or spring in a sunny spot in soil that is non too fertile and somewhat dry. Corn cockle flowers from June to the end of August.

Corn cockle used to be used as a medicine for jaundice, oedema, skin rashes, and haemorrhoid. Present day homeopathic uses include enteritis (infection of the stomach lining).

Ajuga reptans

BUGLE

Bugle's natural wild habitat is the grassy margins at the edge of a wood throughout Europe and western Asia but it is far more commonly found as a ground-cover garden plant. The plant forms a low mat of dark green to purple foliage and in the spring is topped with purple florets.

In the seventeenth century, bugle was one of the favourite herbs of the famous herb expert Nicholas Culpeper. He praised its wound-healing properties. A decoction of the herb was dissolved in syrup and taken internally and an ointment with it spread on the wound.

Today we are far more interested in the toxic properties of bugle which protect the plant against insects. The discovery that white fly larvae are killed once they eat bugle has stimulated research into the plant's potential as a natural weapon against insects.

Ajuga reptans, *bugle, seen among ivy.*

Alcea rosea, *hollyhock.*

Alcea rosea, *hollyhock.*

Alcea rosea syn. *Althaea rosea*

HOLLYHOCK

Only cultivated forms of hollyhock are known, with the original species having come from Asia Minor. This plant has now become the favourite of cottage gardens and in Denmark the 200cm (79in) high flower stems can be seen growing between the joints in paving. Hollyhocks are perennials but are best grown as biennials. After flowering in the second year they should ideally be dug up and burned because they will almost always be infected with

Alcea rosea, *with hollyhock rust.*

hollyhock rust *(Puccinia malvacearum)* which causes orange patches on the leaves (on the undersides) and affects the entire leaf in its more advanced stages. The rust appears in winter at the top of the plant. For those who do not want to get rid of the plant, the disease can be delayed by cutting the flowering stem off close to the ground after flowering.

The flowers of the hollyhock make a delicious herbal tea which is also good for coughs and bronchitis. The sap from the roots can be used to make a cough syrup. Formerly the plant was also used as a remedy for diarrhoea, stomach and kidney ailments, and the roots were given to children to bite on to help them with teething.

A purple dye can be formed from the purple (almost black) *Alcea rosea* 'Nigra'. The spent flowering stems are used for making a yellow dye for wool and other textiles.

🌱 ⚕ ✏

Alchemilla alpina

ALPINE LADY'S MANTLE

Unfortunately the original species from which the lady's mantles of cultivation were formed are all extinct. These left behind hybrids which cannot be

Alchemilla alpina, *alpine lady's mantle.*

Alchemilla conjuncta.

Alchemilla mollis, *lady's mantle.*

fertilised with pollen from another plant (and not even from the same plant). In spite of this seeds capable of germinating are self-sown in abundance. The alpine lady's mantle is best recognised by the deeply lobed leaves often hand-shaped on their stems like the leaves of horse chestnut. The plants are of low habit (20cm/8in). These plants grow in the mountains of central and western Europe but also in the colder northern extremes of Europe and Iceland, where these photographs were taken. For use see *Alchemilla mollis.*

Alchemilla conjuncta

LADY'S MANTLE

Superficially this species resembles *A. alpina* and is often sold under this name but the lobes of the

leaves of this species are fused together for at least a fifth of their length. This species grows in the Alps and the Jura and can be found naturalised in Scotland. It grows about 30cm (1ft) high and bears flowers in slender clusters in June and July.
For uses, see *Alchemilla xanthoclora*.

Alchemilla mollis

LADY'S MANTLE

The most cultivated form of lady's mantle does not exist in the wild but is widely grown in gardens as border edging and sometimes becomes naturalised after escaping. The plant grows well in almost all circumstances and readily self seeds itself, especially where the ground is disturbed. The leaves are relatively large and have felt-like hairs on both sides. The drops of dew on the plant in early morning consist not just of dew but also of the plant's own sap which the plant has expelled. This perennial flowers continuously from May to late autumn. When the foliage looks a bit the worse for wear, the plant can be cut back to just above the ground.
Lady's mantle can be used to dye fabric and wool green, yellow, and brown. For other uses, see *Alchemilla xanthoclora*.

Alchemilla mollis, *lady's mantle.*

Alchemilla xanthoclora

Alchemilla xanthoclora syn. *A. vulgaris*

LADY'S MANTLE, LION'S FOOT

At the break of day, pearly drops of "dew" form on the edges of lady's mantle. Medieval alchemists eyed the magical liquid and added it to their potions that were supposed to deliver the "philosophers' stone" that would turn base metals into gold. These efforts by the alchemists resulted in the biological name of this genus.
Modern analytical chemistry has in a manner of speaking found the "philosophers' stone", earning mountains of gold through the sale of medicines. It is a role in which *Alchemilla* plays almost no role but in folk medicine the herb remains popular, particularly as an infusion of the dried leaves. The herb is particularly considered to deal with women's ailments, with the tannins stemming bleeding and helping with painful menstruation and during child birth. *Alchemilla* should not be used during pregnancy itself. With its ability to stem bleeding, the herb was once a much prized treatment for wounds, and was also used for stemming diarrhoea, internally for cleansing of the blood and externally for the skin. *Alchemilla xanthoclora* is considered by some as the best of the closely related species, others consider *A. alpina* to have better medicinal use. It is best recognised by the funnel-shaped erect leaves with toothed margins with smaller teeth at the point than the rest of the leaf.

Alisma plantago-aquatica

WATER PLANTAIN

The poison of a rattlesnake can be neutralised by water plantain and hence it is used in the United States to treat snake bites. However the plant grows beside water and rattle snakes prefer arid areas so the remedy is not exactly to hand. The plant is also a native in Europe, where it grows best on water margins where the water level changes.

Alisma plantago-aquatica, *water plantain.*

Alliaria petiolata, *garlic mustard.*

The water plantain has been used for centuries in North America, Europe, and Asia (especially in China and Japan) as both medicine and food. The root is edible and the volatile oils and bitter resin from the plant are used medicinally. *Alisma* is prescribed for epilepsy and dysentery. The active ingredients are diuretic (causing urination and perspiration) and help to cleanse the kidneys and bladder. This can help to treat kidney stones and bladder infections.

Alliaria petiolata

GARLIC MUSTARD, HEDGE GARLIC, JACK-BY-THE-HEDGE

When Jack-by-the-hedge is touched, it released a strong garlic-like scent, which explains the other common names. The tops of the shoots and young leaves can be added to herbs to spice them up. The aroma is of garlic but the taste is of a mild mustard. The plant is in no way related to garlic but is a member of the cabbage family and related to mustard.

In addition to culinary uses, *Alliaria petiolata* is used as a remedy for several illnesses that occur together or in sequence one after the other: eczema, asthma, and bronchitis. It is also regarded as a treatment to relieve rheumatism and gout. Garlic

mustard's natural habitat as a wild plant is open soil that retains moisture in partial shade. The plant usually grows as a biennial, flowering in May.

Allium cepa

ONION

With a string of onions around your neck, you need have no fear of the devil according to old superstition. Perhaps not, but regular use of onions will certainly keep you healthy and ward off that "other world" longer, because there is hardly another

Allium cepa, *onion.*

plant that has such healthy properties. The plant works as a diuretic, heals wounds, and is especially useful for colds and throat infections. The onion bulb is most health-giving when chopped and added raw to salads but this leaves a strong after-taste in the mouth. For this reason onions are more frequently cooked but then lose much of their potency. The onion is used in homeopathy for asthma, bronchitis, rheumatism, hay-fever, and ear-ache. Onion essence is sold as a treatment for dandruff and hair loss. Some people are allergic to contact with the juice of an onion and can suffer rashes.

The dry outer peel of an onion provides an orange-coloured dyestuff which can be used to dye wool and clothing red and brown.

Allium cepa 'Proliferum'

EGYPTIAN TREE ONION

The normal onion bears a green and white striped spherical flower in its second summer, but the Egyptian tree onion from the Proliferum group of *A. cepa* only flowers from time to time. Instead of flowers, new onions are usually born at the end of the stems which can be used as fresh onion in salads, pressed for their juice, or pickled in vinegar.

Allium cepa *'Proliferum,' Egyptian tree onion.*

These onions have a stronger taste than normal onions and they are extremely easy to propagate by removing the small "seedling" onions from the stems and getting them to root. The plant has a somewhat unkempt style of growth and no decorative value but looks fine as a specimen in its own right.

Allium fistulosum

WELSH ONION, SCALLION, SPRING ONION

Commonly known now as spring onion, the Welsh onion or scallion is especially popular in Chinese cookery. The "bulb" is no larger than the stem and both are edible. The plant has a distinct onion taste and similar medicinal properties: including the treatment and prevention of influenza, aiding the digestion, diuretic properties, and reduction of cholesterol. This plant is a hardy biennial to short-lived perennial. Seed onions are often formed in the flower cluster which can easily be used to propagate new plants; otherwise propagate from seed in March.

Allium fistulosum, *spring onion.*

Allium fistulosum, *spring onion.*

Allium porum, *leek.*

Allium porum

LEEK

Cooked leeks are a well-known winter vegetable and the thinly-sliced rings of the fresh plant are also ideal for adding to soups. Do not cook leek for longer than five minutes. Leek can also be added raw to salads, using small amounts of finely-sliced leek from the white and pale-green parts of the stems.

Early sown leeks are planted out in hollows in the ground. Once the stalks start to grow the hollows are filled in and then later earthed up to create the long white stems. Leeks need very fertile soil. If they are not harvested in the winter, the plants will flower the following summer with large rounded flower clusters of pink florets. Leeks that have gone to seed are not suitable for eating.

Allium sativum

GARLIC

The ancient Egyptians swore an oath by onion and garlic, according to the Roman chronicler Plinius. Garlic was considered a holy plant and it still is for some people. *Allium sativum* is one of the healthiest of plants, strengthening the entire body with its properties. Heart and circulatory problems are prevented and those who have suffered a heart attack can prevent a recurrence through regularly use of garlic. The cholesterol level in the blood is reduced and the supply of blood to the tissues is

Allium sativum, *garlic.*

improved. Garlic also cleanses the skin, gets rid of worms, and when applied externally can treat acne. The plant contains many vitamins and also helps to reduce inflammation and prevents fungal growth. Garlic also slows the ageing process.

The cloves of garlic are finely sliced or otherwise crushed in a garlic press for addition to dishes. Fresh garlic or cloves stored in oil retain their full potency, but this is partially lost during cooking.

The only disadvantage of garlic is that the breath smells strongly of garlic when it is eaten regularly and the perspiration can also smell of garlic.

The ancient Greeks used garlic and wine together to treat snake bites although I doubt whether this was effective, even though this combination does contain powerful active constituents as anyone who drinks plenty of wine at the same time as eating garlic will know. There is a risk of restless sleep and palpitations from the combination. Otherwise, garlic can be taken in unlimited quantity.

An infusion of garlic can be used to treat mildew on plants.

The plant is no longer found growing wild. The slender stem grows to about 100cm (39in) high and bears fairly small ball-like flower clusters of pink florets. Below the soil the ovoid bulb forms many cloves. These are all protected by a white skin.

♃ ⚕ ✳

Allium schoenoprasum syn. A. sibiricum

CHIVES

Chives are one of the most rewarding plant to grow yourself. This perennial will even survive in a pot on a balcony or window sill. The plant is hardy but does lose its growth above ground with moderate frost. The plant produces countless new green shoots of tubular leaves which are best used when new. The leaves can be chopped and added to salads. The mild onion taste is also delicious in tomato soup and also with bread and cheese.

By early summer, many stems become tough and start to flower tiny flowers (2cm/³/₄in) which attract the bees in droves. Flowering stems are no longer suitable for culinary use. After flowering, cut the plant right back and fresh green shoots will emerge.

Although the plant is rich in vitamin C and aids digestion, it is virtually unknown in medicinal use.

⚕

Allium schoenoprasum, *chives*

Allium schoenoprasum, *chives.*

Allium schoenoprasum *'Album,' white chives.*

Allium schoenoprasum 'Album'

CHIVES

With colour arrangements now being so important in the garden, unusual colour versions of plants are very popular. White flowered forms of *A. schoenoprasum* can be found with names such as *forma album,* 'Albifloss' and 'Album'. This are paler varieties of the normal chives and they have the same culinary properties.

Allium tuberosum

CHINESE CHIVES, GARLIC CHIVES, CUCHAY

Chinese chives have a similar flavour to chives but with a hint of garlic. Pick the tender ribbon-like leaves without hard flowering stems and chop them finely for salads, soups, and sauces. Chinese chives are also excellent with boiled or fried eggs and with potato dishes.

The plant is used in China to improve kidney function, for bladder complaints, and for incontinence. Chinese chives flower in late summer with aromatic white flowers and makes an ideal decorative plant. It originates from South-East Asia, grows to almost 50cm (20in) and is fully hardy.

Allium tuberosum, *Chinese chives.*

Courtesy The Kruidhof, Buitenpost.

Allium tuberosum, *Chinese chives.*

Allium ursinum, *chives.*

Aloe vera, *Barbados aloe.*

Allium ursinum

RAMSONS, WILD GARLIC

The distinctive aroma of ramsons (which many call wild garlic) pervade woods and gardens in May and June with their pungent garlic-like smell. This perennial grows to about 30cm (12in) high and can be found virtually throughout Europe in woods in open but moisture-retaining soils, especially those that are alkaline. Ramsons only require a little light to grow.

For centuries the herb has been taken internally to cleanse the system, particularly to get rid of stomach and gut parasites but is also used to treat the liver, gall bladder, and blood. The plant helps to reduce blood pressure.

The leaves are picked in April, May, and June and then the bulbs are harvested in the summer. Both leaves and bulbs are sliced finely for addition to salads and the strong garlic taste adds aroma to soups and sauces.

The plant is a protected species in a number of European countries and may not be picked or the bulbs lifted. Toxic symptoms can occur with excessive levels of consumption but the strong taste makes this unlikely.

Aloe vera syn. *A. barbadensis*

BARBADOS ALOE, CURACAO ALOE

It is said that Cleopatra owed her beauty in part to the *Aloe vera* plant, which took care of her skin. The gelatinous constituents of the leaves are still widely used in cosmetics: to strengthen the hair in shampoo, for cooling of the skin in sun-tan lotion, but most of all for skin treatment following radio-therapy. *Aloe vera* also has antiseptic properties for infected wounds and skin complaints.

The plant should only be taken internally in measured doses because of the plant's toxicity, which can lead to kidney damage. In low-level doses, the plant enhances the appetite and in higher doses is a laxative. Pregnant women and those in menstruation must not take the plant internally.

Plants of the *Aloe* genus originate from arid regions in Africa and Asia and the plant is unable to withstand any frost and can only be grown out of doors all-year-round in tropical and sub-tropical latitudes. The yellow-flowering plant is grown in northern Europe as a house and container plant.

Aloysia triphylla syn. *Lippia citriodora*

LEMON VERBENA

Lemon verbena can only survive the mildest of winters in mild coastal areas within Europe. The plant is mainly cultivated elsewhere as a container plant. The plant originates from South America where the leaves are added to tea because of their lemon taste. In Europe the plant is mainly used for flavouring desserts. Membranes on the underside of the leaf provide volatile oil that smells of lemon and because the leaf retains its aroma for a long time, it is popularly used in pot-pourris.

Lemon verbena tea aids the digestion, is calming, reduces cramp, and antiseptic. Hang a bag of leaves in bath water for the fragrance and relaxant nature of the herb.

Althaea officinalis

MARSH MALLOW

The marsh mallow proves that a living pharmacy can also be attractive. This perennial grows to about 200cm (79in) with erect stems full of fine grey-green leaves and equally fine pink flowers,

Althaea officinalis, *marsh mallow.*

Aloysia triphylla, *lemon verbena.*

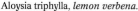

Althaea officinalis, *marsh mallow.*

making it a first class garden plant. Marsh mallow is native throughout much of Europe but fairly rare because its habit is brackish soil. In cultivation, it will tolerate almost any soil.

The plant used to be cultivated on a large scale in the past with its fibres being used to make rope and paper and gelatinous sap from the roots was included in remedies for many ailments. This substance causes tissue softening and it is therefore used to reduce and heal skin inflammations. The root can be chewed as a remedy for sore throats and the dried roots can be used for an infusion (without boiling the water) for mouth and gum disorders, plus treatment of throat, stomach, and intestinal ailments. Marsh mallow syrup with aniseed is a proven remedy for coughs and colds.

 ✳

Amaranthus caudatus

LOVE-LIES-BLEEDING, TASSEL FLOWER

The leaves of *Amaranthus caudatus* are eaten as a vegetable in South America where they are abundant because this annual grows about 100cm (39in) high. The plant becomes easily naturalised in many tropical and sub-tropical countries where it can be a perennial. In northern Europe the plant is grown as a decorative garden annual which does well on poor soil. The purple flowering panicles grow about 45-60cm (18–24in) long and these can

Amaranthus caudatus, *love-lies-bleeding.*

be used with the leaves to dye wool and textiles red.

Anagallis arvensis ssp. *arvensis*

SCARLET PIMPERNEL, POOR MAN'S WEATHERGLASS

If the tiny flowers of scarlet pimpernel close-up in the morning then it is time to go home. The plant even reacts to a passing cloud, hence their other common name. You will need to look closely though because the flowers are miniscule on a plant less than 10cm (4in) high. Every part of the plant is toxic, tasting bitter and causing vomiting.
In the right dose, the herb can help bladder and kidney stones, epilepsy, and constipation. Overdoses can cause kidney damage and inflammation of the stomach lining, so that self prescription is definitely not recommended. The herb is used in homeopathic medicine in safe dilutions for itching rashes and boils.

Ananas comosus

PINEAPPLE

The well-known pineapple is not just a juicy fruit but also has medicinal uses. The plant belongs to the order of Bromeliaceae and a substance bromelaine is derived from the plant which has a number of economic uses plus incorporation in medicines for treating stomach and intestinal disorders. The juice contains the substance so that medicine can be taken in a pleasant-tasting manner.
The pineapple originates from Latin America and can only be grown in moist, warm air. This was achieved in the nineteenth century kitchen gardens of England by using a hotbed of horse manure. The plant cannot withstand temperatures below 15°C (59°F) and is very difficult for non-professionals to cultivate.

Anangallis arvensis *ssp.* arvensis, *scarlet pimpernel.*

Ananas comosus, *pineapple.*

Anchusa officinalis, *alkanet.*

Anchusa officinalis, *alkanet.*

Anethum graveolens, *dill.*

Anchusa officinalis

ALKANET

Alkanet is to be found virtually throughout Europe but is only commonly found in certain places. It has a preference for a sunny position in dry, non acid, and nitrogen rich soil. The plant grows 20–30cm (8–12in) tall and flowers continuously from May to September with reddish pink blooms which turn deep blue later.

The plant has virtually no medicinal uses but was once used to treat boils, inflammations, and sensitive skin. and also taken internally as a laxative and for coughs and stomach ulcers. Alkanet contains caffeic acid, chlorogenic acid, and rosemarinic acid. Its use these days is greater for creating a dyestuff from its roots which can be used to colour textiles and wool red and brown.

Anethum graveolens syn. *Peucedanum graveolens*

DILL

Dill is the herb that can calm the hiccups in children. It is suggested that the smell of the seed banishes the hiccups and children in North America are given a little dill to chew on during lengthy sermons in church. Because of this it is also known as

Courtesy The Kruidhof, Buitenpost.

"sermon seed." Dill aids the digestion, helps guard against wind, stomach cramps in babies, acts as a diuretic, and stimulates milk for nursing mothers. The good associations with dill are perhaps largely owed to its pleasant aroma and the herb was once picked to be strewn on the floor. Today we incorporate it in pot-pourris.

Dill is also one of the most useful of culinary herbs. The fresh leaf is an ideal accompaniment (added after cooking) with fish and egg dishes, in sauces, and salads. The flower clusters and ripe seeds are added to vinegar when pickling onions and gherkins.

The oil from dill is used in soap.

Dill is easily grown as an annual and is often confused with fennel *(Foeniculum vulgare)*. The stems bear foliage divided into thread-like segments and in summer are topped by umbels of golden flowers. These are excellent in bouquets and flower arrangements, making this a popular plant for the decorative garden. Organic gardeners plant dill alongside brassica for larger crops.

Angelica archangelica

ANGELICA

The archangel Michael is supposed to have told monks to chew the roots of angelica to protect them from the plague. It did not protect Medieval man, although the plant does contain active constituents that have antiseptic and fungicidal properties. For this reason, fish are sometimes packed in angelica by the Lapps. The volatile oils and bitter-sweet substance have similar properties as dill: as a disinfectant, diuretic, cramp-relieving, aid to digestion, and relief for the wind.

Although the active constituents are found in the entire plant, the greatest concentration is in the roots and these are dried for use in medicines. Salves containing angelica and baths with the herb dissolved in them provide relief for rheumatism and gout sufferers.

Angelica archangelica, *angelica.*

Angelica archangelica, *angelica.*

The seeds and roots are used to flavour liqueurs such as Benedictine and in northern Europe the stalks are candied for decorating cakes and desserts. The plant is found in these parts growing along the banks of rivers but elsewhere in Europe it is less common, though by no means rare. The plant can be found alongside water or in pasture land growing to about 200cm (79in) tall and topped by a flowering umbel. This angelica is slightly toxic and is best taken as a medicine under expert guidance and is not advised for pregnant women or diabetics. The sap from the plant irritates the skin and can increase sensitivity to ultra-violet light, causing burning. See photosensitivity under *Heracleum mantegazzianum*.

Angelica sylvestris

EUROPEAN WILD ANGELICA

The common wild angelica has a more slender appearance than *A. archangelica.* The stems of this biennial to short-lived perennial often turn reddish-brown. The plant can be found widely distributed throughout Europe in moist, humus-rich, and fertile soils.

Angelica sylvestris, *wild angelica.*

Antennaria dioica, *catsfoot.*

Anthemis tinctoria, *golden marguerite.*

Anthemis tinctoria *'Wargrave', golden marguerite*

The medicinal working of this plant can be compared with *A. archangelica,* though less potent. The plant also has a less pronounced scent and is predominantly used as an expectorant cough remedy.

The same contra-indications apply to the European wild angelica as the larger species: not for pregnant women or diabetics, with care necessary to prevent the sap making the skin photosensitive (see *Heracleum mantegazzianum).*

Antennaria dioica

CATSFOOT, LIFE EVERLASTING, CAT'S EAR

Catsfoot can be found widely distributed throughout Europe but rarely in lowland areas although it can be found on lowland heaths and dunes. The abundant summer-flowering blooms display themselves on stems about 20cm (8in) high above a carpet of sturdy foliage.

Catsfoot once had wide-scale use as a medicinal herb, providing a remedy for diarrhoea, gall-bladder, and liver complaints, jaundice, and coughing but is little used in the present day.

Anthemis tinctoria

GOLDEN MARGUERITE, OX-EYE CHAMOMILE

Golden marguerite grows widely as a weed in European arable land, especially in Scandinavia, central, and eastern Europe.

This perennial is quite easy to grow in the garden from seed. There are numerous cultivated varieties in garden centres, varying from deep yellow to every shade of yellow and cream. The petals of *A. tinctoria* 'Wargrave' are paler yellow than those of the species. Chopped foliage and flowers were once strewn on the floor to spread their aroma in house and to ward off fleas. The plant was used medicinally for spasms, hysteria, and to help asthma and fever

45

patients to sleep but it is now virtually unused medicinally.

The main importance of the plant today is as a dyestuff with the flower buds, flowers, and spent blooms all providing yellow dye for colouring textiles and wool.

Anthriscus cerefolium, *chervil.*

Anthricus cerefolium

CHERVIL

The delicate aniseed-flavouring of chervil has made it an indispensable culinary herb. The herb is regarded an essential ingredient for fine cooking, especially for flavouring of sauces, and for adding to egg and fish dishes. Only the fresh leaves are used and these are added at the end of cooking because both cooking and drying cause the herb to lose its taste.

The true gastronome therefore ensures the plant is available all year round. Chervil seed can be sewn in monthly succession as soon as there are no more ground frosts. The plant is a biennial but is not fully hardy so that the growth usually withers but can usually be kept successfully in an unheated greenhouse or frame. Chervil can also be grown in a pot.

The herb contains vitamin C and minerals that are important for the body; it also aids the digestion, helps to purify the blood, and is diuretic.

Anthricus sylvestris

COW PARSLEY, QUEEN ANNE'S LACE

When the cow parsley begins to flower in May it is a harbinger of summer. The tall plant grows to 150cm (5ft), although shorter in sunny positions and flowers copiously on fertile roadside verges

Anthriscus sylvestris, *cow parsley.*

where the soil is moist. The plant's origins are the edges of woods. The biennial or short-lived perennial flowers in its second year when the flowering grow usually dies back to be succeeded by self-seeded replacements, ensuring there is always cow parsley in the same place.

Cow parsley is not used any more for medicinal or culinary purposes but the entire plant is used in water to dye things yellow.

Anthriscus sylvestris, *cow parsley.*

46

Anthyllis vulneraria, *kidney vetch.*

Apium graveolens, *celery.*

Anthyllis vulneraria

KIDNEY VETCH

Kidney vetch is a low-growing annual or short-lived perennial which is covered from May until autumn with small, rounded flower clusters. The plant is found almost throughout Europe but only in sunny positions on dry, alkaline soil, such as chalk downs and railway embankments.

The dried flowers can be used for an infusion that is a cough remedy and purifies the body. This is why the herb is often added to herbal teas for its cleansing properties. The same infusion can be used for a compress to help wounds heal more quickly.

Apium graveolens

WILD CELERY, SMALLAGE

Celery comes in a variety of forms: the well-known vegetable *(A. graveolens* var. *dulce)* which is excellent raw in salads (especially with cheese). Celeriac *(A. graveolens* var. *rapaceum)* grows an underground tuber that can be as large as a football. It can be sliced and eaten raw in salads or cooked.

Wild celery is both bitter and toxic in large amounts but a cultivated form *Apium graveolens* var. *secalinum* is available in many smooth-leaf and curly-leaf varieties is more useful as a herb. The wild species grows in Europe and neighbouring parts of Asia, especially on coasts and tidal estuaries, and the edges of salt marshes, because they need a brackish habitat. The cultivated forms thrive best in soils that do not dry out too readily. The seed can be sown from March. Celery is a valuable culinary asset, being widely used in stocks, soups, and sauces. Celery is added to dishes just before they are served, and raw in salads. Celery acts as a diuretic and this property is most potent when the juice is pressed from the roots and

Apium graveolens, *celery.*

stems or the volatile oils are used from the seeds. Celery stimulates bladder and kidney function and is also used to treat such diverse ailments as rheumatoid arthritis, bronchitis, asthma, and kidney infections. Pregnant women are advised not to take celery in concentrated form.

Apocynum cannabinum, *dogbane.*

Aquilegia canadensis, *columbine.*

Apocynum cannabinum

DOGBANE, CANADIAN HEMP, BLACK INDIAN HEMP

Dogbane belongs to the same family as the oleander and is equally poisonous. The active glycocides work in a similar fashion to digitalis in foxgloves. The heart beat can be slowed and strengthened but the dosage is a very precise and must be determined by a doctor. Self medication is extremely dangerous. This herb is controlled by law in some countries.

The native Americans were expert in the use of this herb, employing it to induce vomiting for kidney complaints and also as a diuretic. The strong root fibres were also used to make fishing nets and baskets.

Apocynum cannabinum can be grown in a flower garden as a cultivated specimen, becoming about 100cm (39in) tall, and flowering in late summer. Beware of the sap from the plant for it can cause severe skin rashes.

⚕ ✳

Aquilegia canadensis

COLUMBINE

Animals leave the shiny black seeds of this columbine alone because they are highly poiso-

nous. This did not prevent the native Americans from using the seeds as a remedy for headache.

This columbine grows across a broad sweep from north to south of the eastern side of North America. The flowers are pollinated by hummingbirds. *Aquilegia canadensis* has a strong preference for moist, rocky woodland, but grows in gardens in any soil that retains moisture.

⚕

Aquilegia vulgaris

GRANNY'S BONNET, COLUMBINE

The nun and composer Hildegard von Bingen, who lived in the Middle Ages, was mistress of various arts. Among the many skills, she was an expert herbalist who prescribed the wild columbine to reduce the inflammation of swollen glands. In Spain, the root of the plant was chewed while abstaining from other food to treat kidney stones and the plant was also used to treat mouth ulcers but this resulted in some children being poisoned. Granny's bonnet is a toxic plant that contains prussic acid among other substances. Today, the plant has virtually no medicinal uses. Granny's bonnet grows wild throughout Europe on alkaline, somewhat dry soils, in partial shade but is also a

Aquilegia vulgaris, *granny's bonnet.*

Arctium lappa, *greater burdock.*

Courtesy The Kruidhof, Buitenpost.

Arctium lappa, *greater burdock.*

well-known garden plant, which flowers in May and June. The original species has bluish-purple or white flowers but the cultivated varieties found in gardens are a wider range of colours from yellow, through pink and red to blue. Double blooms of two colours are common. The single-flowered sort are usually thronged with bees.

Arctium lappa

GREATER BURDOCK, LAPPA, BEGGAR'S BUTTONS

The mass of prickles and hairs on flowerheads of greater burdock probably gave men the idea of using the plant as a stimulant for hair growth. It is still possible to find hair tonics and lotions containing burdock.

The root of greater burdock contains substances that reduce fungal growth and kill bacteria. These also have diuretic properties so that they have a cleansing effect which helps in treatment of rheumatic problems. *Arctium* helps to purify the blood, is beneficial with internal infections such as gastritis, stomach ulcers, and also for treatment of liver and gall bladder problems and even perhaps

for tuberculosis. Compresses of burdock root help to cleanse the skin of eczema and acne.

Greater burdock can be found throughout Europe growing on clay soil, but also on other soils beside hedges and on the edges of woods. It grows to about 200cm (79in) and flowers in mid-summer with crimson flower bracts with hooked spines or burrs.

49

Arctium minus, *lesser burdock.*

Arctium minus syn. *A. minus* ssp. *pubens*

LESSER BURDOCK, COMMON BURDOCK, LAPPA, BEGGAR'S BUTTONS

It is not easy to tell the greater and lesser burdocks apart so that they are often confused with each other. To check it is necessary to cut one of the bottom leaves from the stem and if this is hollow the plant must be the lesser burdock since the leaf stems of the greater burdock are solid. The flower bracts of lesser or common burdock are less than 2cm (³/₄in) across. Some consider burdock of intermediate size between the greater and lesser species to be a crossing of the two but it has no difference in the uses of the root of the herb which have identical active constituents. See *Arctium lappa.*

Arisaema triphyllum

JACK-IN-THE-PULPIT, INDIAN TURNIP

This secretive plant from the forests of the eastern parts of North America was eaten by the natives and yet it can be deadly poisonous. The native Americans knew how to crush and dry the root to neutralise the toxins. For medicinal use it is essential that the active constituents are not lost and

Arisaema triphyllum, *Jack-in-the-pulpit.*

therefore the preparation of the plant for therapy is skilled. Medicines derived from the plant are used for hoarse throats, and treatment of infections in the mucous membranes, tonsils, and larynx.

Jack-in-the-pulpit makes an interesting curiosity of a plant for woodland gardens with its flowers in early summer that betray their relationship with the arum lily. The botanical name indicates the trifoliate leaves which wilt soon after the plant has flowered.

Aristolochia clematitis

BIRTHWORT, HEARTWORT

In the ancient cultures of Egypt, Greece, and the Roman empire the birthwort was highly regarded for the miraculous way in which wounds that were treated with the herb were healed. Modern scientists have analysed the plant and found it contains a mixture of substances that are effective in healing wounds. The most important active constituent is aristolochic acid which stimulates the growth of white blood cells and causes the immune system to be made more active. The plant also contains a substance which dries up suppuration from wounds and another which disinfects. Infusions of birthwort are often held against the skin with a compress which allows air to reach the skin.

Aristolochia clematitis, *birthwort.*

Birthwort must not be used for pregnant women and others should only use it under medical supervision to prevent poisoning from excessive doses. Birthwort originates from the countries surrounding the Mediterranean but can now be found in other parts of Europe, especially on dry, alkaline soils.

Armoracia rusticana syn. *A. lapathifolia, Cochlearia armoracia*

HORSERADISH

The principal interest with horseradish is the thick root, although the tender leaves are also used in salads and with smoked mackerel. When the roots are cut, volatile oils are exuded which bring tears to the eyes just as with onions but they help to clear blocked airways and sinuses. The medicinal uses include internally for arthritis, gout, sciatica, respiratory, and urinary infections, and when suffering from cold sweats. Mixed with honey and sugar, one teaspoon can be taken three times a day as a cough mixture. Horseradish also contains substances that help to reduce bacterial infections.

Horseradish is of course widely used by cooks with the fresh root grated on its own or with apple as a

Armoracia rusticana, *horseradish.*

51

Armoracia rusticana, *horseradish.*

Courtesy The Kruidhof, Buitenpost.

condiment with fish, or made into a sauce with vinegar and cream with roast beef, cold chicken, egg, and potato dishes. The pungent taste is similar to mustard and horseradish should be taken in moderation.

The plant originates from southern Russia but because of its excellent properties it quickly spread throughout the northern hemisphere, where it can be found naturalised growing in fertile, moisture-retaining soil. This perennial can be easily propagated from root cuttings (provided they have a few eyes). It is best to ensure no root is left in the ground when the plant is harvested because these can grow and become rampant.

Arnica chamissonis.

Arnica chamissonis

Arnica chamissonis originates from the Rocky Mountains of North America but is also cultivated as a perennial in borders and rock gardens. The plant cannot tolerate alkaline soil. This American relative of the mountain tobacco (see following entry) is used in salves to ease the pain of bruising and to stem bleeding. See also *Arnica montana.*

Arnica montana

ARNICA, LEOPARD'S BANE, MOUNTAIN TOBACCO, MOUNTAIN DAISY

Mountain tobacco is a poisonous plant but is widely used in medicine. A tincture is applied externally in a compress for bruising, strains, sprains, traumas, bleeding, swollen arteries, and mumps. It can be used to gargle for gum disorders but must be spat out. An infusion of mountain tobacco improves blood circulation and supply of blood to the heart. The herb is used in homeopathic medicine for similar treatment but for a wide variety of other ailments, such as concussion, tennis elbow, and for painful operation wounds or after tooth extraction.

Take great care with mountain tobacco because it contains toxic substances such as helenaline. The plant is taken internally in some countries but considered unsafe in the United Kingdom for other than external use and deemed unsafe in the USA. The herb irritates the lining of the stomach and gut. Its external use can lead to allergic reactions for some people. This can also occur when using massage oils containing *Arnica.*

Substances within the plant appear to inhibit the development of insects such as the feared grain weevil, which can wreak havoc to the yield of a harvest. *Arnica montana* grows in mountain pasture but also in lowlands, peat moors, and heaths, especially where nutrients are improved by burning. Ovate leaves are formed on the root rhizome followed in June to August by yellow daisy-like flowers. The

Arnica montana, *mountain tobacco.*

Artemisia abrotanum, *southernwood.*

plant, which does not tolerate alkaline soils, grows mainly in mountainous areas of southern Scandinavia southwards through central Europe.

Artemisia abrotanum

SOUTHERNWOOD

Even sparrows and starlings are aware of the protection against insects of southernwood of the sage brush or wormwood family. They like to incorporate its branches into their nests to ward off fleas and lice. Humans too quickly learned the plants useful properties. Once the branches were used to brush the skin to protect against midges and placed in drawers and wardrobes to guard against moths. The plant continues to be valued for its natural insect repellent characteristics. Organic gardeners spread the foliage between rows of carrots and cabbages to keep their pests at bay. The leaves have a delightful lemon smell and consequently used to be strewn on the floors in houses.

The herb is used in small amounts for salads, fish, and chicken dishes. The herb was once highly regarded in folk medicine, being said to protect from the plague, increase potency, and put hair back on a bald head. Today somewhat less exaggerated claims are made: heightening of appetite, aid to digestion, destroys worms, is antiseptic, and reduces fever. Pregnant women should not use the herb because of its astringent nature.

The herb is sometimes added to shampoo and soap (for greasy skins). Stems with foliage can be used to make a yellow dye for woollens and fabrics.

The perennial can be easily propagated from cuttings and makes an ideal foliage plant for borders with its grey-green pinnately divided leaves.

Artemisia absinthium

WORMWOOD

Anisette owes its popularity to the ban by the French (and other governments) of absinthe. Addiction to absinthe became a major problem in the nineteenth century with regular drinkers suffering muscular cramps, followed by damage to the central nervous system. This was more than addiction to alcohol but to thujone which is toxic. It is still contained in some vermouths and liqueurs but in much lower and safe amounts.

When the production of absinthe was terminated, the large-scale cultivation of wormwood ceased so that it was less likely to become naturalised by escaping from cultivation. The plant is now mainly found growing wild along the coasts of western Europe where the winters are mild. The plant is frost tender.

Artemisia absinthium, *wormwood in spring.*

The essential oil of wormwood, which is abundant in the plant, appears to be an excellent medicine for gall bladder disorders and stomach problems. The substance also increases the appetite. Infusions of the plant do not suffer from high levels of thujone because this dissolves less readily in water than alcohol. The tea is bitter tasting and is therefore usually combined with other herbs such as peppermint. Pregnant women should not uses the plant in any form because it can abort the foetus.

Wormwood is used as a culinary herb mainly when roasting meat and poultry and has a beneficial effect on the digestion.

The plant is also used to produce a yellow dye, which with additional treatment can also be used to create green in woollens and fabrics.

The tips of the plant used to be used between clothes and under the bed to repel insects.

Artemisia absinthium *(wormwood) in flower.*

Artemisia annua

SWEET WORMWOOD, SWEET ANNIE

Sweet wormwood is one of the tallest growing annual plants, reaching 200cm (79in) and can serve as a temporary hedge. The plant resembles a conifer.

Recently it was discovered that the plant can play an important role against malaria. The drugs used to protect westerners from malaria have been so widely dispensed that malaria parasites are becoming immune, requiring ever stronger drugs to protect travellers and tourists from malaria. Artesunate is produced from sweet wormword and

Artemisia absinthium *(wormwood) in flower.*

Artemisia annua, *sweet wormwood.*

54

appears to be a promising alternative medicine. The effectiveness of the herb against bacterial infections has been known very much longer. Sow the seeds in situ outdoors in spring.

Artemisia dracunculus

TARRAGON

Tarragon has been cultivated for centuries for its unusual but strong flavour. There are two types which very slightly from each other but French tarragon *A. dracunculus* ssp. *sativa* has the better taste but is less hardy. It almost never flowers in northern Europe and needs to be renewed by propagating from cuttings about every two years. Russian tarragon *(A. d.* ssp. *dracunculoides)* is fully hardy, grows taller (to 150cm/59in) but does not have the same subtlety of taste.

The grey-green leafed shoots of tarragon are harvested before flowering and these are often immediately added to vinegar. Tarragon vinegar has at the same time a sweet and sour aroma and is widely used in sauces. Both fresh and dried tarragon is used in omelettes, salads, and with fish, poultry, and meat dishes but its strong taste makes it most

Artemisia dracunulus, *tarragon.*

Artemisia ludoviciana, *western mugwort.*

suitable for incorporation with cold sauces, herb butter, and dressings.

Tarragon increase the appetite and is used medicinally for indigestion and worms.

Artemisia ludoviciana

WESTERN MUGWORT, WHITE SAGE, CUDWEED

Western mugwort is often grown in gardens for its decorative grey foliage. There are numerous varieties, some with finely pinnate leaves. When the leaves are touched a delightful absinthe aroma is released, making the herb ideal for use in nosegays and pot-pourris.

The plant was once used in its countries of origin (USA and Mexico) to treat diarrhoea. Western mugwort is a perennial that grows to between 100–150cm (39–60in). To ensure the silver hairs on the plant, plant it in a sunny spot in a well-drained soil.

Artemisia vulgaris

MUGWORT, FELON HERB, CHINESE MOXA

Mugwort grows as a weed on the edges of arable fields and in hedges, especially on sandy soils. Its name of felon herb is derived from the practice of using nose-gays of the herb in court to protect others from jail fever. The sturdy stems easily reach 150cm (59in) high. These are often reddish in colour with rectangular pinnate green leaves that have white hairs on their underside.

The plant has similar medical and culinary uses as wormwood *(A. absinthium)* but has a less pronounced aroma, more subtle taste, and is less potent. Mugwort increases the appetite, and stimulates the gall bladder and liver. The culinary use is directly related to these medicinal properties, with the herb being added to food to aid the digestion.

Artemsia vulgaris, *mugwort.*

Courtesy of The Kruidenhof, Buitenpost.

Arum italicum, *arum.*

Pregnant and lactating women should not use the herb.
The plant supplies a yellow dye which can be used to colour wool and fabrics a dull green.

⚕ 🍴 /

Arum italicum

ARUM, LORDS AND LADIES

The flowering spathes emit a scent which attracts flies and midges. These land on the flower form which is slippery on the inside and thereby pollinate the pistil if they have previously visited a similar plant.
This species of arum grows wild as a woodland plant in southern Europe and in coastal areas but has escaped from cultivation here and there elsewhere. The leaves characteristically have white veins which stand out from the forest floor in autumn. The flower forms are borne in spring with white to pale yellow spikes.
For the berries, toxicity, and uses, see *Arum maculatum.*

⚕ *

Arum maculatum

CUCKOO PINT, LORDS AND LADIES

The cuckoo pint or lords and ladies is extremely poisonous. Every part of the plant contains several extremely toxic substances and others which cause irritation. Self-medication with this plant is extremely dangerous but the plant is used by apothecaries and homeopaths to produce medicines against cold, hoarseness, chronic bronchitis, and inflammation of the membranes, in the mouth, nose, throat, and stomach.
Because the toxicity is largely removed by drying

Arum maculatum, *cuckoo pint.*

or cooking, the cooked roots of cuckoo pint used to be (and still are) eaten and also used to produce starch.

The cuckoo pint is a native woodland plant of fertile soil that is rich in humus. The leaves and flower form appear in spring. The greenish flower form has a chocolate brown to purple spike at its centre. This develops during the summer into a stem with berries which are green at first but become reddish orange by autumn. By this time the green leaves (often with brown patches) have withered.

♄ ✳

Asarum europaeum

WILD GINGER, ASARABACCA

Asarabacca has been used to turn alcoholics off drink by putting it in a glass but since this is not good for the liver which is already under threat there must surely be better ways to come off the drink. This wild ginger is actually poisonous and should only be used under medical supervision. The plant has been known for its healing properties since Roman times. The volatile oils from the root are the most important medicinal substance from the plant. These are used to induce vomiting and to excite the kidneys. *Asarum* is also used to treat migraine. The root has to be used when fresh. Asarabacca grows in broad-leaved woodland in most European countries, having a preference for alkaline soil with ample humus. The plant has little light needed with its shiny evergreen foliage. The foliage is replaced in spring with new leaves. Barely noticeable small brown florets appear in April to May. The plant cannot be used as a culinary substitute for ginger *(Zingiber officinale)*.

♄

Asclepias curassavica

MILKWEED, SILKWEED

The milkweed is used in the Caribbean as a powerful expectorant. The use is not without its risks be-

Asarum europaeum, *wild ginger.*

Asclepias curassavica, *milkweed.*

cause of the substance asclepiadine contained in the plant. This highly toxic substance can cause muscle paralysis and even death through heart failure. *Asclepias curassavica* is sometimes offered as a container plant which bears yellow ochre to orange flowers on the ends of 100cm (39in) long stems. The plant is evergreen but cannot withstand temperatures below 10°C (50°F).

♄

Asclepias incarnata

MILKWEED, SILKWEED

A smelly milky sap is oozed from the roots of this plant that has healing properties in the right dose. This is used among other things to stimulate the heart in much the same way as digitalis from foxgloves. Depending on the level of the dose, the powdered root acts as a diuretic, serves as an expectorant, or treats worms. Medical supervision in its use is essential.

This milkweed originates from marshes in the USA. The perennial plant grows about 150cm (59in) tall and makes an ideal plant for flower borders, preferably in wet soil, such as by a pond. The flowers in summer smell of vanilla.

♄

Asclepias incarnata, *milkweed.*

Asclepias syriaca, *milkweed.*

Asclepias syriaca, *milkweed.*

Asclepias syriaca

MILKWEED

This American milkweed has the same healing power as the tuber rooted milkweed *(Asclepias tuberosa)*. The root provides a treatment for asthma among other disorders. The plant has been and still is cultivated on a large scale in the USA. The silken down of the seed plumes is so abundant that they are used as filling for cushions and the long fibres of the stems are used to make fine white rope. In Canada the young shoots are cooked in the same way as asparagus.

Asclepias syriaca is a fully hardy plant for the flower border that grows 200cm (79in) high. It prefers a sunny position in well drained soil.

 ✳

Asclepias tuberosa

PLEURISY ROOT, BUTTERFLY WEED

The vernacular name of *Asclepias tuberosa* of pleurisy root is derived from the use of decoctions of the plant for treatment of pleurisy. The plant is toxic.

The plant closely resembles *A. curassivica* but this can only be grown in northern Europe as a container plant. Pleurisy root can be tried in a sunny spot with well-drained soil but will probably not survive a hard and wet winter.

Asparagus officinalis

ASPARAGUS

The new shoots of garden asparagus *(Asparagus officinalis* ssp. *officinalis)* are on sale in greengrocers in the spring of each year but this sub species is different to the wild asparagus. The shoots are cut while they are still below ground so that they are pale and tender as people prefer them. More mature shoots are rather stringy.

Many people find that their urine has a strong smell after eating asparagus. This is caused by asparagin a diuretic but the odour only occurs with people who do not possess the gene to break it down.

Perhaps this experience with urine led to asparagus being used as a cleansing herb to shed liquid, get rid of worms, and as a laxative. Medicinally, asparagus or asparagusic acid is used to treat bladder and kidney complaints, rheumatism, arthritis, gout, oedama from heart failure, and schistosomiasis. Generally, the roots are used rather than the shoots but this differs from culture to culture. Some people suffer an allergic reaction to asparagus which causes a rash if they touch the plant. Internal use increases the allergic reaction.

Asparagus is a native plant throughout almost all of Europe, except the north, and grows as a 200cm (79in) tall perennial, mainly on open, sandy soils.

Asparagus officinalis ssp. officinalis, *cultivated asparagus.*

Asparagus officinalis, *wild asparagus.*

Asperula tinctoria, *dyer's woodruff.*

After the nondescript flowering, red berries with black seeds are formed on the female plants.

Asperula tinctoria

DYER'S WOODRUFF

The roots of this woodruff are used to create a red dye for colouring textile and wools. The stems of the plant support themselves in nature on grasses in coarse grassland or on branches of bushes, in which they can climb to about 100cm (39in) high. The plant bears small white flowers between June and September. The plant is a native of woodland and mountain sites in Europe and Asia but is threatened in many of its natural habitats.

Asplenium scolopendrium syn. Phyllitis scolopendrium, Scolopendrium vulgare

HART'S TONGUE FERN

The tongue-shaped foliage of this fern is evergreen and can be found right up into the colder reaches of Europe (except the north-east and higher mountains). The fern grows protected from drying winds in moist broad-leafed woodland, on rocky hills

Asplenium scolopendrium, *hart's tongue fern.*

Atriplex hortensis *var.* rubra.

and valleys, and in lowland areas, sheltering behind walls, around wells, and at quay-sides. The fern was once held to have supernatural powers. Those who sprinkled the seeds (or rather spores) in their tracks would instantly become invisible.
The hart's tongue fern was once a popular folk remedy but is little used today. Infusions are made for diarrhoea and dysentery, and the leaves are used to wrap burns. The fern is still used in homeopathy for diabetes.

Atriplex hortensis

RED MOUNTAIN SPINACH, RED ORACHE

Red mountain spinach or red orache originates from Asia but has been cultivated for so long in Europe and self-seeds so readily that it is widespread. The plant is cultivated as an annual and is popular as an ornamental plant in the form *Atriplex hortensis* var. *rubra*. The leaves can be eaten or cooked just like spinach but some may have an allergic reaction to the plant. The precise working of the substances in the plant is not entirely understood.
Back in the Middle Ages, the plant was prescribed for liver and lung ailments. The plant is used to purify the blood and also increases resistance to disease. Because of this it is sometimes used for infu-

sions for these purposes, particularly as a spring tonic.
The stems can be used to make a yellow dyestuff for textiles.

Atropa belladonna

DEADLY NIGHTSHADE, DWALE

Renaissance Italian ladies realised that cute animals always have large eyes, so to make themselves

Atropa belladonna, *deadly nightshade.*

Courtesy The Kruidenhof, Buitenpost.

more appealing, they put drops of deadly night-shade sap in their eyes. The sap contains the alkaloid, atropine, which dilates the pupils of the eyes. Hence the ladies could go to their balls as a "bella donna" or beautiful lady. Atropine is still used as drops by ophthalmologists when they need to examine the eye in detail.

The name *Atropa* is derived from the goddess of Greek mythology who determined one's lot or luck. Atropa cut the thread of life and became goddess of the dead. This name points to the deadly toxins of deadly nightshade. The plant contains a range of poisonous alkaloids, of which atropine is the best known. The berries above all are extremely dangerous because they do not taste bad. Eating just five berries can cause serious and even fatal consequences for children, although the sensitivity to the toxin varies from person to person. Animals too react in different ways to the toxins. Birds happily eat the berries without consequences and rabbits eat the foliage but cats and dogs are extremely susceptible to the poisons.

Once the plant was smeared on the skin as a sedative before operations. For its use as a salve against witches, see *Hyoscyamus niger.*

Deadly nightshade is still cultivated in order to produce medicines. These are particularly used for muscular cramp and tension, stomach, and intestinal cramp, and menstruation pains. There are also medicines for bronchial asthma and stomach ulcers but self-medication is life threatening, as is its use as "soul liberating narcotic". Ecstasy pills have been laced with atropine, making them even more dangerous because of severe hallucinations and panic. The plant is widespread throughout Europe, especially where trees have been felled and on marginal land.

 ✳

Avena sativa

OAT, GROATS

Oat is an annual cereal plant that is given to horses as fodder and eaten by humans as oatmeal. The

Avena sativa, *oat.*

Avena sativa, *oat.*

use of oats in medicine is less well known. Oat contains avenine which is used as a sedative for those with sleeping problems, anxiety, nervous tension, and bed-wetting but also for nervous tremors. Oat also helps to subdue cravings for those trying to break addiction to nicotine and other drugs.

Oats are also a healthy food containing many useful amino acids, alkaloids, glycosides, fixed oils, minerals, and trace elements. A decoction of chopped oat straw can be used in bath water for treatment of rheumatism and gout.

Atropa belladonna, *deadly nightshade.*

ℬ

Baptisia australis, *wild indigo.*

Ballota nigra *ssp.* foetida, *black horehound.*

Ballota nigra ssp. *foetida*

BLACK HOREHOUND

Cattle will not eat this foul-smelling horehound and therefore large clumps of the nettle-like plant can be found in pasture land. The plant originates from the countries surrounding the Mediterranean but it is now widespread in Europe. The plant flowers between May and October and it is this, together with its rounded, compact form (approx. 50cm/20in high), which makes *Ballota nigra* a not uncommon garden plant. It is unfortunate that the plant emits an unpleasant odour.

The herb was once widely used for its expectorant and cramp relieving properties. It is useful for sickness, vomiting, indigestion, and breathing difficulties. The herb is also used to treat those prone to hysteria.

Baptisia australis

FALSE INDIGO, WILD INDIGO

The native American Mohicans used the roots of *Baptisia* species to disinfect wounds. Subsequent

Baptisia australis, *wild indigo.*

Courtesy The Kruidhof, Buitenpost.

Courtesy The Kruidhof, Buitenpost.

research has proven that the plants do indeed possess substances which reduce infection. These substances from the roots increase resistance to bacterial infection, reduce fever, and in stronger doses induce vomiting. The leaves can be used to dye fabrics blue.

Baptisia australis is a perennial originating from the south of the United States (the Latin *australis* being used here merely to denote "southern", not Australian origins. The plant prefers fertile, rich in humus, moisture-retaining soil in sun or partial shade. Given these conditions, it will sometimes grow as tall as a man. Normally, plants grow to about 100cm (39in) and they flower in summer with blue, lupin-like blooms.

Baptisia tinctoria

WILD INDIGO, INDIGOWEED, RATTLEWEED

Wild indigo has been used to dye wool and textiles since ancient times. The leaves provide a blue dye that closely resembles indigo, leading to the use of indigo or false indigo in the common names. The roots are used medicinally as disinfectant and antiseptic (see *Baptisia australis*) but especially for

Baptisia tinctoria, *wild indigo*.

Baptisia tinctoria, *wild indigo*.

Courtesy The Kruidhof, Buitenpost.

treatment of typhoid, dysentery, malaria, cholera, and intestinal 'flu. Because of side-effects from using the herb medicinally, the herb is rarely used these days.

Wild indigo is a perennial that grows upwards and spreads outwards to about 100cm (39in). It originates from the northern parts of North America. It flowers from spring with arching clusters of yellow florets followed by blue-black pods.

Barbarea vulgaris

ST. BARBARA'S HERB

St. Barbara's herb smells of watercress and can be used as a culinary replacement. The leaves can be

Barbarea vulgaris, *St. Barbara's herb*.

Courtesy The Kruidhof, Buitenpost.

picked in the first summer after sowing and even during mild winters. The plant is rich in vitamin C and therefore a particular benefit for health during the dark winter months. The fresh leaves can be used to taste to flavour salads and with fish but the taste is fairly strong.

Barbarea vulgaris grows throughout Europe as a biennial or perennial on moist soil, arable, and pasture land, and alongside ditches. The plant can be sown from seed in spring, preferably in fertile soil that is rich in humus and moisture-retaining. In such soil, the plant will freely self seed.

Bellis perennis

COMMON DAISY

Daisies' yellow centres with white petals flower in grass from early spring. The flowers close-up towards evening and the undersides of the petals are almost always red. The plant used to be associated with warfare: they flowered on the grassy battle fields and were used to staunch bleeding wounds and the herb does indeed have an antiseptic property which helps wounds to heal.

Infusions of the flowers or leaves are purifying and diuretic and therefore good for arthritis, gout, acne, and other skin complaints. Such infusions stimulate the function of the gall bladder and increases the appetite.

Daisies are regarded as weeds by some and doggedly removed from lawns but others regard the yellow and white flowers as cheerful. Children have long made daisy chains and although their stems are too short for vases, they can be used to decorate a dish.

Bellis perennis, *common daisy.*

Berberis vulgaris

COMMON BARBERRY

The common barberry is a native shrub in most European countries but is generally more readily found in gardens. The viciously thorny bush is almost impenetrable and has few demands in cultivation. The shrub is covered in spring with clusters of yellow flowers and these are succeeded by elongated berries which turn bright red in autumn. Every part of the shrub except the berries is moderately toxic. The outer part of the roots in particular contain a high concentration of the alkaloid berberine.

The ripe berries can be readily made into a sharp-tasting conserve or sweetened by the addition of

Bellis perennis, common daisy.

Berberis vulgaris, *common barberry.*

Berberis vulgaris, *common barberry.*

Betula pubescens, *downy birch.*

other fruit. This conserve stimulates the appetite and can help women to prevent miscarriage.

Infusions of the leaf and outer "bark" of the roots are diuretic and purifying and can be prescribed for liver and gall bladder ailments. The herb should only be used under medical supervision. In homeopathy, *Berberis vulgaris* is prescribed for colic of the gall bladder and kidneys, haemorrhoid, and rheumatic joints. The outer root is used to made a yellow dye for wool and textiles.

Betula

BIRCH

Downy or white birch and silver birch are quite difficult to tell apart especially as they cross with each other and there are consequently many of their hybrids. Generally, the branches of silver birch hang down more than those of white birch and this latter species thrives best in marshy places.

Both species of birch can be used as herb in the same way. The best known is the tapping of the sap. The sap stream starts to flow in December and in early spring (March–April) will pour out of any wound. Large cuts at this time must be avoided or the tree will bleed to death. By boring a small hole of 1cm ($^3/_8$in) diameter and inserting an appropriate tube, the sap can be tapped and used for mainly cosmetic purposes, such as against greasy hair, or to get rid of dandruff or stem hair loss.

Young birch leaves make a mild and purifying infusion, much used for spring tonics. The infusion is diuretic and aids bladder and kidney problems and rheumatism and gout. The leaves are also used to make a yellow dye for fabric and wool.

Betula pendula, *silver birch.*

Borago officinalis, *borage.*

Borago officinalis, *borage.*

Borago officinalis

BORAGE

Even if we had forgotten the value of borage, the plant would still be important. The blue flowers produce an abundance of nectar which attracts hosts of bees. Humans also find borage a delicacy. The flowers detach easily from the plant and can be added to salads as an edible garnish and flavouring or frozen in cubes of ice.

Tender new leaves can be finely chopped and added to salads or strewn in soups just before serving. The taste is of fresh cucumber. Stems that are sliced in half lengthways or are crushed add the same flavour to drinks. The taste is lost in cooking and drying of this watery plant is not possible.

Medicinally, it is mainly the new shoots of the herb before flowering that are used when fresh to make infusions or chopped finely and added to milk. The plant has long been regarded for its ability to lift the spirits. It is an anti-depressant that prevents palpitations and strengthens the heart beat. The herb is used for these purposes in homeopathic medicine.

There are a number of varieties of the species, such as *Borago officinalis* 'Alba' with white flowers and *B. o.* 'Variegata' with yellow markings on the leaves.

Borago originates from the countries surrounding the Mediterranean but has become naturalised fur-

Borago officinalis *'Alba'.*

Borago officinalis *'Variegata'.*

ther afield through escape from cultivation. Where conditions are right, borage will self-seed on a massive scale, especially in gardens. The seedlings, which germinate in late summer, can withstand severe frosts and will survive most winters to flower in May. The seed can be sown early in spring in moisture-retaining soil for flowering from the end of June until autumn.

Ⴟ ‖ ✳

Botrychium lunaria

MOONWORT

Moonwort is a secretive fern that only shows itself above ground in late spring. Just the one "leaf" is formed and one spore-bearing plume each year. The "leaf" is fringed with a double "beard" and series of half-moons that resemble an old-fashioned key. People used to believe the fern capable of opening locks and pulling the horseshoes off a horse's hooves if it trod on the plant.
Horse's have nothing to fear from the fern because is only grows about 10cm (4in) high and is always surrounded by other low plants. Moonwort is quite rare and found mainly in dry upland pastures and on rock ledges.

Botrychium lunaria, *moonwort.*

Legend has it that the moonwort was much favoured by witches and others who practised black magic. The fern had to be gathered by moonlight when it possessed its magical powers. In folk medicine the fern was widely used to treat wounds and particularly internal haemorrhages.

Ⴟ

Brassica nigra, *black mustard.*

Courtesy The Kruidhof, Buitenpost.

Brassica nigra

BLACK MUSTARD

Mustard used to flavour food is prepared from both white and black mustard seeds which are soaked in vinegar for twenty-four hours before grinding. The resulting sauce is very pungent and widely used with savoury dishes.
Crushed mustard seed soaked in water stimulates supply of blood to the skin and is applied to the skin with a compress for rheumatism, slipped disc, gout, pneumonia, and bronchitis. Do not leave the mustard on the skin too long (no longer than three minutes with children) because mustard contains a skin irritant that can cause blisters.
Brassica nigra originates from around the Mediterranean but escaped from cultivation in more northern countries where it is grown for oil and mustard. The plant is an annual and grows about 100cm (39in) high.

Ⴟ ‖

Brassica nigra, *black mustard.*

Brugmansia arborea

ANGELS' TRUMPETS

The Amerindians of South America were told if they sat under an angels' trumpets to stay alert, for they would see an eagle fly over them and then disappear. The plant originates from that part of the world but can be grown in Europe as a container plant if kept protected from frost. Anyone who grows one of these plants with their large flowers and heady sweet perfume can well imagine those stories. The perfume can cause headaches.

The plant contains very poisonous alkaloids such as atropine, hyoscyamine, and scopolamine. The last of these causes hallucinations for anyone who ingests the plant. The Amerindians use the plant to go into a trance to put them in touch with the spirit world.

But it is an unpleasant and dangerous trip because

Brugmansia arborea, *angels' trumpets.*

of the harmful side effects of the toxic substances. *Brugmansia aurea, B. sanguinea, B. suaveolens,* and *B. versicolor* and their hybrids have similar properties.

✳

Bryonia cretica, *white bryony.*

Bryonia cretica

WHITE BRYONY

The corkscrew-like ranks of white bryony grasp hold of anything in order that their stems can climb high into hedges and bushes. The native plant bears white flowers from June and these are succeeded in autumn on the female plants by poisonous reddish-orange berries. The thick root ball is used medicinally as a powerful laxative, for pleurisy, rheumatism, and gout. Because of the plant's toxicity, very precisely determined doses are essential and treatment with the plant can have unpleasant side effects, which is why white bryony is rarely prescribed these days. In homeopathy though *Bryonia* is an important treatment for influenza, fever, inner ear infection, and also for bronchitis, arthritis, ruptures, pre-menstrual tension, headache, and migraine.

Buxus sempervirens

COMMON BOX

This well-known evergreen shrub which is commonly grown as a hedge, in particular low partitioning for herb gardens, is also an active herb. Both the leaf and bark provide a substance used to bring down high temperatures such as malaria attacks, to deaden rheumatic aches, taken as a laxative, and to kill intestinal parasites. For all this, box is rarely used medicinally because of its extreme toxicity which in high doses can even prove fatal. In homeopathic medicine though it is not dangerous and is used for rheumatism and a hair-growth tonic. The leaves produce a red dyestuff.

Buxus sempervirens, *common box.*

Studying herbs at the herb garden at the Netherlands Open Air Museum, Arnhem.

C

Calamintha nepeta *ssp.* nepeta, *lesser calamint.*

Calamintha nepeta, *lesser calamint.*

Courtesy Netherlands Open Air Museum, Arnhem.

Calamintha nepeta syn. *C. nepetoides, Satureja nepeta*

LESSER CALAMINT

The various types of calamint grow mainly in the warmer parts of Europe, preferring dry, lime-rich rocky habitats. Outside these natural growing areas, calamint is cultivated as a herb and ornamental plant and some have escaped from cultivation to become naturalised. This herb was already highly regarded around the birth of Christ, when it was reputed to drive off snakes, cure jaundice and leprosy, and lift the spirits. The delightful scent certainly banishes melancholia but the other uses of the herb are no longer recognised. The plant's wonderful scent is of mint. Nowadays, the herb is mainly used for infusions to relieve cramp and calamint tea is considered to be useful to treat indigestion and stomach cramps, even when these are caused by nervous tension. It is also used for depression and period pains. Both the leaf and twigs are used as a culinary herb, specially for meat dishes. Pregnant women are advised not to take the herb in any form.

Calamintha nepeta ssp. *nepeta*

LESSER CALAMINT

The binomial designations of the calamints is not transparent, with botanists making regular changes and introducing new names. This has led to tremendous confusion. The sub species *Calamintha nepeta* ssp. *nepeta* bears more axillary flower cymes per stem but otherwise is identical to the main species. For uses, see *Calamintha nepeta.*

Calamintha sylvatica syn. *C. ascendens, C. officinalis*

COMMON CALAMINT

The pale lilac flowers of this species, of which the *sylvatica* name means "of the woods," are flecked with darker pink to purple. They flower closer to the stem, so that the growth is more compact. The young shoots and leaves are added to game. For further culinary and medicinal uses, see *Calamintha nepeta.*

Calamintha sylvatica, *common calamint.*

Calamintha sylvatica ssp. *ascendens*

GREATER CALAMINT

The greater or climbing calamint is particularly distinguished by the downy hairs of the stems. The leaves are dark green and they appear more succulent than the woody impression of *Calamintha nepeta.* The scent and flavour of this species is less pronounced than with *C. nepeta.* The northern boundary of this species is Britain, Belgium, and more rarely, in Germany.

♀ ‖

Calendula arvensis

FIELD MARIGOLD

The field marigold is in every way smaller than the well-known garden marigold and also a lighter colour: yellow ochre to pale orange. The field marigold can be used in much the same way as the marigold (see *Calendula officinalis).* The recognised herb sort *(officinalis* indicates a useful herb) is more widely used, not least because it contains more oil. The field marigold does have the additional value of a substance that helps to reduce blood pressure.

♀ / ‖

Calamintha sylvatica *ssp.* ascendens, *greater calamint.*

Calendula arvensis, *field marigold.*

Calendula officinalis, *marigold.*

Calendula officinalis

MARIGOLD

The common or garden marigold has an important role in the prevention of illness in painters, carpet layers, printers, and others who work regularly with solutions refined from oil. These people run the risk of permanent damage to the brain and central nervous system, with difficulty to concentrate being one of the major symptoms. The oil in marigold seeds are used to create a "reactive solution" which oxidises on contact with the air, thereby preventing harmful vapours being released. This oil is also an excellent substitute for the scarce turpentine oil. Fields are likely to be filled with the orange of marigolds in the near future. The plants also grow well in soils that are low in nitrogen.

The plant thrives too quite happily in the garden in poor soil, provided its position is sunny. Marigolds self seed themselves readily under these circumstances.

Marigold has been in use for centuries, with people dyeing their hair yellow with it in the sixteenth century. Today, marigold is a food colouring for rice, soup, butter, and cheese. The wilted flowers are used to dye textiles and wool matt yellow.

Infusions of the flowers and decoctions of marigold leaves have a wide range of medicinal uses. *Calendula* has a purifying effect and is particularly used to deal with fungal infections, bacteria, and viruses. The herb is antiseptic, healing wounds, treating eczema, and inflammation of the

Calendula officinalis, *marigold.*

skin, ears, eyes, and gums. Some people also maintain it is useful for treating skin cancer. Blood purifying infusions of marigold relieve period pains, and complaints associated with child birth. A cream of marigold is smeared on the belly for stomach ache.

The leaves of marigold are ideal as a garnish with various dishes.

Caltha palustris, *kingcup.*

Caltha palustris, *kingcup.*

Caltha palustris

KINGCUP, MARSH MARIGOLD

The buds of the kingcup or marsh marigold used to be picked before they flowered in April. The buds were placed in salted vinegar and used instead of capers, while the young leaves were added to salads. Excessive consumption however, led to instances of poisoning which caused people to appreciate that the plant is slightly toxic. The main irritant in the herb is the volatile oil protoanemonine, which disappears when the plant is dried.

It is not advisable to use the fresh plant for either culinary or medicinal use. *Caltha palustris* is used in homeopathic medicine for whooping cough, infections of the mucous membrane in the bronchi, and skin rashes.

Kingcup is a perennial plant which grows on water margins (especially at the sides of streams and marshes). The yellow flowers, which resemble large buttercups, open in April to May.

Calystegia sepium

HEDGE BINDWEED, BELLBINE, CONVOLVULUS

Hedge bindweed can easily climb 15m (50ft) with its winding stems. The plant readily seeds itself in moist

Calystegia sepium, *hedge bindweed.*

hedges and at the foot of bushes to develop rampant growth. The large white flowers open in June and remain until early in autumn. The flowers are attractive but not welcomed in the garden because once established, it is almost impossible to get rid of. The plant is sometimes cut and dried to make an infusion with strong laxative properties, or decoctions of the roots are used for the same purpose. Infusions are also used in a compress to hasten healing in slow to heal wounds but because of potentially drastic side-effects, self medication is inadvisable.

Camellia sinensis, *tea.*

Cannabis sativa, *hemp or marijuana.*

Courtesy The Kruidhof, Buitenpost.

Camellia sinensis syn. *Thea sinensis*

TEA

Tea has been cultivated for so long that it is difficult to be certain where the plant originated. Most consider this was western China. Tea has been one of the most important herbs since prehistoric times in China and Japan. The young leaves are steamed and then dried: this is then known as green tea. Decoctions of green tea revitalise, aid digestion, and reduce tooth decay. Moistened leaves or a wet compress of tea help to prevent itching and reduce infections in grazes and reduce irritation from insect bites.

Tea only became known to Europeans in the seventeenth century and the herbal drink became very fashionable, so that many cool hilly areas in the sub-tropics are used for wide scale cultivation of the tea bush. The plant prefers cool and pure air, but not frost, with ample moisture. Tea was once only picked by hand, leaf-for-leaf, with only the new young leaves being suitable but in many areas to bushes are clipped to produce cheaper tea.

Europeans mainly drink black tea. The leaves are allowed to ferment before drying. Black tea is more bitter, contains more tannin, and has stronger and more concentrated active constituents. Strong black tea helps treat diarrhoea. Tannin also has disadvantages, increasing the risk of oesophageal cancer but this can be neutralised by drinking a little milk with tea.

Cannabis sativa

HEMP, MARIJUANA, MARIHUANA, HASHEESH

Hemp is the most controversial of all herbs. Glandular hairs on the tops of plants (especially with female plants just before flowering) discharge a resin, also known as hashish, which contains hallucinogenic substances and makes the user mildly befuddled. Images are formed in the mind in quick tempo but in no logical sequence. The user can become excited and speak gibberish, but does not become aggressive. Marijuana is not addictive.

Most experts consider that marijuana is not any more harmful than alcohol but in spite of this, *Cannabis* products are banned in almost every western nation. This has led to a double standard in many countries, where the authorities do little or nothing to prevent its use while international trade is actively fought because of the criminality that flows from the illegality of cannabis.

Because of this illegality, a sub-culture has grown up surrounding the use of *Cannabis* with its own slang: hashish is termed "stuff" or "shit". The term "weed" refers to the dried tops of the plant, while "kif" is lower quality hashish.

The use of *Cannabis* is not a modern phenomenon: the Chinese Emperor Shen-Nung wrote about it in 2737 BC. The plant was used as a stupefying incense, the seeds were eaten for their nutrition, and the fibres from the stems were used to make ropes. Hemp is still a valuable economic fibre for rope. A special type was cultivated which grows to 6m (20ft) in one year and it can also be used as a

Cannabis sativa, *hemp or marijuana.*

Capsella bursa-pastoris, *shepherd's purse.*

Capsella bursa-pastoris, *shepherd's purse.*

windbreak. Another variety was developed for the seeds: bird food often contains hemp seeds.

Medicinally the plant was deemed very important until it was banned. Marijuana is an extremely effective treatment for queasiness, particularly for use with cancer patients undergoing chemotherapy. Pressure has been growing on governments to at least permit the controlled medical use of *Cannabis sativa.*

☤ ✳

Capsella bursa-pastoris syn. *Thlaspi bursa-pastoris*

SHEPHERD'S PURSE, WITCHES' POUCHES, PICK-POCKET

Shepherd's purse can be found growing almost everywhere as an inconspicuous weed. Flowering stems spring from the leaf rosette with miniscule white flowers. The leaf is at its most tasty in the spring when it makes a mellow addition to salads.

Shepherd's purse is important medicinally in stopping bleeding, and is particularly used to stem bleeding of the uterus but because the active constituents vary from plant to plant, other means are now more widely used. Herbal tea (often in combination with other herbs) is still widely used to purify the blood and for its beneficial effect on blood pressure, blood circulation, heart stimulation, urinary and bladder infections, period pains, and induces shorter child labour. Because of this last property, the herb must not be used during pregnancy.

Capsicum annuum

SWEET PEPPER, BELL PEPPER, CHILLI PEPPER, PAPRIKA, CAPSICUM, PIMENTO, CAYENNE PEPPER

Peppers (red, green, yellow) and chilli peppers are cultivated varieties of the same species, which once grew in tropical America but no longer grows wild. After its discovery in the Americas, the Spanish brought several cultivated forms, that had been developed by the indigenous population, to Europe. These plants were considered as the greatest of treasure after gold and were widely eaten in southern Europe but in recent decades, these plants have increasingly found their way into the cuisine of northern Europe.

Depending on the cultivar, peppers are sweet, pungent, or extremely pungent. The sweet varieties, known as peppers, paprika, pimento, or capsicum are used as a vegetable but the cayenne or chilli peppers are only used to spice dishes. *Capsicum* is a very healthy plant because it is rich in vitamins

Capsicum annuum, *pepper.*

Capsicum annuum, *pepper.*

76

(especially vitamin C). The plant also acts as a tonic, awakes the appetite, aids digestion, acts as a diuretic and antiseptic (especially for inner ear infections or mastoiditis). The herb is used externally in a compress to treat rheumatism and gout.

Grow the plant as an annual in a warm, sunny position (preferably in a greenhouse), in fertile soil that retains moisture without becoming waterlogged. The plant grows about 150cm (5ft). Cultivation is similar to growing tomato plants but peppers need slightly more warmth.

♀ ⚕

Carica papaya

PAWPAW, PAPAYA

The pawpaw or papaya is so soft that it is difficult to transport over long distances. Because of this they are rarely seen on fruit stalls outside their natural growing areas but travellers to places where it never freezes, such as the Canary Islands and places further afield will certainly enjoy the tender flesh of this fruit. The foliage and fruit grows at the top of fibrous trunks that become steadily taller, reaching 8m (26ft) high. Only the female plants bear the fruits which can be 30cm (12in) or longer and weigh 3–4kg (6lb 10oz–8lb 13oz) each. The fruits have pinkish red flesh. The white milky sap of

Carica papaya, *pawpaw or papaya.*

Carica papaya, *pawpaw or papaya.*

the plant, found predominantly in the leaves and unripe fruits, is used medicinally. It contains an enzyme, papain. Apply a little of the sap to a burn as quickly as possible to prevent blisters forming. All manner of uses were previously prescribed for the sap including the reduction of cancerous tumours. Today the claims have been moderated but papain still has many uses: the enzyme stimulates digestion, especially the conversion of proteins, and helps to prevent worms. Its external application helps to heal deep wounds.

The Amerindians knew of these properties and tenderised meat by wrapping it in papaya leaves.

Carthamus tinctorius, *safflower.*

Papain is also used to clarify beer, to coagulate milk, and in the production of chewing gum.

₹ ‖ *

Carthamus tinctorius

SAFFLOWER, SAFFRON THISTLE, FALSE SAFFRON

Many women over the ages will have made themselves up with safflower without knowing it because it is incorporated with talcum powder to make rouge. Not that this need cause women any concern, since safflower contains substances that heal skin inflammation.

Safflower is used for heart and coronary artery disease and these can be safely and tastily prevented by cooking with safflower oil which helps to reduce cholesterol. Pregnant women are advised not to use safflower internally.

The colour from the flowers has been used since the ancient Egyptians to dye clothes and is still used to dye the robes of Buddhist monks. The plant is still widely used to dye textiles, silk, and decorative feathers red, pink, or yellow and is also a widely used food colouring.

₹ / ‖ ☕●

Carum carvi

CARAWAY

The soft leaves of caraway are added to salads and also, just before serving, to soups and sauces. The seeds, containing volatile oils with the aroma carvone, are used to impart a strong flavour to potato and cabbage dishes but also sprinkled on bread and cakes, and provide the flavour in kümmel liqueur.

Carum carvi is prescribed for digestive problems above all, including wind, stomach cramp, and period pains. Carvone appears to slow germination of potatoes that are stored and they prevent scabs forming when potatoes are damaged. Caraway probably originated from the cooler parts of Europe and Asia, where it still thrives best, also having a preference for alkaline clay soil. The plant is grown as a biennial that stays so low in its first year that farmers plant another annual crop alongside it which is then harvested, leaving the caraway to grow on. After flowering in the second year in May to June, the seeds are harvested in July to August.

₹ ▲ ‖ *

Carum carvi, *caraway.*

Carum carvi, *caraway.*

Castanea sativa, *sweet chestnut.*

London during the winter. The nuts can be eaten boiled or roasted as a snack or vegetable and used in sauces, soups, and stuffings.

The sweet chestnut was brought north of the Alps by the Romans because of its importance as food and medicine. The strong tree can grow to an old age. The elongated, lobed leaves becomes yellow in autumn and it is about this time that the chestnuts are ripe. They fall from the tree in their extremely prickly outer shells. These outer shells can be used to make a dye for colouring textiles and wool brown-bronze or even beige.

Castanea sativa

SWEET CHESTNUT, SPANISH CHESTNUT

The leaves of the sweet chestnut reduce spasms and disinfect. For this reason, it was used to treat fever, specially, bouts of malaria. The substances in the leaf have a concentrated action which stems both diarrhoea and internal haemorrhages.

Chestnuts themselves are a tonic for those feeling out of sorts or suffering from a cold, so it is not surprising that traders in hot chestnuts do good business in the streets of major cities such as

Catha edulis

KHAT

In Somalia, Ethiopia, Djibouti, and the opposite side of the Red Sea in Arabian Yemen, khat is the most important stimulant. In Yemen, life almost ceases after midday, when the adult inhabitants start to chew the leaves of the khat tree. The substances in the leaves have a mild stupefying effect, making the user feel calm and relaxed; hunger and anxiety disappear.

Khat has never become popular outside the area

Catha edulis, *khat.*

Catha edulis, *khat.*

where it grows because the active constituents in the leaves are only available when the leaves are fresh. The leaves are picked fresh each day and can be kept for about one day if wrapped in cool, moist banana leaves. Khat has recently arrived in Europe, being flown in by aircraft to groups of Somalian and Ethiopian refugees who eagerly await the mild legal narcotic at airports in order to sample again a taste from their home land.

In its countries of origin, *Catha* is used medicinally to treat coughs and asthma. The low tree with its arching branches will only grows where there is no frost.

Catharanthus roseus syn. *Vinca rosea*

MADAGASCAR PERIWINKLE, ROSY PERIWINKLE, CAYENNE JASMINE

The Madagascar or rosy periwinkle contains a cocktail of toxic alkaloids. The leaf of this plant is sometimes smoked in the USA. The narcotic substance has a spiritually uplifting but also harmful effect. *Catharanthus* contains substances which inhibit the division of cells (cytostatica) but those who use the substance for "fun" undermine their immune system.

This same cyostatica effect is important in preventing unwanted cell growth and is an important treatment for cancer, in particular for leukaemia and Hodgkin's disease. The plant had been used in folk medicine for centuries to treat diabetes, high blood pressure, constipation, asthma, and men-

struation problems. It should only be used under medical supervision.

The plant originates from Madagascar but grows rampantly as a weed in many tropical lands. It can be grown in northern Europe as an ornamental container or pot annual and is often sold under the old name of *Vinca rosea*. The minimum temperature that the plant can withstand if 12°C (53°F).

Centaurium erythraea syn. *Erythraea centaurium*

CENTAURY, FEVERWORT

Centaury improves the appetite, quells fevers, and aids the digestion. The herb, minus the roots, is picked just before or during flowering and then dried in order to make infusions. Infusions of the herb also help in treatment of jaundice and liver and gall bladder complaints.

In homeopathic medicine, centaury stimulates production of gastric juices and the appetite. Pregnant women should only use the herb in homeopathic doses.

The plant grows as a biennial, mainly in an open position in moisture-retaining soil. A short flowering stem rises in summer from the leaf rosette. The delicate pink flowers only open when the sun shines. In those areas where centaury is rare, it is best not to collect the plant. The seed germinates well in almost any garden soil.

Calaranthus roseus, *Madagascar or rosy periwinkle.*

Centaurium erythraea, *centaury.*

Centranthus ruber, *a white form of valerian.*

Centranthus ruber, *red valerian.*

Centranthus ruber

RED VALERIAN

The French like to put the roots of red valerian in soups and in some countries, the leaves are added to salads but any medicinal properties the plant is deemed to have are probably due to confusion with valerian *(Valeriana officinalis)*. That plant calms the nerves but red valerian does not have these properties.

Centranthus originated in the lands around the Mediterranean and was brought north as an ornamental plant. In areas with a mild climate, such as southern England, red valerian has become naturalised, clinging to walls in sunny spots. The colour of the flowers varies from red to pure white.

Chamaemelum nobile syn. *Anthemis nobilis*

CHAMOMILE, ROMAN CHAMOMILE

Chamomile heals other plants. If chamomile is placed next to an ailing plant it will perk up before your eyes. Cut flowers too benefit from the proper-

Chamaemelum nobile, chamomile.

garden soil that is not waterlogged. The yellow and white flowers appear in summer.

♄ 🜩 ⚔ 🍶 ✳

Chamaemelum nobile 'Flore Pleno'

Numerous cultivars have been selected from *C. nobile* for their different characteristics. *Chamaemelum nobile* 'Flore Pleno' is a cultivar with double button-like flowerheads in which the fertile button of the species is changed to a sterile floret. The characteristic is only retained through propagation by cuttings.

Chamaemelum nobile 'Treneague'

Chamomile was used to sit on from the Middle Ages. Turfs were piled up to form a bench and then planted with chamomile which covered the turfs entirely. When people sat on the chamomile, a wonderful apple scent was released. "This lifts the spirits and heals the body," was written in ancient herbals.

Chamaemelum nobile 'Flore Pleno.'

ties of this plant. Add some infusion of chamomile in the water with the flowers and they will stay fresh looking longer.

Chamomile or Roman chamomile and wild or German chamomile have very similar properties and effects. They are among the most important of herbs, used since ancient times for much the same purposes. The tasty chamomile tea is an effective sedative, useful for sleeplessness and nightmares. The herb relaxes cramped muscles and is therefore widely prescribed for constipation, stress, colic, and period pains. It calms hyperactive children.

Chamomile oil is one of the important volatile oils and dried flowers are used in pot-pourris. The oil, or decoction of the flowers, is added to water for both a rejuvenating but also relaxing bath. Steam inhalations with the plant help to open blocked airways and to relax the skin.

Infusions used in compresses soften scabs, soothe and help to heal wounds, and treat eczema.

Decoctions of chamomile are also used to lighten and strengthen blond hair.

Pregnant women are advised not to use chamomile and some people are allergic to the sap of the plant which can cause irritation and a rash.

Chamomile grows as a perennial in clumps that grow no higher than 40cm (16in). It grows in any

Chamaemelum nobile *'Treneague.'*

Chelidonium majus, *greater celandine.*

Chamaemelum nobile *'Treneague.'*

This cultivar remains low and roots where its recumbent stems touched the ground providing a mat of ground cover that can be used to form a lawn, which releases the wonderful apple scent when trodden on and while mowing. Chamomile cannot withstand constant foot traffic or competition from weeds, so requires regular maintenance.

Chelidonium majus

GREATER CELANDINE, SWALLOW WORT, TETTERWORT

If the stems or leaf stalks of greater celandine are broken, a drop of bright orange sap is released with which it is possible to write on your skin; but what is written cannot easily be removed. The sap contains slightly toxic substances that do not penetrate the skin but will irritate the mucous membranes if taken internally.

Fresh sap, or a tincture was once daubed on warts to hamper cell growth but for as many miracle cures of warts that were recorded, there were as many cases where nothing happened. Warts do disappear spontaneously of course but the sap does have bactericidal properties.

The highest concentrations of the active substances are contained in the roots and these are used both for folk medicine and homoeopathically to reduce cramp and for inflammation of the gall bladder. Infusions of greater celandine are used for gall bladder, stomach, and intestinal disorders but should not be used during pregnancy.

The entire plant can be used to create a golden yellow dye for textile and wools.

The perennial plant grows wild on the edges of woods and close to bushes in good, moisture-retaining soil. Because of the lengthy period of flowering from May to October, the plant is ideal for the "natural looking" garden. Greater celandine self-sows itself profusely with the help of ants which carry the seeds.

Chelidonium majus, *greater celandine.*

Chenopodium ambrosioides *var.* anthelminticum, *wormseed*

Chenopodium ambrosioides *var.* anthelminticum, *wormseed.*

Chenopodium ambrosioides var. anthelminticum

WORMSEED, MEXICAN TEA

When Europeans arrived in North America, they noticed that the indigenous population chewed the leaves and seeds of the native variety of goosefoot plant, which became known as wormseed. The plant contains very active substances that destroys intestinal parasites and *Chenopodium* oil is widely used for this purpose. The parasites are stunned by the substance and then flushed from the system about two hours later using a purgative.

Only use *Chenopodium* oil under medical supervision because too much can have serious consequences and there have been numerous fatal accidents.

The herb is widely used in veterinary medicine to treat intestinal parasites in pigs.

☤ ✳

Chenopodium bonus-henricus

GOOD KING HENRY

The leaves of good King Henry are rich in iron, vitamins, and iron. The plant is a forgotten vegetable which disappeared together with the big estates. Previously, the gardeners cultivated the plant by sowing its seed in spring. The plant was then left to grow for a year and the following year the shoots

Chenopodium bonus-henricus, *good King Henry.*

Courtesy The Kruidhof, Buitenpost.

of the new growth were blanched by earthing up or covering with a pot. The blanched shoots were prepared just like spinach or steamed until tender. The arrival in the west of stir-fry has seen a revival in the vegetable's use. The young leaves are ideal for brief cooking in a wok, which also retains the health-giving properties. Leaves can also be add raw to salads.

Good King Henry is a wild plant of fertile, moisture-retaining soil, preferring alkaline clay soil or good loam. The medium height plant self seeds itself vigorously in gardens.

Chrysanthemum segetum

CORN MARIGOLD

Once the golden appearance of corn might not have been due to the ripe ears but the corn marigolds growing between them. The plant originates from the warm region surrounding the Mediterranean but it found the fertile arable soils of northern Europe an excellent habitat. The plant became a noxious weed for farmers and in some countries farmers faced fines to encourage them to get rid of the "nuisance". This was so successful that it is now a rare sight to see a corn marigold amidst crops. Today, one has to seek them on fertile verges or uncultivated patches of good but fairly dry soil. Corn marigolds can also be found growing as annual bedding in gardens, where they flower right through until late summer.

Corn marigold has long been considered one of the best sources of yellow dye for wool and textiles.

/

Cichorium intybus

CHICORY, SUCCORY

Chicory or endive is a cultivated form of the wild chicory which is the ancestor of this vegetable that is popular in continental Europe. The original species grows as a perennial to 200cm (79in) high in verges and open places. The purple to sky blue flowers only open in the morning on fine days, between July and October.

The roots are baked and can be used as a replacement for coffee, albeit with a somewhat bitter taste. Results are better when blended with real coffee and this also neutralises the adverse effects of sleeplessness and nervousness that coffee can cause.

Leaves of wild chicory collected in spring form a pungent addition to salads and the flowers can be uses to garnish dishes. The flowers are edible but have a rather bitter taste.

Chrysanthemum segetum, *corn marigold.*

Cichorium intybus, *chicory.*

Courtesy The Kruidhof, Buitenpost.

The plant, flowers, and infusion of the dried root stimulate the appetite and purify the blood. They are taken as preventive medicine for thrombosis, rheumatism, gout, and liver complaints.

꿁 ꞁꞁ ✳

Cimicifuga racemosa

BLACK COHOSH, COHOSH BUGBANE, BLACK SNAKEROOT

The native Americans called this bugbane "squaw-root" because they dug up the roots in late autumn to make medicine to relieve menstruation and labour pains. Today, decoctions of the root are used for the same purposes and black cohosh appears to be the most useful plant for easing post delivery problems for women. Several hours after use of the homeopathic remedy *Famosan* most women find that the flushes cease, while associated post partum problems such as tiredness, nervous headache, depression, restlessness, and rheumatic pains are eased.

The black cohosh originates in North America. It is grown elsewhere as a stately perennial of up to 200cm (79in) high, with elongated flowering racemes in late summer.

꿁

Cimicifuga racemosa, *black cohosh.*

Cinnamomum camphora, *camphor tree.*

Cinnamomum camphora syn. Laurus camphora

CAMPHOR

By steaming the wood of the camphor tree, camphor is released. The substance is well-known for its use in mothballs to deter moths. There were also stories that camphor was added to soldier's food to reduce their appetite for sex.

Camphor was once widely used to strengthen the working of the heart and nervous system and as a disinfecting cough medicine but because of its toxicity, it is now rarely used internally. Camphor oil spirit is used externally for muscular aches, camphorated oil relieves rheumatism, and salve of camphor prevents and treats chilblains. In China and Japan, where the camphor tree grows naturally, it can reach 40m (130ft). In northern Europe the evergreen tree has to be grown as a pot plant.

꿁 ✳

Cistus laurifolius

ROCK ROSE, SUN ROSE

Cistus shrubs help to protect whales because a comparable oleo-resin to the strong-smelling wax-like intestinal secretion, known as ambergris, that

Cistus laurifolius, *rock rose.*

Cistus ladanifer, *rock rose.*

was harvested from sperm whales for the perfume industry can be derived from these plants. The substance is known as ladanum or labdanum. The resin is harvested from the rock rose, removing one more reason for hunting whales.

Harvesting the ladanum excreted by the shrubs used to be a by-product of keeping sheep because when the sheep grazed between the bushes of rock rose, the resin adhered to their fleeces. Shepherds combed the fleece to remove the resin. Today, leaves are steamed to harvest the resin.

Cistus laurifolius mainly grows on the Iberian peninsula where the low evergreen bush has sticky branches on which, in summer, it bears 5cm (2in) wide white flowers with a yellow centre. Grown on well drained, well-worked soil, the shrub will survive frosts to -18°C (- 0.4°F).

For medicinal properties, see *Cistus ladanifer.*

Cistus ladanifer

ROCK ROSE, SUN ROSE

The sticky branches of *Cistus ladanifer,* which is a native of the south-western parts of the Mediterranean, are a source of the oleo-resin ladanum (see *Cistus laurifolius).* The substance acts as an expectorant and is also used to treat infections of the mucous membranes, diarrhoea, and dysentery. The leaves are placed on wounds to disinfect them and stem bleeding. *Cistus ladanifer* originates from south-west Europe and can be grown in mild climates as an ornamental shrub for the large white flowers with a maroon basal blotch on each. Planted in a well-sheltered, dry, sunny position, the shrub can withstand -18°C (- 0.4°F).

Citrus limon

LEMON

Lemon is a very well-known fruit that is rarely eaten, instead being used as a bitter and sour flavour-

Citrus limon, *lemon.*

ing and as garnish. Lemon before a meal stimulates the appetite, which is why slices of lemon are added to cocktails, mineral water, and tonic. During a meal, lemon neutralises fat and oil in a dish and is therefore widely used in fish dishes. The fat neutralising effect can be readily seen if finger bowls with lemon water are used. Lemon after a meal aids the digestion of fat in the food.

The fresh scent of the volatile lemon oil is widely used in countless cosmetic and cleaning products.

The principal medicinal use of lemon is as a drink, often with sugar or honey, against colds. If a slice of lemon is pressed against an insect bite, the swelling will be eased.

Lemon trees can only withstand temperatures down to 5°C (41°F) so that they are grown as container plants in harsher climates. The plant can be kept manageable by pruning. The white blossoms have a wonderful sweet scent. To ensure fruiting following the blossom, special varieties developed for cooler climates are available for those outside the normal climate range for lemon trees.

Clematis recta

CLEMATIS

The clump-forming clematis does not climb but grows to about 100cm (39in) high as a hardy perennial in central and southern Europe. Elsewhere it is increasingly grown as a decorative plant

Clematis recta, *clematis.*

88

because of its grey-green foliage and clusters of white flowers from mid-summer to autumn.

The sap of the plant causes irritation to the skin and is toxic if ingested, causing inflammation of the stomach and intestines. The toxicity is lost through drying. The plant was previously used as a dried herb for impotence and this is still the case in homeopathic medicine. *Clematis recta* provides medicine to treat inflammation of the testicles and gonorrhoea.

℥

Clematis vitalba

TRAVELLER'S-JOY

The French call traveller's-joy "beggar's herb" because beggar's smeared themselves with the sap of the plant to gain sympathy. The sap irritates and inflames the skin, causes a red rash and blisters. Taken internally, the herb is toxic, causing inflammation of the stomach and intestines.

Taken in moderation, traveller's-joy has healing properties, so that a compress of the leaf helps to promote healing of boils and inflamed skin by improving the supply of blood to the area. Preparations of the herb are also used in homeopathic doses for skin mites, migraine, and rheumatism.

The plant is widely distributed as a wild plant throughout large parts of Europe and North America and is also found elsewhere as a naturalised garden plant. The curling leaf stalks grasp hold to enable the plant to climb up to 30m (100ft) high. After flowering, clusters of seed plumes are formed.

℥

Cnicus benedictus syn. *Carbenia benedicta, Cardus benedictus*

BLESSED THISTLE, HOLY THISTLE

The blessed thistle has readily earned its name as a medicinal herb. The stems are plucked just before

Clematis vitalba, *traveller's-joy.*

Cnicus benedictus, *blessed thistle.*

flowering and quickly dried. Because of the irritating properties of the herb's active substances, it is wise to wear gloves and safety glasses when doing so. The dried herb is used in infusions with other herbs (such as sweet flag or sedge) to stimulate the appetite, improve the digestion, and aid bowel movement. Excessive use can cause nausea and vomiting.

The blessed thistle grows on open, barren places around the Mediterranean, and Asia Minor. The plant can be grown as an annual in northern Europe in a sunny position in well-worked soil.

℥

Cochlearia danica

SMALL SCURVY GRASS

Small scurvy grass has discovered a new habitat: the central reservation of dual carriageways and motorways, where the earth is salt laden from the grit spread during the winter to prevent ice. The plant's origins as salt-loving plant are along the coasts of the North Sea and European Atlantic coast. Small scurvy grass is a health-giving herb that is used in the same way as common scurvy

Cochlearia danica, *small scurvy grass.*

Cocos nucifera, *coconut.*

grass, except it cannot be harvested in winter and self seeds itself to grow anew each year.

♊

Cochlearia officinalis

COMMON SCURVY GRASS

Sailors used to take a barrel of scurvy grass with them on long sea voyages. The herb was eaten to prevent scurvy because the herb contains very high levels of vitamin C, making it extremely healthy. The herb is not eaten as a vegetable because of the pungent mustard-like taste, instead it is added as a flavouring to salads.

Common scurvy grass awakens the appetite, and improves digestion, the functioning of the gall bladder, and liver. These purifying actions also help to soothe the effects of rheumatism and gout.

Common scurvy grass is an evergreen perennial that grows in the wild in brackish soil where the salt water and fresh water meet. *Cochlearia officinalis* can be cultivated in ordinary garden soil, resulting in larger leaves than in coastal sites. The herb can be harvested in summer and winter.

⚕ ♊

Cochlearia officinalis, *common scurvy grass.*

Cocus nucifera

COCONUT

The coconut is the main cause of death in some tropical countries because each of the giant seeds is encased in a shell up to 35cm (14in) long, which fall to the ground from a height of up to 30m (100ft) when they are ripe. Those hit on the head by such a falling coconut are often killed.

Apart from this, the coconut is one of the most useful plants for man. Inside the hard shell of the nut there is delicious coconut milk which as the nut matures becomes glutinous and later fibrous. These fibres are ground and form an important side dish in oriental cooking, especially Indian and Indonesian food. The ground coconut is also used in all manner of desserts, cakes, and biscuits. The milk is drunk as an extremely refreshing and nutritional drink in tropical countries.

The thick shell surrounding the seed consists of long brown fibres and these are used to produce matting, rope, and more recently as a compost and mulch for the garden. The composted fibres make an excellent sterile growing medium for other plants and the fibres are also pressed into mats for hanging baskets to replace moss.

The powdered root of coconut palms appear to help in treating certain fevers, diarrhoea, and dysentery.

Coconut palms only grow within the zone between 20 degrees north and 20 degrees south of the equator. The range is further restricted to coastal areas where the climate is equable, needing an even temperature range to grow. The trees do not thrive at temperatures below 18°C (64°F) and are very difficult to cultivate in northern Europe.

⚕ ♊ ✳

Coffea arabica

COFFEE, ARABIAN COFFEE

The coffee bush originates from Ethiopia but was first cultivated in the Yemen, where the bushes can still be seen growing on small terraces on the steep, cool mountains. For a long time the only source of coffee was from these mountains, from where it was shipped through the port of Mocha to the rest of the world. After Dutch merchant venturers smuggled the beans, coffee cultivation was established in other parts of the world, such as Brazil, and Indonesia. In poor countries producing coffee, the beans are almost all exported, so that the local population has no coffee to drink. In the Yemen, the locals make very weak coffee using the soft outer fruit surrounding the beans.

The aromatic blossoms are succeeded by berries, rather like cherries, containing two beans or seeds. The beans are briefly roasted and subsequently ground to make granular coffee. Coffee has been the most important stimulant and pleasure-giving drink for centuries. It also has medicinal properties. The carbon derived from roasting coffee beans and the raw beans are both of importance in medicine. Carbon or charcoal is used as an absorbent agent for stomach upsets and in cases of poisoning. The

Coffea arabica, *coffee bean.*

Coffea arabica, *coffee bush.*

Coffea arabica, *sale of the coffee beans.*

raw beans are used homoeopathically to treat just those symptoms which occur from excess coffee: restlessness, hyperactivity, sensory overload, and sleeplessness (especially when ideas keep turning over in the mind).

Coffee can only be grown as a container plant in Europe, requiring a minimum temperature of 12°C (54°F).

Colchicum autumnale

AUTUMN CROCUS, MEADOW SAFFRON, NAKED LADIES

The meadows in certain central and southern European countries are filled in autumn with tufts of large, leathery leaves. The cattle graze carefully around them because they are extremely poisonous. The leaves of the autumn crocus wither during the summer and are replaced by pinkish-purple flowers without foliage. After pollination, the seed capsules form under ground and push up new leaf sheaths in the following spring. The plant is native throughout much of Europe to northern Germany.

Colchicum autumnale, *autumn crocus on the window sill.*

Colchicum autumnale, *soil-less flowering.*

Every part of the autumn crocus contains the extremely toxic colchicine, with the highest concentrations in the ripe seeds and bulb. This is no reason not to plant this species because cases of poisoning are extremely rare. The plant does not form any attractive berries, so that once children have passed the age where they investigate everything by placing in their mouth, it is actually sensible to get them used to the fact that some plants are poisonous, so that the parents can teach them that they need to be careful with nature, which can be just as dangerous as the most toxic chemicals.

Autumn crocus will also flower even when the bulb is not in the soil and are often sold as house plants to flower on window sills without the benefit of soil. After flowering, plant the bulb in the garden (in soil that does not dry out too readily, therefore often in partial shade). Colchicine is a successful treatment for gout, but has nasty side-effects, such as diarrhoea, and is rarely prescribed. Pregnant women and kidney patients must not use it, and given its toxicity, self medication can prove fatal. Homeopathic remedies based on autumn crocus are entirely safe. They are in fact prescribed to treat diarrhoea, and also for gout, rheumatic joints, and stomach and intestinal complaints.

Colchicum autumnale, *leaves of autumn crocus in spring.*

Conium maculatum

HEMLOCK, POISON PARSLEY

Socrates was required to drink from a poison cup in 399BC. The final moments of the famous Greek philosopher were described by Plato: how at first he could no longer stand and then how his lower body lost all sense of feeling until the poison paralysed his muscles and heart. It is probable that Socrates died of hemlock with its poisonous coniine alkaloid. This was the customary method of execution in ancient Greece.

Hemlock is deadly poisonous and does not betray its toxicity with a warning taste. Unfortunately other edible umbel-flowering plants are sometimes confused with hemlock or the equally dangerous water hemlock or cowbane *(Cicuta virosa)*, water dropwort *(Oenanthe crocata)*, and fool's parsley *(Aethusa cynapium)*. Expert herbalists and doctors can refine the dose so that the herb can be used medicinally: as a sedative (it was also given to those sentenced to death), for asthma, dry and painful coughs, and nerve pains. Hemlock is rarely used because of its high toxicity. *Conium* is prescribed in homeopathic medicine for depressive illness, pre-menstrual tension, anxiety, and dizziness. The outer flesh of the stems can be used to create a dye that can be used to colour wool and textiles orange-brown to grey-brown.

Conium maculatum, *hemlock.*

Hemlock is an umbelliferous flowering biennial which grows in all areas with moderate climates. During the first year, a rosette of foliage is formed from which the up to 200cm (79in) high flower stems are formed in the second year.

Consolida ajacis, syn. *Delphinium consolida*

FIELD LARKSPUR

Field larkspur flowers earliest on sandy soils, where it also thrives best. This annual is making a come back as an ornamental plant for the garden. The blue, white, and pink cultivars are sown in position in the soil in either autumn or very early spring. They flower from June to September.

Field larkspur is poisonous, with the seeds in particular being very toxic, which is why their former use to get rid of intestinal worms fell into disuse. Present day uses include a tincture of delphinine for hair lice and nits, and skin lice. The flowers are less poisonous and can be taken in small doses added to herbal tea and to add colour to such teas. Sap from the petals provides a blue colouring which can be used in combination with alum to create a green food colouring.

Consolida ajacis, *field larkspur.*

Consolida ajacis, *field larkspur.*

Convallaria majalis, *lily-of-the-valley.*

Convallaria majalis

LILY-OF-THE-VALLEY

It is a custom in many countries to hand each other bouquets of lilies-of-the-valley on May Day. The flowers appear, together with the leaves, from creeping roots. *Convallaria* grows throughout Europe in woodland and gardens, where it can become rampant.

The entire plant is so poisonous that a child who drank the water in which the flowers stood died. Experts can use the active constituent convallamarine to save heart patients. The working of the substance is similar to the glycocides in foxgloves (*Digitalis*) used to stimulate the heart and to treat congestive heart failure. Because convallamarine does not accumulate in the body in the same way, it can be used over a longer period than digitalis. In homeopathy, *Convallaria* is used for the same purposes.

The flowers have a wonderful sweet scent and the fragrance is popular for soap and other cosmetic products, including perfume. A green dye can be created from the leaves.

Coriandrum sativum

CORIANDER

The Romans rubbed coriander into meat to keep it longer and indeed they were right to do so, for modern analysis shows that the plant contains natural fungicidal and bactericidal substances.

The disinfectant properties of coriander were also known to Chinese herbal medicine. The herb is used to treat food poisoning. Coriander contains volatile oils. Internally, these act as an expectorant, reduce cramps, stimulate the appetite, and externally provide some relief from rheumatic complaints and haemorrhoid.

The oils from coriander seeds add aroma to perfumes, soap, pot-pourris, and are used as an aromatic in liqueurs.

The most important function of coriander though is culinary: as flavouring in liqueurs, and for baking, but also as a kitchen herb. The fresh leaves add flavour to salads, soups, and sauces, and are added to stock-pots and curries. Coriander is widely used in oriental cooking.

Coriander originates from Asia Minor. This annual plant was introduced by the Romans. Sow seed directly in the soil where it is to grow between

Coriandrum sativum, *coriander.*

Coriandrum sativum, *coriander seeds.*

Coriandrum sativum, *coriander.*

Courtesy The Kruidhof, Buitenpost.

Corydalis cava syn. *C. bulbosa, Pseudofumaria*

FUMITORY, LADY'S HEN

The difference between *Corydalis cava* and *C. solida* is best determined by removing the tuberous root and slicing in through. The tuber of *C. cavus* is hollow (denoted by the Latin name "cavus" as opposed to the solid roots of the eponymous *C. solida.*

The tubers of both plants, regardless of whether hollow or solid contain alkaloids such as corydaline and bulbocapnine. For uses, see *Corydalis solida.*

The hollow-tuber species is a striking spring flowering plant on the wooded slopes of central Europe, especially on those sites where earthquakes have brought minerals close to the surface. The plant requires a moisture-retaining and humus-rich

March and May. Depending upon the variety, coriander grows 40–100cm (16–39in) high with large umbrella like flowers, with soft, finely pinnated foliage that is strongly aromatic.

95

Corydalis cava, *fumitory*.

tions than the related *Corydalis cava*, loosely known as fumitory in common with many other plant of the *Fumaria* genus. The flowers appear in March, together with the leaves. The plant is native to large parts of Europe and is popular in gardens. The active substances in the tubers have been used as a painkiller, and to treat cramps and convulsions for at least 1,200 years. The herb is not suitable for pregnant women and because of the toxicity of the alkaloids in the tubers, it should only be used under medical supervision. Bulbocapnine is synthesised in modern medicine for use during brain scans.

Cosmos sulphureus

The annual *Cosmos sulphureus* originates from Central America where it grows to the height of a man. In Europe the plant reaches about 100cm (39in) high and has orange or yellowish flowers on long stems that are ideal as cut flowers. Sow seed under cover in March, or directly in the ground from May. The plant flowers from July and can continue blooming until October. The flowers are picked as they open or after flowering and provide yellow, orange, and red dyestuff for colouring textile and wool.

Cosmos sulphureus.

soil. Elsewhere the plant has become naturalised through escape from cultivation, and is grown best in gardens on fertile, moisture-retaining soil beneath broad-leafed trees. *Corydalis cava* flowers in April.

Corydalis solida syn. C. halleri, C. transsylvanica, Pseudofumaria

FUMEWORT

Fumewort is less fussy about its growing condi-

Corydalis solida, *fumewort*.

Crataegus monogyna, *common hawthorn.*

Crataegus laevigata *'Paul's Scarlet', cultivar of may.*

Crithmum maritimum, *samphire.*

Crithmum maritimum, *samphire.*

Crataegus

HAWTHORN, THORN, MAY, QUICK, QUICKTHORN, QUICKSET

Hawthorn has been rediscovered. Once the native shrub come tree served as medicine against diarrhoea, and period pains. Today, its use to improve blood circulation blood and heart function is of greatest interest. Substances in the blossom and fruit are very beneficial to the supply of blood to the heart, aiding recovery following heart attack. Hawthorn or may is available for sale as a homeopathic remedy but it is also possible to pick the blossoms in spring and dry them. The pungent infusion of the dried blossom is usually sweetened. The herb has best effect when taken over a longer period. The substances in *Crataegus* help prevent such disorders as angina pectoris, weak heart, and irregular heart beat, and also improve the circulation.

Blossoms are suitable for use from both the common hawthorn *(Crataegus monogyna)* and may *(Crataegus laevigata)*.

Crithmum maritimum

SAMPHIRE, ROCK SAMPHIRE, SEA FENNEL

Samphire grows on rocks on the edge of the Atlantic Ocean and the Mediterranean . This peren-
nial succulent cannot survive without salt and is therefore virtually impossible to grow away from the coast. Coast dwellers collect the juicy leaves, with their pungent and salty taste, for use in salads. In Britain, samphire is often pickled, or cooked in butter. This tasty herb is also healthy: acting as a diuretic, thus cleansing the body, and aids digestion.

Cruciata laevipes

CROSSWORT

Rheumatism, oedema, and sprains were once treated using crosswort. The plant is suitable for both

97

Cruciata laevipes, *crosswort*.

Cucurbita pepo, *pumpkin*.

Cryptotaenia canadensis syn. C. japonica

HONEWORT, JAPANESE WILD CHERVIL

The now disregarded *japonica* tag for this genus is perhaps more appropriate because this herb is greatly appreciated as a vegetable and herb by the Japanese. The plant is native to Japan, but also parts of East Asia and North America. The herb, with its trifoliate leaves, prefers moist semi-shady places.

The Japanese pick the leaves (that taste like celery) while young and add them to salads but they are far more commonly cooked as a side vegetable. The red-leafed cultivated variety is illustrated.

§

internal and external use although today herbs are known with much more effective healing properties. Today crosswort is principally an attractive herb found in the by-ways of chalk soil landscapes in Europe. The leaves are born in wreathes of four crosses around the square-section stem. The warm yellow flowers appear in spring and early summer.

§

Curcibita pepo

PUMPKIN, WINTER SQUASH

The pumpkin or winter squash helps men through the male menopause. After about 45 years old, the prostrate gland begins to grow, and this can cause difficulties with urinating. Pumpkin seeds contains a mixture of oils, vitamins, and minerals, including zinc, which work together to prevent urinary disorders in the event of an enlarged prostrate gland. The husks of the seeds in particular are used to prepare medicines.

The oil from the seed was once used to treat worms. Today the husked and roasted seeds are regarded as a delicacy.

Pumpkins can be grown by sowing the large seeds in spring under glass and then transferring to extremely fertile soil in a sunny position in June. Placing a brick, stone, or plank of wood under the pumpkin prevents it from rotting.

§

Cryptotaenia candensis, *honewort*.

Cupressus sempervirens

ITALIAN CYPRESS, MEDITERRANEAN CYPRESS

Cyprus was a young man in ancient Greece. He tended a much loved giant deer but accidentally pierced it with his spear. The giant deer died and Cyprus begged Apollo to let him mourn for ever. Hence the young man became a cypress tree, the symbol of sadness. The cypress is found by cemeteries in southern Europe, which are regarded not just as places of mourning, but also of eternal life. Hence the cypress tree is symbolic in both Greek and Roman mythology but also in Islam. The slender cypress, with yielding but resilient tip, is often portrayed on the gravestones of women in Turkey.

The evergreen tree contains volatile oils which are aromatic, especially when the foliage is pressed. The oil is the major constituent of chypre perfume. The extremely strong wood also contains the volatile oil. The wood is barely touched by funguses or wood-boring insects. Blanket and linen chests were often made of the wood because the scent kept moths at bay. The aroma has a beneficial effect for lung patients. Substances in the cones are astringent and treat diarrhoea, varicose veins, and haemorrhoid. They also help to staunch bleeding and are antiseptic.

Although the home of the cypress is the warmer lands surrounding the Mediterranean , it can also grow in northern parts of Europe. The languid column can withstand -20°C (-4°F) but will only survive in well-sheltered places because it cannot withstand bitter cold winds.

Cupressus sempervirens, *Italian cypress.*

Cupressus sempervirens, *Italian cypress.*

Cupressus sempervirens, *Italian cypress.*

Curcuma zedoaria, *zedoary.*

Curcuma zeodaria is sometimes sold as a house plant. In traditional folk medicine the species is a known treatment for stomach disorders and increases gall bladder activity. *Curcuma* is also used for this same purpose as a homeopathic medicine.

♃ / ⚕

Cyclamen hederifolium syn. *C. neapolitum*

CYCLAMEN, SOWBREAD

Cyclamen starts to flower in August to September. This is the best time to blossom in its lands of origin (the eastern Mediterranean), since it rains in the region predominantly during autumn. In northern parts of Europe, cyclamens are hardy and can be tried as garden plants in shaded places, preferably under broad-leafed trees on alkaline soils. The bulbs must be disturbed, by digging or being moved, as little as possible.

Cyclamens such as that illustrated and the sowbread *(Cyclamen purpurascens* syn. *C. europaeum)* contain cyclamine which is a toxic alkaloid that can cause inflammation of the stomach lining. The former use as a strong laxative and to treat worms has to be advised against because of the plant's toxicity.

Cyclamen is used for a wide range of ailments in homeopathic medicine, such as gout, rheumatism, chronic headache, migraine, and nerve or period pains.

♃

Curcuma zedoaria

ZEDOARY

Foods sold within the European Community often bear E numbers to denote food additives which are permitted to be used in food production. The average consumer has little interest in these details about all manner of additives from pectin to aluminium but they are very important to those with an allergy to specific substances so that you can avoid foods with specific E numbers. The designation E100 stands for curcumine which is the yellow colouring from *Circuma.*

The genus originates from southern Asia, is of the *Zingiberaceae* or ginger family, and has a creeping root or rhizome, just like ginger. Curcumine is contain in the rhizome. The best known form of *Curcuma* as a food colouring and flavouring is *Curcuma longa,* or tumeric. Tumeric provides a moderately pungent spice and contains yellow colouring which is used both as a dyestuff for wool and textiles and as food colouring in sauces, piccalilli, curry dishes, egg, and chicken dishes. The substances from the root have similar medicinal properties to ginger.

Cydonia oblonga

QUINCE

The large yellow fruits of quince have a sharp or tart taste, except when they are cooked to produce a preserve or jelly. Slices of raw quince are also used to garnish meat dishes.

Cyclamen hederifolium, *cyclamen.*

Cydonia oblonga, *quince.*

Cydonia oblonga, *quince.*

The raw fruit in particular is extremely healthy, being rich in minerals and vitamins.
The pips or stones are used medicinally. The husks of the poisonous seeds contain a viscous substances which heal infections in the mouth and throat. The substances are added to cough and throat medicines. The healing properties are also widely used in skin ointments.
Cydonia oblonga originates from Asia Minor but has long since been cultivated in lands with hot summers. The low tree bears only modest fruit in northern parts of Europe but is hardy.

Cynara cardunculus

CARDOON

The cardoon is becoming better known, not just as a vegetable, but as an ornamental plant for the garden. The deeply lobed leaves are extremely large but are outshone in the second year by the 200cm (79in) high flowering stems topped by superb flowers. The giant thistle attracts swarms of bees to it.
Those who want to eat the plant will not wait for the flower to set. Instead, a strong non-flowering plant is wrapped in spring with cardboard, paper, or

Cynara cardunculus, *cardoon.*

Courtesy The Kruidhof, Buitenpost.

plastic to blanch the leaves. These provide a tasty and healthy vegetable.
The cardoon is a perennial from the western parts of the Mediterranean and it requires a sunny position and ample feeding to get it to grow well. The plant can withstand frosts of -18°C (-0.4°F) but if protected can withstand the hardest winter.

Cynara cardunculus, *cardoon.*

101

Cynara scolymus, *globe artichoke.*

Cynara scolymus, *globe artichoke.*

Cynara scolymus

GLOBE ARTICHOKE

The artichoke is probably a cultivar of the cardoon (see *Cynara cardunculus)* and is sometimes known as *C. cardunculus* Scolymus Group. Globe artichokes are not found in the wild but often in gardens, especially in southern Europe. The climate in northern Europe is less suited to their growth, although cultivation is possible in warm, sheltered places in well worked soil, with the roots protected in winter with an airy, insulating layer, such as leaves or straw. If fed with sufficient manure, artichokes can grow to 200cm (79in) high. The leaves are greyer and less deeply lobed than cardoon. The flower bulb is the principal point of the globe artichoke. The bottom and surrounding scales are eaten as a delicacy. The roots and leaves contain substances which are used to make medicines which aid the digestion, working of the gall bladder, and liver, and which are also diuretic, helping to release urine, thereby purifying and lowering cholesterol in the blood. The extremely healthy plant also helps with certain geriatric ailments.

Cytisus scoparius syn. *Sarothamnus scoparius*

BROOM, SCOTCH BROOM

The yellow flowers of broom spread their stunning fragrance in May to June. The shrubs grow wild throughout Europe, especially on acid, sandy soils but broom is also a popular garden shrub which has no special demands. The shrub, which grows to about 150–200cm (59–79in), is toxic. The poisonous substances in broom are used in medicine, especially for irregular heart rhythms and palpitations. The former use as an astringent and blood staunching agent following child birth has been replaced by other means. Pregnant women should not use the herb and others should only do so under medical supervision. Broom provides a yellow dyestuff for colouring wool and textiles.

Cytisus scoparius, *broom.*

Dactylopius coccus, *cochineal beetle.*

Dactylopius coccus, *cochineal beetle.*

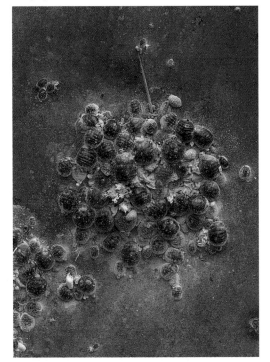

Dactylopius coccus

COCHINEAL BEETLE

This is a plant encyclopaedia but we make one exception: the cochineal beetle which lives on the prickly pear cactus *(Opuntia)*. The prickly pear originates in the Americas but has been brought to warmer countries around the Mediterranean to cultivate for their edible fruits and the cochineal beetles. In Australia the plants have grown out of control to plague proportions.

Before Columbus, the Aztecs used the cochineal for dyeing cloth. They collected the beetles from the plants, plunged them briefly into boiling water, and then dried them. The bodies are filled with carmine red colouring. By plunging wool, cotton, or silk into baths of mixtures of cochineal and indigo, dyers can create any colour between red and blue.

Cochineal is used in homeopathy for coughs, asthma, and bronchitis.

Daphne mezereum

MEZEREUM

The red berries of mezereum seem very attractive to children but are extremely poisonous. Fortunately accidents are few because the berries have a ghastly taste. The sap from the bark is also dangerous for gardeners who prune the shrub or break off any branches. The sap causes severe skin irritation followed by open wounds which do not heal readily.

Daphne was once given to induce vomiting but the active constituents are far too dangerous for this use. In homeopathic use, *Daphne* is safe for treatment of rheumatic disorders, and to treat skin complaints.

Daphne mezereum grows wild in much of Europe, preferring humus rich alkaline soil and partial shade. The shrub grows to a maximum of 100cm (39in) high and flowers early in March to April with blossoms that have a scent reminiscent of lilac. It is not surprising that *Daphne* is popular in the garden.

Daphne mezereum 'Rubra', *mezereum.*

Datura metel, *thorn apple.*

Datura metel

THORN APPLE

When an Indian Hindu man died, his widow used to be consumed in the fire together with her husband. The widow would squat alive in the flames to keep her man company. The widow's one consolation for this act of suttee was that she would be stupefied by drinking *Datura metel.* The fruit and seeds contain substances which initially induce a stupor and then cause hallucinations.

Because of this latter property, thorn apple has been used since ancient times to create visions and enable contact with greater powers. Added to wine, thorn apple increases the effects of alcohol and removes all inhibitions from the drinker so that they speak their mind. The herb was therefore sometimes secretly added to wine as a "truth potion". The dosage of thorn apple is extremely critical, because of the highly toxic nature of the substances it contains, which in excess can cause madness or death.

For use as a medicine, see *Datura stramonium.*

Datura metel originates from southern China, but has become naturalised in areas where there is no frost. It is grown as an annual ornamental garden plant because of its velvety foliage and erect white flowers. There are also cultivars with yellow, pink, or blue tinted flowers.

Datura stramonium

JIMSON WEED, THORN APPLE, DEVIL'S APPLE

The unripe fruits and seeds of the jimson weed or thorn apple contain a mixture of toxic substances, which are similar to deadly nightshade and henbane. They have the same stupefying and hallucinogenic properties as described for *Datura metel.*

The herb *Datura* was once used as a narcotic painkiller for operations but today the active constituents are only available in many countries on

Datura stramonium, *jimson weed.*

Datura stramonium *var.* tatula, *thorn apple.*

Daucus carota, *wild carrot.*

prescription because of their misuse as a drug. Thorn apple can only be used under medical supervision because of its highly toxic nature with the exception of homeopathic doses.

In the right dosage, *Datura* can relieve spasms. The plant is cultivated in order to win the active constituents for use in medicine to treat Parkinson's disease, convulsive coughing, asthma, whooping cough, and nervous disorders.

Datura stramonium originates in the USA and Mexico. After its introduction to Europe, the annual plant quickly became naturalised, especially in very fertile areas, such as refuse tips. The white flowers are not erect as with *Datura metel*, but hang to one side. The variety *Datura stramonium-* var. *tatula* has lilac blue flowers.

 ✳

Daucus carota

WILD CARROT

Eating carrots helps you to see better, especially in the dark, so that they are a suitable treatment for night blindness. Carrots contain carotene, which is

Daucus carota, *wild carrot.*

converted in the human body into vitamin A, which is the vitamin that helps to increase the sensitivity of the eyes.

Carrots from the greengrocer are a cultivated form of the wild carrot. They are especially healthy when raw. Grated carrot or carrot juice can be used in large quantities to get rid of worms and to correct nutritional deficiency in small children. The substances in carrots have a diuretic effect, help resistance to cancer, and to ease an irritated gut. Internal use is good for healthy skin. Externally, a puree of carrot or grated carrot aids healing of burns.

All manner of cultivated varieties of *Daucus carota* ssp. *sativa* are grown. The juice from the roots of wild carrot and infusion of the dried foliage have similar properties. Carrot juice is incorporated in perfumes among other uses.

Wild carrot is a native plant in sunny places, preferring alkaline soils. The 100cm (39in) high plant grows for one year, sometimes two, before flowering. The white flower umbels, usually with one purple coloured flower at the centre, curl once the seeds ripen.

Daucus carota, *wild carrot.*

Dianthus deltoides, *maiden pink.*

The maiden pink remains dwarf in habit and grows on dry, sandy, sparsely populated soil from Siberia through to western parts of Europe, although it is less common in coastal areas.

Dicentra formosa syn. *D. eximia*

WILD BLEEDING HEART

The bleeding heart flowers in late April–early May in many gardens. The perennial originates from North America and thrives best in Europe in partial shade and slightly moist soil. The leaves of this plant wither by early summer but it has stored sufficient nutrition in its roots to survive until the following spring. The thickened roots are used for a homeopathic remedy to lift the spirits, as a diuretic, to heal genital ulcers of syphilis, and cure infection of the stomach lining, and were used to treat scrofula (an ancient disease that was probably a form of tuberculosis).

Dianthus deltoides

MAIDEN PINK

The maiden pink was once a well known expectorant, now its use is culinary, although preparation of the flowers requires much patience. Each petal consists of a coloured part and a white heel. This latter part has a bitter taste and has to be removed. Then the fresh, coloured petals can be added to salads and such like. An infusion of the petals has a calming effect when added to wine. The entire flower can be dried for use in pot-pourris.

Dianthus deltoides, *maiden pink.*

Dicentra formosa, *bleeding heart.*

Dictamnus albus *'Purpurea', dittany.*

Dictamnus albus *'Albiflorus', dittany.*

Dictamnus albus var. *'Purpurea'*, syn. *D. dasycarpus, D. fraxinella*

DITTANY, BURNING BUSH

Dittany or burning bush shows its best trick after hot summer days. Hold a lighted match to the flowers or seed capsules and the volatile oils which evaporate from the plant will burn. The plant's natural range is a broad belt from Spain, through southern Europe, to Asia, and China. Elsewhere it is cultivated in gardens for the white, pink, or mauve flowers. These are borne by the slow-growing perennial, which in a sunny position can reach 70cm (27$^{1}/_{2}$ in) high.

Handle the plant carefully, especially during hot weather when the hot oils are secreted, because some people have an allergic reaction which increases the skin's photo-sensitivity, making the skin more vulnerable to ultra-violet light, and causing blisters.

Previously, decoctions from the roots and leaves were used to ward against the plague which may not have been such a bad idea, since modern analysis shows that the plant contains substances which are bactericidal. The plant was also used as a herb to rid themselves of worms and as a tonic and an aid to the digestion. In the present day, *Dictamus albus* is only used in homeopathic med-icine for irregular periods, and stomach or intestinal disorders.

℞ ✳

Dictamnus albus, *burning bush, burning.*

Digitalis grandiflora, *yellow foxglove.*

Digitalis lanata, *woolly foxglove.*

Digitalis grandiflora syn. *D. ambigua, D. orientalis*

YELLOW FOXGLOVE

The yellow foxglove grows beside streams and at the edges of woods throughout Europe, with its northern boundary in Belgium, although it is rare in that country. Elsewhere it is known as a garden plant. The large greenish yellow flowers later turn yellow ochre and flower from June to August. The biennial to perennial thrives in ordinary moisture-retaining garden soil. The medical properties are identical to *Digitalis purpurea*.

Digitalis lanata

WOOLLY FOXGLOVE

Woolly foxglove has stronger medicinal properties than the common foxglove. The small leaves of the woolly foxglove contain between 1–1.4 per cent of the glycoside digitalis, which is extremely toxic but can cure people when used in very small doses. The common foxglove rarely exceeds 1 per cent,

even under the most favourable conditions and has a wide variation in the amount of the glycosides it contains. There is another reason though why woolly foxgloves are cultivated: the plant contains a higher amount of digoxin. The body breaks this substance down so that the treatment can be taken over a longer period without accumulation in the body. Woolly foxglove is cultivated on a large scale for the production of digoxin (for the medicinal properties, see *Digitalis purpurea*).

Woolly foxglove originates from the Balkans and Asia Minor. The slender biennial to perennial grows between 150–200cm (59–79in) high, depending on conditions. Elsewhere, woolly foxglove is an eye-catching evergreen plant in gardens. Plant in well-worked and well-drained soil to prevent the leaf rosette from rotting.

Digitalis lutea syn. *D. eriostachya*

FOXGLOVE

Although *Digitalis lutea* contains the same substances as common foxglove, it is rarely grown for medicinal purposes. The plant is an ideal ornamental garden perennial though for attractive borders. It grows to about 100cm (39in) and flowers from June until August with small yellow flowers that sometimes have small brown flecks in the front of the mouth of the flower.

Digitalis lutea grows naturally in large parts of Europe with its northern boundary in the Belgian Ardennes. It also flowers in the wild from June to August.

☤

Digitalis purpurea

COMMON FOXGLOVE

The cover of almost any book about poisonous plants features the common foxglove. This has made it the best known toxic plant and in gardens where there are children the plant is expressly removed. You can save yourself the effort, since foxgloves are less dangerous than was once thought. The substances contained in the plant are certainly highly toxic but the chances of children ingesting them are minimal. Children rarely eat flowers (they are attracted to berries) and if they should try to eat a foxglove, the plant will warns them thoroughly.

As co-author of a book about fun plants for chil-

Digitalis purpurea, *common foxglove.*

Digitalis lutea, *foxglove.*

Digitalis purpurea, *common foxglove.*

Bell-shaped flower of Digitalis purpurea, *common foxglove.*

edges of woods and in clearings, and where timber has been felled. The flower stems develop in late May. They grow, already in flower, to a height of up to 200cm (79in). The drooping bell-like flowers attract countless bees.

Diospyros kaki

CHINESE PERSIMMON, JAPANESE PERSIMMON, KAKI

One of the more than one thousand cultivars of persimmon is *Diospyros kaki* 'Sharon', sometimes know as the Sharon fruit, which is orange coloured, the size of a beef tomato, and sold as a delicacy. The flesh of the fruit is firm and therefore easy to transport but the thicker skin of the Sharon fruit is less tasty than the less frequently offered persimmon. The fruits of this Japanese tree are soft, with gelatinous parts. They are eaten when overripe because the tannin which affects the gums has then broken down.

Preserves can be made from Chinese persimmons but the fruit tasts best raw or as a dessert.

Chinese persimmons help a wide range of ailments: when cooked, for diarrhoea and constipa-

Diospyros kaki, *Chinese persimmon.*

dren, I volunteered to act as guinea pig by eating a foxglove flower. When I bit into the flower a very bitter and astringent substance was released which irritated the mouth and caused a flood of spittle. Several attempts were made to chew the plant but I found it impossible to swallow the plant because the plant made me retch. After I spat the flower out, my mouth continued to produce bitter-tasting spittle for several hours and felt fiery as though inflamed. Drinking milk got rid of the taste and fiery sensation. Following this we decided to include the plant in the children's book. The flowers are in any event too large for small children to swallow whole. See also "Children and poisonous plants" earlier in this book.

Common foxglove can provide a treatment for heart patients. The plant contains the glycoside digitalis which is used in treating heart disorders. The substance improves supply of blood to the heart and helps to treat heart weaknesses and it is also prescribed for irregular heart beat. The substances are accumulated in the body, so that digitalis cannot be taken for a prolonged period. The medicine is also diuretic and is used externally for treatment of ulcers.

Digitalis purpurea is a biennial to perennial and it grows wild throughout Europe, especially at the

tion; the juice of unripe fruit lowers the blood pressure, and consumption of the fruit helps to get rid of hiccups. The calyx surrounding the fruit is cooked and taken internally to stem internal haemorrhages. Although the tree can withstand considerable frost, a bountiful harvest is only possible where the climate is hot or after a long hot summer. The tree is sometimes planted in mild areas, such as by the coast, for the fine autumn colours of its leaves. It requires a sunny position that is sheltered.

♃ ♊

Dipsacus fullonum

FULLER'S TEASEL

Insects are unable to climb up the stem of the fuller's teasel because they fall into a channel of liquid surrounding the stem. This "cup" is always filled with liquid, partly from rainwater but also from a discharge from the plant itself. The viscous discharge from the plant prevents the liquid from evaporating. Comparatively recently it was discovered that the plant is insectivorous. The insects fall into the "cup" and are unable to get out because it is too smooth. The insects drown and are digested

Dipsacus fullonum, *fuller's teasel.*

Dipsacus fullonum, *fuller's teasel.*

by the fluid. Glands in the plant derive nutrients from the liquid.

This liquid was once used to treat eye disorders. These days, salves and ointments are made using the roots and leaves to relieve the pain of rheumatism and gout, and also for an internal medicine for tuberculosis. The fuller's teasel grows throughout Europe as both a wild plant and naturalised escapee from cultivation. The plant prefers sunny positions on alkaline soil but can readily self seed itself in almost any garden soil. In the first year, the plant forms a rosette of green leaves which remain pressed close to the ground. In the second year, the plant shoots to about 200cm (79in) high and then flowers in late summer with a characteristic honeycomb flower form. The first blue to pink flowers are formed on the central "cells" of the honeycomb. Gradually the cells above open too, followed by the lower ones, so that two rings of petals are formed, the upper one moving upwards, and the lower moving downwards.

Dipsacus sativus is a cultivated form grown for the hooked spines on the ends of the bracts which were once used for raising the nap of woollen cloth.

♃ ✳

Dodonaea viscosa *'Purpurea'*.

Doronicum pardalianches, *leopard's bane.*

Dodonaea viscosa

STICKY HOP BUSH, NATIVE HOPS

The leaf of the sticky hop bush is covered with resin glands, which produce so much resin that the branches can be burned as a torch. In hot, dry areas, the shrub is used as a windbreak to prevent soil erosion. The roots take a firm grasp and the wood is extremely hard and ideal for fencing, while the fruit can be used as a replacement for hops in brewing beer.

In addition to all these benefits, the shrub from Central America also has medicinal properties. The leaf is chewed for toothache; the resultant liquid has to be spit out because it is extremely high in tannin. The tannin is also useful for its astringent nature as a gargle for toothache, and externally to heal wounds and insect bites. Some cultures ingest the herb internally as a remedy for fever.

The sticky hop bush now grows in many arid areas, such as South Africa and Australia. In Europe they are available as a container plant. The "red" cultivar, *Dodonaea viscosa* 'Purpurea' is particularly attractive as an ornamental plant. Protect well from frost.

 ✳

Doronicum pardalianches syn. D. cordatum

LEOPARD'S BANE

Leopard's bane is a somewhat obscure plant. The botanical name *pardialanches* literally means "leopard strangler", akin to the vernacular name, but nobody knows why. There has been a case of pigs being poisoned by the plant. It is likely that they grubbed up the thickened bulbs and ate them. It was these bulbs which brought the plant from the south-western parts of Europe to the north, as a powerful medicinal herb that was planted in monastery gardens. From these places, the plant became naturalised in large estates, and subsequently elsewhere, so that in many parts of Europe it now grows widely as a "wild" plant. The root tubers were once used to treat dizziness but not any more.

The *Doronicum* genus are popular ornamental plants because they flower early in April to June with large yellow flowers. The herb prefers humus-rich soil that retains moisture in partial shadow.

Drimys winteri

WINTER'S BARK

At the southern tip of South America the climate is moderate so that the winter's bark form of pepper tree from Chile can be grown in mild climate zones of Europe. It is best grown in northern Europe as a container plant with the most suitable variety being the comparatively dwarf *Drimys winteri* var. *andina*, which grows as a shrub.

Winter's bark was once highly regarded as an excellent remedy for scurvy. These days, the bark is added to remedies for dysentery, stomach complaints, colic, and indigestion.

Drosera rotundifolia

ROUND-LEAVED SUNDEW

Plants struggle to derive nutrients from the ground in acidic peat bogs. The sundew therefore finds its

Drimys winteri, *winter's bark*.

Drosera rotundifolia, *round-leaved sundew*.

nutrients in the air. The leaves are covered by hairs with glands at their tips, which secrete a liquid that attracts insects but is so sticky that the insects become trapped. The plant then bends more hairs towards the victim and enzymes digest the nutrients from the body. Where conditions are right, round-leaved sundews can grow in large colonies.

Pharmaceutical use extends to the entire plant, with droseron being extracted for the relief of spasms and therefore also for spasmodic coughs

and retching, asthma attacks, and bronchitis. *Drosera* has the same uses in homeopathic medicine.

Dryopteris filix-mas syn. *Aspidium filix-mas*

MALE FERN

The male fern grows naturally in moist ground in open canopy broad-leaved woodland. The feathery fronds only remains green in mild winters. Generally, new growth uncurls from the rhizomes each year.

In the past these rhizomes were dug up to make a very effective worm treatment that was especially useful for dealing with tapeworms. The plant is little used in the present day because small doses are not of any use and large doses can be dangerous for the patient. Overdoses can cause blindness or even death. Pregnant women, children, and liver patients should certainly not use the herb.

Dryopteris filix-mas, *male fern*.

Courtesy The Kruidhof, Buitenpost.

113

The squirting cucumber can be grown as an annual plant for the garden, requiring a sunny position in well-drained soil.

Echballium elaterium, *squirting cucumber.*

Echballium elaterium

SQUIRTING CUCUMBER

The plant gets its vernacular name from the strange way the fruit splits open when ripe and spurts a jet of liquid. The squirting cucumber resembles a gherkin. While the plant grows, pressure builds up in the liquid within the fruit. If the fruit are pressed around their middle, the fruit splits open where it is attached to the stem and the seeds are ejected with such force that some books warn of eye damage, although in my own experience I find this somewhat exaggerated.

The herb can certainly be dangerous if taken without due care. The herb is prescribed for oedema and as a purgative. Small overdoses of decoctions from the dried fruit act both as a laxative and induce vomiting, while higher doses can cause serious poisoning. Hence the herb should only be used under medical supervision.

Echinacea purpurea

PURPLE CONEFLOWER, PURPLE ECHINACEA

When the white man arrived in North America, the purple coneflower was one of the most important medicinal herbs. The native North Americans

Echinacea purpurea, *purple coneflower.*

Echinacea purpurea, *purple coneflower.*

Echinacea purpurea *'White Swan'*.

Echium vulgare, *viper's bugloss.*

chewed the root of the flower which turned the prairies red. The sap provided a local anaesthetic which was useful in the case of wounds or insect bites. The herb also disinfected the wound and provided an anti-toxin to treat rattlesnake bites. The native Americans used the herb internally for coughs, headache and stomach ache, and swollen glands.

Later, when the properties of the purple coneflower and other related species had been researched, it was found that the native people had been absolutely right in their uses of the herb. It contains painkilling, antiseptic, and blood purifying substances that are kill bacteria and fungi, and increase the body's natural resistance.

The purple coneflower is a fine summer-flowering herbaceous perennial which grows about 100cm (39in) high and bears its purple blooms from mid summer. There are also white-flowering varieties such as *Echinacea purpurea* 'White Swan'.

Echium vulgare

VIPER'S BUGLOSS

People used to believe that a tongue of pollen stuck out of the mouth of viper's bugloss which could heal a snake bite if placed on the wound by sucking out the venom. The plant does contain antiseptic substances but today it has no uses beyond that of a decorative garden plant and as edible garnish in drinks and candies.

Viper's bugloss is a biennial plant of sunny places in very well worked or disturbed ground. It flowers virtually throughout Europe on sandy verges and embankments. The seeds can remain dormant deep in the ground for a long time but germinate as soon as they are once more exposed to sunlight.

Equisetum arvense

FIELD HORSETAIL, BOTTLEBRUSH, SHAVE GRASS

There is no other plant about I am more fanatical to prevent gaining a foothold in my garden than field horsetail. This horsetail can quickly become a pernicious weed when it pops its head up in moist, disturbed sandy soil.

Equisetum arvense, *field horsetail.*

Equisetum telemateia, *giant horsetail.*

The roots creep deep under the soil and continually push up new shoots in different places. Pulling them out has little point because this spore-forming plant cannot be weeded or successfully chemically treated.

Perhaps the gardener should make the best of horsetail's positive points. Once, the herb was used to treat tuberculosis. In the present day it is chiefly used as a diuretic to help treat rheumatism, gout, swollen limbs, and bladder and kidney problems. It is also useful to treat coughs. The herb is used to make an infusion. The active substances are flavone, saponin, and silicic, which can be dissolved in bath water to strengthen connective tissue, promote better circulation, reduce swellings and rheumatic disorders, and raise the general resistance of the body.

The above ground parts of the plant are harvested to produce green dyestuff for wool and textiles. Other horsetails are also used for this purpose, such as giant horsetail *(Equisetum telemateia).* Because some horsetails are more toxic, such as marsh horsetail *(Equisetum palustre),* they are best avoided for self medication. Homeopathic medicine mainly uses Dutch rush or rough horsetail *(Equisetum hyemale).*

Erica tetralix

CROSS-LEAVED HEATH

Cross-leaved heath does not grow naturally in the driest places as does bell heather *(Erica cinerea),* instead preferring moist heaths and in wet hollows. Understandably the plant is common on Britain's many wet moorlands with their boggy places. Cross-leaved heath flowers with small balloon-like flowers during the summer and attracts hosts of bees.

Erica tetralix, *cross-leaved heath.*

The properties of cross-leaved heath are similar to those of bell heather: diuretic, used to cleanse the system and to treat ailments such as gout.

℞

Conyza canadensis syn. Erigeron canadensis

HORSEWEED, CANADIAN FLEABANE

Horseweed is tougher than it first appears. It escaped from a botanical garden in the seventeenth century and has subsequently conquered much of Europe. Prior to this is grew in Canada. The plant liberally self-seeds itself in dry, disturbed soil and is regarded as a pernicious weed that is difficult to eradicate because of its resistance to chemical treatments.

The plant itself contains tannin and volatile oils which are used in North America to treat diarrhoea, stem internal haemorrhages, and as a diuretic to treat rheumatism and gout. Homeopathic medicine uses the blood clotting properties of horseweed to treat internal bleeding, for example of the uterus.

℞

Conyza canadensis, *horseweed.*

Eriobotrya japonica, *Japanese medlar.*

Eriobotrya japonica

JAPANESE MEDLAR, LOQUAT

The large corrugated leaf of the Japanese medlar contains natural bactericidal agents which also kill viruses. Theses substances are well used to fight infection, especially in loquat cough mixture for colds and bronchitis. The Japanese medlar or loquat originates from both Japan and China (where the medicinal properties are most widely used). Today, the tree grows in all sub-tropical areas for its plum sized orange fruit which are made into fresh but sharp tasting jams and jellies.

The Japanese medlar can just about survive winter in some European coastal areas. In this case, the tree sheds its leaves and since the flowering period is in winter, the tree does not set fruit in northern latitudes. The tree can be grown as a container plant and if kept above 10°C (50°F) will not shed its leaves.

℞ ||

Eruca vesicaria

ROCKET

Countries in the south of Europe in particular are especially fond of rocket in salads and it is ideal

Eruca vesicaria, *rocket.*

Eruca vesicaria, *rocket.*

Rocket is extremely health-giving: it acts as a tonic, purifies the blood, and aids digestion. It was once used to prepare cough mixture. The entire plant is edible and the seeds are used to produce oil, which is used with mustard. The most general form in cultivation is *Eruca vesicaria* ssp. *sativa.*

♀ ‖ ✳

Eschscholzia californica

CALIFORNIAN POPPY

Californian poppies look very innocent, yet they contain substances with properties similar to opium. However infusions of Californian poppy are much milder in effect than opium and without the same degree of after-effects. The flowers originate from the western side of America, where the indigenous population used the plant for toothache long before the white man arrived in their land. Californian poppy is still used today for this purpose and also for nervous pains and spasms, plus the calming of hyper-active children. In homeopathy *Eschscholzia* is used both as a tonic and sleeping draught.

The Californian poppy is grown as an annual in Europe and in milder areas it self-seeds itself in winter. Elsewhere, sow the seeds in early spring.

Eschscholzia californica, *Californian poppy.*

when added to vegetable stir-fry. The annual is cultivated mainly in winter in milder climates because it runs quickly to seed and becomes too tough during hot weather.

Sow the seed as early as possible in spring in northern Europe, when only milder frosts are to be expected. Ensure there is plenty of nitrogen in the soil to encourage the leaves to grow rapidly. If the plant grows slowly, the herb will taste bitter. It is possible to sow in autumn and then harvest several weeks later until moderate frosts will kill the plant off.

The plant grows to about 20–60cm (8–24in) tall and flowers from June until later autumn with orange flowers. There are selected cultivars with white, creamy-yellow, and pink flowers, that are either single or double.

Eucalyptus

GUM TREE

The largest plants on earth are trees, and the largest tree is a *Eucalyptus* of more than 100m (328ft) high. Gum trees originate from Australia where the woods smell strongly of the aroma of their volatile oils that is discharged by the leaves. This oil of eucalyptus is found in inhalers and vapour rubs for blocked noses and it is also added to both scented and bath oils. Eucalyptus oil is also added to massage oils to help to relax muscles. The gum from the tree was formerly used in pigment manufacture. Strips of bark can be used to dye wool and textiles brown, the leaves for green-yellow, and the twigs for reddish-orange.

Eucalyptus, *gum tree.*

Euonymus europaeus *'Fructo-coccineus', spindle tree.*

Euonymus europaeus

SPINDLE TREE

When head lice were still commonplace, the pulverised fruit and the leaves, or oil from the fruit of the spindle tree were used to kill the lice. Today, there are much simpler remedies. This is also true of the other medicinal uses which spindle once provided: the native shrub acts as a laxative and heart stimulant. Or at least they can have these properties when used under expert guidance. The alkaloids and glycosides in spindle are extremely toxic, making self-doctoring extremely dangerous.

The wood from the deciduous shrub is extremely hard and can be used to make wooden dowels and pegs and spindles for use in spinning.

After the somewhat unremarkable flowering in spring, the fruit change colour during the summer from pink to red. When they burst, bright orange seeds are exposed which are eaten by birds.

Eupatorium cannabinum

HEMP AGRIMONY

Hemp agrimony flowers alongside water and at the edges of moist woodland from June. The pale flesh-

Eupatorium cannabinum, *hemp agrimony.*

Eupatorium cannabinum, *hemp agrimony.*

Eupatorium maculatum 'Atropurpurea', *joe pye weed.*

coloured flowers draw many butterflies, and bees. The flowers are born in packed corymbs. Hemp agrimony grows about 150cm (5ft) high and is a welcome native plant in the garden for a moist corner.

The plant contains *eupatorine* which acts as a diuretic that is used for oedema, and swollen legs. Hemp agrimony purifies the blood, acts as a tonic, stimulates liver and gall bladder function, and in higher doses acts as a laxative and expectorant.

Eupatorium maculatum 'Atropurpurea'

JOE PYE WEED, GRAVEL ROOT, QUEEN OF THE MEADOW

The *Eupatorium* genus is named after King Mithrades Eupator who as well as being king of Pontus, was also a great herb expert, who used *Eupatorium* medicinally.

Eupatorium maculatum is regarded by some as synonymous with *Eupatorium purpureum*. Both species grow wild in marshy ground in North America. The 'Atropurpurea' form bears larger flower corymbs and has darker red shoots, which grow about 200cm (79in) long. The leaves are also more red than olive green.

For use see *Eupatorium purpureum*.

Eupatorium purpureum

JOE PYE WEED, GRAVEL ROOT, QUEEN OF THE MEADOW

The purple Joe Pye weed is the American equivalent of the hemp agrimony which grows in Europe. *Eupatorium purpureum* grows across North America in moist or wet ground, flowers in summer, and can reach 2–3m (79in–10ft) high in fertile soil.

The native Americans gained a red dye from the plant for colouring leather and clothing. They used the roots of the plant as medicine, especially against typhoid. Both Joe Pye weed and hemp agrimony have similar properties. Decoctions and tinctures, especially from the roots, are diuretic and act as a tonic. The herb is ideal for oedema, difficulty in urinating, gout, rheumatism, and particularly used for kidney stones.

Eupatorium purpureum, *Joe Pye weed*.

Euphorbia amygdaloides, *spurge*.

Euphorbia amygdaloides, *spurge*.

Euphorbia

SPURGE

The approximately thousand species of spurge originate in the main from hot regions of Africa and Asia but a considerable number also grow in more moderate climates as either native or garden plants. When the plant is damaged, a white milky sap is released, which contains poisonous substances. If the sap comes into contact with the skin or eyes, the affected part must be irrigated immediately with plenty of water. Sap in the eye is especially dangerous as this can cause blindness.

Every part of these plants – but particularly the sap and seed – are also extremely toxic if ingested, so that medicinal use is only possible under medical supervision.

Because of this toxicity, spurge is rarely used these days. Previously, the sap was dabbed on to warts to remove them. It is possible this works, in view of the way the sap aggressively erodes skin. Internal use as a drastic purgative and medicine for oedema has probably long since ceased because of the high toxicity of the substances in the herb. The substances in purge are used homoeopathically to treat diarrhoea, stomach spasms with vomiting, skin irritations, and irritation of the mucous membranes.

Euphorbia amygdaloides

WOOD SPURGE

The milky sap from *Euphorbia amygdaloides* in particular has aggressive eroding properties, so that this type is chosen to get rid of warts. For general use, see *Euphorbia*.

This species grows in open canopy broad-leaved woodland, especially in southern parts of Europe, North Africa, and western regions of Asia. This perennial of the woodland and shady banks is found in southern parts of Britain. The 50–90cm (20–36in) high plant flowers in early summer and is also widely planted for its ornamental value in gardens.

Euphorbia cyparissias

CYPRESS SPURGE

The stems and leaves of cypress spurge resemble tiny coniferous trees. They grow to a maximum of 50cm (20in) high and bear yellow flower clusters on the ends of their shoots in May to June. The main native range of this plant is southern and central parts of Europe but is also regarded as a native plant of chalky soils in the extreme south-east of England. Elsewhere is grows as a naturalised es-

Euphorbia cyparissias, *Cypress spurge.*

capee from cultivation or in gardens. It prefers open grassland and the edges of woods.

Cypress spurge was once used medicinally for its ability to reduce fever temperatures. This species though is especially toxic, so that any medicinal use other than homeopathic is ill advised. For use and toxicity, see *Euphorbia.*

Euphorbia lathyris, *caper spurge.*

Courtesy The Kruidhof, Buitenpost.

Euphorbia lathyris

CAPER SPURGE

Voles and moles are banished by caper spurge according to those who sell the plants and the rather rigid biennial is planted in gardens for this reason. It grows to about 100cm (3ft 6in) high (higher on very fertile soil). The long stems bear straight rows of elongated leaves and the top of the plant flowers in the second summer. The fairly large flowers form fruits the size of peas from which the seeds spring. The seeds germinate also outside gardens, especially in dry, sun-baked places. The plant naturalises most readily in southern and central parts of Europe, together with North Africa, and subtropical America. The plant is a native of the lands surrounding the Mediterranean but it precise origins are unknown. It may also be native to southern England ancient woodland.

For use and toxicity, see *Euphorbia.*

Euphorbia palustris.

Euphorbia palustris

SPURGE

Euphorbia palustris likes to have its roots in wet soil. This species grows in southern and central parts of Europe, especially along the big rivers. The plant can cope well with flooding, even during the summer flowering period. In the wild the plant grows about 100cm (39in) high but in gardens, where the soil is extremely fertile, it can grow as tall as a man. The plant does not have to be planted in waterlogged soil: humus rich moist soil will also do. For use and toxicity, see *Euphorbia.*

Herb garden at the Dutch Open Air Museum, Arnhem.

Euphrasia stricta, *eyebright.*

Euphrasia stricta

Plants of the *Euphrasia* genus, in particular *Euphrasia officinalis* were once used to treat eyes by the doctrine of signatures and modern research has proven the plant to have beneficial properties for such use. Infusions of *Euphrasia* (of the eyebright family) are often used with chamomile as disinfectant and also used warm in compresses held against the eye for tired or weeping eyes. This causes any burning feeling to disappear. Drinking the infusion has a similar effect and also increases resistance to colds. *Euphrasia* is widely used in homeopathic medicine for a range of eye problems.

This species of *Euphrasia* is a native of northern Europe and Asia (to Siberia) where it grows on poor grassland, having a preference for light loam or sand. The plant is less common in southern Europe. There are numerous species of eyebright and as many more hybrids resulting from crossing. This species of annual can be found in Jersey and grows 10–20cm (4–8in) high, flowering in late summer and autumn.

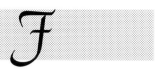

𝓕

Fagopyrum esculentum, *buckwheat*.

Fagopyrum esculentum

BUCKWHEAT

When bees have visited buckwheat, they bring the nectar with its marvellous aroma to their hive where they make strong tasting honey from it. In Asia, where the plant originates, and among vegetarians, the roasted grain is often prepared as a main dish or incorporated into buckwheat pancakes or biscuits.

Apart from its role as food, the plant has medicinal properties. Substances, chiefly from the flowers and foliage, improve bloody supply and strengthen the blood vessels. The plant is prescribed for varicose veins. Side effects are possible, even from consuming buckwheat as food, which can cause an allergic itch. The plant also contains substances which can cause over-sensitivity to sunlight. With cattle that suddenly eat a large amount of buckwheat this can cause severe problems, causing parts of the body not covered by hair to become inflamed.

Buckwheat is part of the Polygonaceae family. It is an annual, originating from Asia, and cannot withstand any frost. Sow buckwheat therefore only after the last frost. The rapid-growing plant reaches about 50cm (20in) by July when it flowers and the grain ripens by October.

꽃 ⚕ ✻

Ficus carica

FIG

Figs are mildly laxative and have a smoothing effect on the oesophagus, stomach, and throat, which is why they are often added to cough syrups. Having to eat figs is certainly no punishment be-

Ficus carica, *fig.*

Ficus carica, *fig.*

cause the false fruits are sweet and sour when fresh, or sweeter and sticky when dried. Figs originate from a tree which grows in the Mediterranean region but will grow in sheltered spots in milder coastal regions in northern parts of Europe. Those who want to grow the figs must choose special varieties though. Fig trees do best trained against a south-facing wall or in a conservatory or greenhouse. There are varieties which will fruit without pollination. The figs are normally pollinated by wasps which creep into small openings in the fleshy flower receptacle and pollinate the blossoms on the inside. The fig is in reality a flower calyx which entirely surrounds the blossom.

꽃 ⚕

Filipendula rubra

MARTHA WASHINGTON

The roots of this plant were used by the native Americans for heart disorders. The plant contains toxic prussic acid compounds. This perennial grows in moist pasture land in America.

In Europe, the herb is solely cultivated as an ornamental plant and can be grown as a perennial, reaching about 200cm (79in) if given fertile moisture-retaining soil.

꽃

Filipendula rubra.

Filipendula ulmaria, *meadowsweet*.

Filipendula ulmaria, *meadowsweet*.

Filipendula ulmaria

MEADOWSWEET, QUEEN OF THE MEADOW

The word aspirin was derived from the former botanical name of meadowsweet, which was formerly *Spirea ulmaria*. The plant was found to contain salicylic acid which was subsequently synthesised to form aspirin.

The herb had long been used in folk medicine for its properties, especially to reduce rheumatic pains. The flowers were strung together and dried and then used to prepare an infusion, which reduces fevers and is diuretic. This helps to cleanse the body and thereby reduces the effects of rheumatism.

Meadowsweet is still used by herbalists and homeopaths, with the homeopathic medicine *Spirea ulmaria* being used for rheumatism and sciatica.

Meadowsweet in a native perennial that grows to 100–200cm (39–79in) high in wet meadows and close to water. The creamy white flowers spread a sweet scent reminiscent of almonds. Once the fresh plant was strewn on floors to create a pleasant smell in the house. These days, flower buds are used in production of perfume.

The entire plant can be used to form a yellow dye for wool and textile. The roots are also used to create a black dye.

Foeniculum vulgare

FENNEL

If you suddenly find yourself short of money, you can try chewing fennel seeds. This is what the poor used to do to banish their hunger pangs. Nowadays the seeds are used in baking and for such culinary purposes as pickling gherkins. The fine foliage and seeds of fennel have a delicate aniseed aroma and taste. Finely chopped leaves can be added to salads and crushed seeds of oil of fennel can be used to flavour sauces. The foliage is especially prized as a garnish with fish and eating fennel neutralises the oil in fish.

In herbal folk medicine fennel seed in particular was used as an expectorant for coughs and bronchitis, and also for stomach and intestinal spasms, for constipation and wind, and as a means of calming children. Homeopaths use fennel mainly for treating eyes and to increase milk yield for nursing mothers.

Foeniculum vulgare *'Giant Bronze'.*

Foeniculum vulgare, *fennel.*

Fennel originates from the lands surrounding the Mediterranean . The variety which grows in more southerly latitudes *(Foeniculum vulgare* var. *dulce)* can be difficult to cultivate. The slightly less sweet tasting *Foeniculum vulgare* 'Giant Bronze' is more easily cultivated and grows tall with bronze-coloured stems. The Florence fennel *(Foeniculum vulgare* var. *azoricum)* is often grown as a vegetable. This forms a ball of fleshy bulb-like stem bases that in southern parts of Europe are short and broad but longer and narrower further north. The "bulbs" are cooked and eaten as a vegetable.

Florence fennel is grown as an annual with seeds sown in April ready to harvest by summer. Sow also in July and August for an autumn crop. Florence fennel can barely withstand any frost.

Normal fennel grows as a biennial to perennial in places with mild winters and sets seed itself. All fennels prefer light but fertile soil.

Fennel and dill are often confused with each other and the related species do cross with each other.

Foeniculum vulgare *var.* azoricum, *Florence fennel.*

Fragaria vesca, *wild strawberry.*

Fragaria vesca

WILD STRAWBERRY

Sugar is absolutely unnecessary with a wild strawberry. The taste is sweet with a delicate strawberry scent which has been lost with the majority of cultivated strawberries. The only disadvantage is that wild strawberries are so small that you need to pick many to make a helping for one. *Fragaria vesca* grows readily in any moisture-retaining garden soil, preferring partial shade. The plant makes runners and eventually become rampant so you might prefer to grow them in a strawberry pot which prevents the runners reaching the ground.

Some people can eat their fill of the fruit while others have an allergic reaction which causes a skin rash. This indicates that the plant contains remarkable substances. The leaves are used for infusions for a range of disorders, such as stopping diarrhoea, and treating stomach and intestinal ailments. The substances in wild strawberries improve kidney function and prevent anaemia. A decoction of the roots acts as a diuretic and therefore aids rheumatism and gout. Infusions also helps to cleanse oil skin and slices of strawberry help to soothe the face, especially after sunburn.

Fragaria vesca, wild strawberry.

Fraxinus excelsior, *common ash.*

Fraxinus excelsior

COMMON ASH

Ash trees bear striking black buds in winter and the blossom burst first in spring, before the pinnate leaves emerge. The flowers have in the mean time changed into winged fruits. This deciduous tree grows slowly at first but can reach 40m (130ft). It has a preference for good soil that is rich in nitrogen.

The leaflets are harvested in May, then the central vein is removed and the rest dried. This can be used for infusions which have diuretic properties and improve kidney function, cleansing the body and consequently also beneficial for rheumatic complaints. The bark was once used to treat malaria. Ash is highly prized for its timber, which is used to make tool handles and shafts for hammers and spades etc.

 ✳

Fucus vesiculous

BLADDERWRACK, BLACK-TANG

The leaves of bladderwrack are both floppy yet tough. They yield fluidly with the waves in the

Fucus vesiculous, *bladderwrack.*

ocean but are seldom torn apart by even the fiercest storm. The seaweed grasps with a firm hold to the rocks along the Atlantic coast. The plant frequently dries out when the tide is out. The strong tissue of the plant copes with this regular change in conditions. *Fucus vesiculous,* or bladderwrack, is olive green and has conspicuous air bladders along its fronds.

In common with other species of *Fucus,* this seaweed contains high concentrations of iodine which affects the working of the thyroid. This can be used to treat goitre and activation of the thyroid can held prevent obesity.

Fumaria officinalis

FUMITORY, EARTH SMOKE, WAX DOLLS

Fumitory, which grows unobtrusively on sandy soil, has been used as a medicinal herb for thousands of years. The herb helps to purify the blood, stimulates gall bladder and liver function, and cleanses the entire body, among other means, by driving out fluid. Excessive use of the herb can lead to toxic reactions, so that the herb should be used under supervision of experts.

Fumaria officinalis flowers from May until autumn throughout Europe and the adjoining parts of Asia and Africa, especially as a weed with a low growth habit in arable land. The delicate plant appears in some of the strangest places in gardens and readily germinates in crevices between paving and in gaps in walls.

Fumaria officinalis, *fumitory.*

G

Galega officinalis, *goat's rue.*

Galega officinalis

GOAT'S RUE, FRENCH LILAC

Cows that eat goat's rue either give more milk or never give milk again. If they eat the herb before it has flowered, they produce more milk but when the plant flowers, it secretes a nervous toxin (galegin) from the roots throughout the plant which can kill cattle.

The botanical name is derived from Greek and refers to the lactation stimulation of the herb. The herb was used from early times to help women lactate and also to reduce the blood sugar level, aid digestion, and as a diuretic. The plant can be dangerous and is virtually unheard of in present day medical use.

Despite this, goat's rue is often planted in informal or "natural" gardens, where its unkempt appearance does not jar. The plant originates from southern parts of Europe and Asia Minor. The colour of the flowers varies widely: from purple to white but is usually pink. The plant is fully hardy and prefers a sunny position for its 100cm (39in) high growth.

℞ ✳

Galeopsis segetum

HEMPNETTLE

Hempnettles contain substances which are beneficial for recovery from chronic lung problems such as emphysema, and brown lung disease. Painful coughs are eased and stubborn phlegm cleared up. The herb's effect is relatively mild though so that it needs to be taken over a period of time. That can be in the form of a homeopathic tincture, which helps to prevent damage to lung cells.

The pale yellow hempnettle grows wild in western parts of Europe on poor sandy or stony soil that is acidic. This annual grows to about 40cm (16in) and flowers from June to autumn with its small, pale blooms.

℞

Galeopsis segetum, *hempnettle.*

Galeopsis speciosa, *Edmonton hempnettle.*

Galeopsis speciosa

LARGE-FLOWERED HEMPNETTLE

The large-flowered hempnettle has yellow with lilac flowers and a rather rigid appearance, growing about 100cm (39in) tall. The plant grows mainly in hedgerows and nitrogen rich but acidic arable land, often where there is a transition from peat to sand. It is less common in Britain than the common hempnettle.

The large-flowered species contains the same medicinal properties as the other hempnettles.

Galeopsis x *tetrahit* syn. *Galeopsis tetrahit*

COMMON HEMPNETTLE

The common hempnettle is considered to be a natural crossing of the large-flowered hempnettle *(G. speciosa)* and the hairy hempnettle *(G. pubescens)* but this is not universally recorded in flora. The annual grows wild throughout almost the whole of Europe, except the extreme south. In Britain the plant is mainly found in arable land but also in woods and fens and on wet heathland.

The common hempnettle has the same medicinal properties as the other hempnettles.

☤

Galeopsis *x* tetrahit, *common hempnettle.*

Galeopsis x tetrahit, *common hempnettle.*

Galium aparine, *goosegrass.*

Galium aparine

GOOSEGRASS, CLEAVERS, STICKY WILLIE

The stems of goosegrass become stuck to you if you brush against them because of the tiny hooks on the stems which attach themselves to clothing. These help this annual plant to climb. The herb grows mainly at the edge of woods and in hedgerows, where it can scramble on other plants to about 100cm (39in). The plant is widely dispersed throughout Europe.

The fruits of the plant have been found in prehis-

toric settlements, where they were possibly used during cheese making. The herb is still used today to help to curdle milk. The roasted seeds can be used as an alternative to coffee.

Goosegrass has astringent properties and is particularly prescribed for reducing swellings in swollen glands. Inflamed tonsils, benign tumours, and cysts are reduced and in addition, goosegrass is also used to treat a long list of other disorders, including crystals in the urinary tract and kidney stones.

Galium boreale, *northern bedstraw.*

Galium boreale

NORTHERN BEDSTRAW

Northern bedstraw flowers as far south in Europe as the Alps but is found in Britain mainly in the north in rocky places. The plant forms rather stiff and bristly growth with stems of about 50cm (20in) which always have a cross of four leaves at intervals and are topped off when the flowers emerge by a tuft of white blooms. The roots can be used to produce a fine red dye.

Galium mollugo, *great hedge bedstraw.*

Galium mollugo

GREAT HEDGE BEDSTRAW

Great hedge bedstraw grows in a wide variety of different places in those parts of Europe that enjoys a moderate climate with a clear preference for fertile soil. In moist, open places, it forms whole cushions of wiry stems which in summer are covered by masses of little white flowers. The properties of great hedge bedstraw are virtually identical to those of goosegrass (see *Galium aparine).*

Galium odoratum, *sweet woodruff.*

Galium odoratum syn. *Asperula odorata*

SWEET WOODRUFF

Bruise the leaves of sweet woodruff and the smell of new mown hay is given off. This is because cumarin is released when the plant is wounded. This is used as an aromatic in food production and also added to alcoholic beverages such as Rhine wines, vodka, and Champagne. An excessive use of cumarin-containing drinks can cause headaches and dizziness. Rats which eat a lot of the substance suffer liver damage. It is therefore understandable that the substance is currently added less frequently to drinks. The dried herb is used for infusions that provide a relaxing tea, which also helps reduce retained fluid, irritability, depression, and sleeplessness. In medicinal form, the herb is used for intestinal spasms, thrombosis, and varicose veins. The dried herb has been one of the most popular aromatics for centuries. Mattresses and pillows were filled with the herb for a better night's rest and a scent of new mown hay. Pomanders were also filled with the herb to be hung between clothes, which also helped to keep moths away. The roots can be used to produce a red dye for colouring wool and other textiles. Sweet woodruff is a perennial which remains low in habit. It is found throughout European woods, especially beech woods growing on alkaline soil. The herb flowers in May to June. The plant is native in Britain.

Galium odoratum, *sweet woodruff.*

Galium verum, *lady's bedstraw.*

Galium verum, *lady's bedstraw.*

Galium verum

LADY'S BEDSTRAW

When lady's bedstraw flowers in July and August, it spreads a wonderful fragrance from its masses of little yellow flowers. In places where the plant grows abundantly, such as grassland, hedge banks, and old sand dunes, the air can be pregnant with the scent. Lady's bedstraw thrives in coastal areas, along rivers, and grassland throughout Europe. The herb has been used since ancient times to curdle milk for cheese making with the cheese acquiring a pleasant taste and attractive colour as a result. Lady's bedstraw is one of the favourite natural dyes with the roots, which are difficult to harvest, providing red dye and the rest of the plant providing yellow.

Galium verum has broadly identical medicinal properties to goosegrass (see *Galium aparine*). Lady's bedstraw is primarily used for kidney stones and problems of the urinary tract.

Gardenia augusta syn. *G. florida, G. jasminoides*

GARDENIA, CAPE JASMIN

The small container shrub which is grown in northern Europe as a house plant can grow into a tree 10m (32ft) high. In China, the strongly-scented blossom is dried and used to make tea because of the wonderful fragrance. The plant also provides a yellow dyestuff that was used by the mandarins and intelligentsia to colour their robes. In Asia in particular, substances from the buds of the plant are used for fevers, toothache, infections, and haemorrhages. Grow gardenia as a house plant, ensuring it is kept well watered in summer, but the water must not be alkaline. The plant starts to flower in mid summer and continues until autumn. Prune the shrub after flowering to keep it to shape and size. The minimum winter temperature is 12°C (50°F).

Gardenia augusta, *gardenia.*

Gaultheria procumbens, *wintergreen.*

Gaultheria procumbens

WINTERGREEN, CHECKERBERRY, TEABERRY

The native Americans used wintergreen for three different purposes. The volatile oils from the plant were used to keep airways open, as a disinfectant, and painkiller. The plant also contains methyl-salicylate, which is very similar to aspirin.

Today the oils and salves of wintergreen are smeared on painful joints (with rheumatism) and muscles. The leaves are used to make an infusion which acts as an expectorant and diuretic, but also helps to reduce inflammations. Take care with the internal use of the oil because overdoses can cause kidney and liver damage.

The aromatic oil is utilised by the perfume industry as a basis for perfumes.

Wintergreen remains a low shrub that grows wild in North American in acid soil. The plant is grown ornamentally in Europe for its evergreen foliage and red berries (which ripen in winter), often as a container-grown specimen.

Genista tinctoria, *dyer's greenweed.*

Genista tinctoria, *dyer's greenweed.*

Genista tinctoria

DYER'S GREENWOOD, BROOM

Dyer's greenwood is very popular for use as a dyestuff for wool and other textiles. The tips of the branches are clipped off with their buds or yellow flowers in June to August and turned into dye. The plant can produce yellow or – depending on the other treatment – shades of brown or green.

The branches contain volatile oils and alkaloids which have medicinal properties which have not yet been fully researched. The herb is often used as a diuretic and to purify the blood as treatment for oedema and kidney stones. The presence of alkaloids makes dyer's greenwood toxic, so that precise dosing is essential and similar results can be achieved with less hazardous herbs.

Dyer's greenwood is a native of most of Europe, including southern Scandinavia and grows in grassland, and heaths, but also on heavier soils where it reaches 100cm (39in) high with a similar span. The shrub flowers in June to July with clusters of golden yellow "butterfly" blooms. It is an ideal garden plant for a sunny position.

Gentiana lutea

GREAT YELLOW GENTIAN

The yellow gentian grows on the grassy slopes of central Europe's mountains, where its large leaves stand out above the encircling growth, especially in June when the yellow flower clusters are born on stems of up to 100cm (39in) long. The gentian can stick out like this because the cattle do not fancy eating it. For this reason hill farmers regard the plant as a weed.

Gentiana lutea, *great yellow gentian.*

Gentiana lutea, *great yellow gentian.*

Geranium maculatum, *American cranesbill.*

Geranium robertianum, *herb Robert.*

The roots contain an extremely bitter substance which is used as a medicinal tincture for ailments such as production of too little stomach acid, lack of appetite, indigestion, wind, defective gall bladder, and liver complaints. The pungent substances are also used as extracts in herbal bitters and other aperitif drinks.

Geranium maculatum

AMERICAN CRANESBILL, ALUM ROOT, SPOTTED CRANESBILL, WILD GERANIUM

The roots of the American cranesbill contain between ten and eighteen per cent tannin, which is at its highest just before flowering. The Sioux in North America knew the effect of this substance and pulverised the root and dried it to form a powder that they used for first aid in dealing with wounds. The tannins have a strong astringent effect, causing the wound to close.

This same effect is also true of internal usage. The herbs was and still is used to treat diarrhoea, dysentery, internal haemorrhages, and excessive menstruation.

American cranesbill flowers from April to June (sometimes right through until autumn) in the moist woods of North America. It is grown in Europe as an ornamental plant and is best planted in moisture-retaining soil in partial shade.

Geranium robertianum

HERB ROBERT

Herb Robert self seeds itself readily in moist, humus-rich soil, especially alongside walls and embankments, at the edges of woods, and in hedges. In shade, herb Robert can easily grow to 50cm

135

Geranium robertianum, *herb Robert.*

Geum rivale, *water avens.*

Geranium robertianum *'Celtic White'.*

(20in) high but in open positions it remains at 10cm (4in). The stems and leaf stalks are reddish and covered with tiny hairs. If the plant is crushed it releases a very unpleasant smell. The herb is an annual or short-lived perennial which flowers from late April until later summer (except in the extreme north and in arid areas).

Besides the usual pink flowers, there are also cultivars with white flowers, such as the large-flowered variety *Geranium robertianum* 'Album' and the dwarf *G. robertianum* 'Celtic White', which flowers profusely. Herb Robert has similar properties to cranesbill but despite that is only used in folk medicine, for the same ailments as *Geranium maculatum.*

Geum rivale

WATER AVENS

When the roots of water avens are bruised they release an aroma of cloves. The roots contain eugenol as found in cloves, and just like that spice, decoctions of the root are used as a painkiller for toothache. The root also contains antiseptic substances and tannin, so that decoctions are also used to treat diarrhoea, internal haemorrhages, and inflammation.

Geum rivale, *water avens.*

Geum rivale grows principally in the northern European countries, in Canada, and northern parts of Russia.

The plant prefers moist soil where it can withstand the full sun. In drier soils it is better planted in partial shade. The drooping flowers bloom from lay May until early July.

Geum urbanum

AVENS, WOOD AVENS, HERB BENNET

According to Medieval legend "devils and poisonous creatures" would not trouble you if you have avens in your pocket. The root contains volatile oils and a high proportion of tannin (sixteen per cent). Decoctions from the root are used to flavour beer, added to perfume, and used medicinally for diarrhoea, dysentery, fever, inflammation (of throat and gums), and vaginal bleeding and discharges.

Avens is only found growing in fertile, moisture-retaining soil. It is evergreen and bears small yellow flowers from spring until the onset of winter.

Geum urbanum, *avens.*

Geum urbanum, *avens.*

Each seed bears a little hook which attaches itself to passing animals (and humans).

Gillenia trifoliata syn. Porteranthus trifoliata

INDIAN PHYSIC, BOWMAN'S ROOT, AMERICAN IPECAC

Indian physic is perhaps best known as an ornamental plant for its white flowers which droop on the ends of thin but strong, woody stems. The plant spreads out but grows to about 50cm (20in) high.

The native Americans in its land of origin knew how to derive substances from the root which induced vomiting, could be used as an expectorant, or laxative, or general stimulant. The effect of the herb was confirmed by Mrs M. Grieve, the famous English herbalist, who described the Indian physic as "a safe and reliable" medicine. Medical supervision is however necessary, because of the powerful effect of this herb.

Gillenia trifoliata, *Indian physic.*

Ginkgo biloba *'Variegata', variegated ginkgo.*

Ginkgo biloba

GINGKO, MAIDENHAIR TREE

The ginkgo is regarded as a living fossil because it belongs to a family of plants that flourished 180 million years ago but which are now extinct, except for this one species. Western visitors saw the trees outside Japanese temples and dubbed it the "temple tree". Searches were made for forests of the tree without success and it later became clear that the tree originates from China, where wild specimens were subsequently found. Specimens were sent from Japan to the Europe in 1727, where it has subsequently grown happily. The fan-shaped leaves turn butter yellow in autumn before falling. The leaves of the tree are used to create medicines that are used above all for improving blood circulation, strengthening arteries, and reducing thickening of the arteries during ageing. *Ginkgo* is used in homeopathic medicine for improving circulation, and reducing thickening of the arteries. The improvement of the circulation helps to prevent chilblains, bedsores, and tinnitus. The herb lowers blood pressure and reduces problems from diabetes associated with ageing.

An infusion of leaves dabbed on the affected areas helps to treat haemorrhoid and varicose veins.

Ginkgo biloba *'Variegata', variegated ginkgo.*

Glaucium flavum

YELLOW HORNED POPPY

The yellow horned poppy is typically found on European coasts, especially on the shingle beds of the Baltic but more sporadically along North Sea coasts. In Britain it is found on shingle beds, sand, and cliff tops. The short-lived perennial flowers from June to September with striking large yellow flowers.

The herb has diuretic properties and is particularly used for treating gall bladder and kidney stones.

Glaucium flavum, *yellow horned poppy.*

Gloriosa superba *'Rothschildiana', glory lily.*

Glechoma hederacea syn. *Nepeta glechoma, N. hederacea*

GROUND IVY, ALEHOOF

Ground ivy will steadily spread itself by runners on moisture-retaining soil in partial shade. The runners root where they touch the ground. The more upright stems bear blue flowers from April and these are harvested in spring to be dried for medicinal use.

The herb contains a host of useful substances such as tannin and other bitter substances which are astringent and antiseptic. The herb is mainly used for these properties in treatment of diarrhoea and for dressing wounds. The leaves of ground ivy are also being increasingly added these days to salads as a tonic, specially in spring. In addition to organic fatty acids, the plant also contains vitamin C but must not be consumed in quantity.

Gloriosa superba

GLORY LILY, MALABAR GLORY LILY, MOZAMBIQUE LILY

The toxins from the root of the glory lily were used in Africa for poison arrows. In India the poison is used to hunt smaller prey: the herb is used to treat lice.

The entire plant is poisonous with the root in particular containing colchicine, which slows cell growth and can reduce the spread of cancer. The substance is also used in genetic engineering.

Colchicine is used to treat attacks of gout, acts as a diuretic, and is used in small doses to induce and speed labour. Given the highly toxic nature of the plant, the herb must only be used under medical supervision.

The glory lily originates from tropical Africa and Asia and is grown in Europe as a climbing house or container plant. It only thrives when warm and the root tuber without foliage is unable to cope with temperatures below 10°C (50°F). Plant in fertile soil and water copiously during the growing period.

Glechoma hederacea, *ground ivy.*

Glycyrrhiza glabra, *liquorice.*

Gratiola officinalis, *hedge hyssop.*

Glycyrrhiza glabra

LIQUORICE

The sweet taste derived from the root of liquorice is fifty times sweeter than sucrose or sugar. The substance which provides this sweetness is glycyrrhizin but there is no dental health problem from the sweetness for children's teeth because chewing liquorice root is just as healthy as using toothpaste.

Children do need to clean their teeth though after eating liquorice derived from the root. Glycyrrhizine is used in food as a sweetener and has been used medicinally for thousands of years. The Egyptians wrote long ago of the healing properties of the plant. Extracts from the roots are still used medicinally for a wide range of ailments. The most important use is the ability to clear mucous from the airways which results in the substances from the plant being regularly added to cold remedies. Excessive use can have side effects, such as high blood pressure.

The plant also provides a yellow dye for colouring wool and other textiles.

Liquorice is a hardy plant from Asia and the area surrounding the Mediterranean . The sturdy stems reach 150cm (5ft) high and bear superb mauve "butterfly" flowers in July and August.

Gratiola officinalis

HEDGE HYSSOP

The hedge hyssop used to be regarded as a rich gift to people from God. The plant was a proven remedy for weak hearts and oedema which was associated with the ailment. The plant contains the glycoside gratiotoxin which works in much the same way as digitalis in foxgloves. Its use as a laxative has particularly subsided due to the availability of much safer remedies. Hedge hyssop is very toxic and must only be used under medical supervision. *Gratiola* is used in homeopathy for gastro-intestinal disorders. *Gratiola officinalis* is a native perennial of central and eastern parts of Europe where it grows in damp meadows, on heaths, and alongside water.

Gratiola officinalis, *hedge hyssop.*

Grindelia squarrosa, *gumplant.*

Grindelia squarrosa, *gumplant.*

Grindelia squarrosa

GUMPLANT, GUMWEED, TARWEED

The buds of the gumplant glisten with a white sticky resin which can also be seen when the flowers open. The plant, with its large yellow flowers, originates from the central and western parts of North America, where it grows in a dry, warm climate. Despite this, the plant is hardy in northern Europe.

The leaves and flowering shoots of the plant and the related *Grindelia camporum* and *Grindelia robusta* can be used to form medicine used to clear stubborn mucous. The herb clears the airways for asthma, bronchitis, and emphysema sufferers. The medicine is also available in homeopathic form.

Hyocyamus niger, *henbane.*

Hamamelis virginiana, *Virginian witch hazel.*

Hedera helix, *ivy.*

Hamamelis virginiana

VIRGINIAN WITCH HAZEL

The Virginian witch hazel blossoms in autumn, with sweetly-scented yellow flowers, just before it sheds its leaves. The shrub originates from moist places in the United States. These days the plant is mainly of importance as an ornamental shrub and as root stock for other species of witch hazel which are more difficult to grow. The native north Americans soaked the bark of the young twigs in water to make a healing eye bath. The bark is high in tannin which is both astringent and antiseptic. Gargling with solutions of witch hazel help sore throats and both mouth and throat infections. A more important use is in salves for haemorrhoid, varicose veins, and treatment of wounds. Witch hazel is widely used in cosmetic products, such as skin creams, and soap for those who perspire profusely.

Hamamelis virginiana, *Virginian witch hazel.*

Hedera helix

IVY

The Greek and Roman gods of good living, Dionysos and Bacchus, are illustrated with wreaths of ivy. The plant signifies drunkenness. In northern Europe, ivy is the only climbing evergreen. It grows wild in woods throughout Europe on alkaline soils where it climbs up the trunks of trees. Healthy trees and well-maintained walls do not suffer from the activities of this climber. The native *Hedera helix* has numerous cultivars with different leaf forms.

The leaves, flowers, and fruit all contain toxic substances which are also used medicinally. These kill bacteria and fungi, reduce spasms, lower fevers, and are used as expectorants. The herb is used in both folk medicine and homeopathy for treating coughs, colds, infected mucous membranes, whooping cough, emphysema, and asthma. Both internal and external use must be under medical supervision because of the toxicity of the plant and potential for skin irritations.

Hedera helix *'Deltoidea', ivy.*

Hedera helix *'Gold Forever', ivy.*

The black berries of ivy can be used to form both pink and grey dyes for colouring wool and other textiles.

Helianthus anuus

SUNFLOWER

Sunflower oil is one of the most important edible oils. It is used for cooking and incorporated in many foods, such as margarine. The oil is both tasty and healthy: the cholesterol level in the blood is reduced by sunflower oil. Sunflower oil is also used in soap, paint, and massage oil and for producing green dye for colouring wool and other textiles.

Helianthus anuus, *sunflower.*

Helichrysum arenarium, *everlasting flower.*

Helichrysum italicum, *curry plant.*

Courtesy The Kruidenhof, Buitenpost.

Sunflower seeds are edible when the husks are removed either fresh or baked and are ideal added to vegetables for stir-fry and other oriental dishes. Sunflower meal is very nutritious and can be used to make bread. Substances from the petals and the top shoots of non-flowering plants help to reduce fever and are specially useful for attacks of malaria. Sunflowers are an annual that originates from Central and South America. The Stem of the plant grows upwards for several months to several meters high (with large coarse leaves). Once the flower develops at the top of the stem, the upwards growth ceases. Sometimes thinner stems that bear smaller flowers shoot from the leaf axils. The sunflower is in reality a composite flower consisting of a cluster of small brown to purple disc-florets surrounded by a ring of yellow ray-florets, which we regard as the petals. After flowering the seeds can be seen formed in extremely uniform spirals in the flowerhead.

    ✳

Helichrysum arenarium

EVERLASTING FLOWER

Plants with white felt-like leaves mainly grow in hot, dry regions, such as that surrounding the Mediterranean. The everlasting flower grows in

eastern and central parts of Europe and was once found as far north as far north as the Netherlands and Belgium. The plant requires a sunny position in dry sandy soil and will grow to 40cm (16in) in such conditions, flowering from June to August with clusters of small yellow flowers. The flowers are perfect for drying by picking them when they first start to bloom and then hanging in an airy place.

The bitter substances, tannin, and small amount of volatile oils in the flowers have diuretic properties and are therefore used as a remedy for oedema, kidney ailments, rheumatism, and arthritis. The antiseptic herb was previously used to treat worms but these days relieves bladder infections and is especially useful for gall bladder infections and in treating gall stones.

Helichrysum italicum syn. H. angustifolium

CURRY PLANT

Sprigs of the curry plant can be used to impart a mild curry flavour to rice and meat dishes, soups, and sauces. The sprigs are added during cooking and removed before serving. The plant has a higher concentration of volatile oils than the related ever-

145

lasting flower and it is therefore used in herb mixtures, cosmetics, and to ease problems with the airways.

The curry plant grows as a low bush of no more than 50cm (20in) high in the countries of the western Mediterranean. It needs to be planted in well-drained sandy soil and the drier the soil, the better will be the plant's resistance to frost. Where frost below minus 10°C (14°F) can be expected, the plant is better grown as a container plant. Prune back extensively in autumn to keep the plant compact.

Helleborus foetidus

STINKING HELLEBORE, STINKWORT, BEAR'S FOOT, DUNGWORT

When the roots of stinking hellebore are dug up a foul stench is released. These roots were once harvested for medicinal use. The roots were dried and crushed for use as snuff that "induced sneezing and hence cleansing of the body."

Currently the plant is rarely used because every part of the plant is extremely toxic. The literal translation of *Helleborus* is "deadly fare" and the crushed and powdered root is apparently effect in killing head lice.

Helleborus foetidus, *stinking hellebore.*

Helleborus foetidus, *stinking hellebore.*

Taken in the right dosage, the substances in stinking hellebore can be medicinal. The roots contain 1.4 per cent protoanemonine which irritates the mucous membranes, acts as an expectorant, is diuretic, bactericidal and fungicidal, and purge worms. Tinctures were once used to calm anxious patients. All these functions can be replaced by less poisonous medicines.

Helleborus foetidus is a native plant throughout much of Europe, found in Britain mainly in chalk and limestone scrub and woods in the south and west. The plant is also grown in milder areas as an undemanding evergreen decorative plant that prefers partial shade. The flowers often appear as early as December.

Helleborus niger

CHRISTMAS ROSE

The Christmas rose is far more difficult to cultivate than the stinking hellebore. *Helleborus niger* originates from the eastern Alps and flowers there as soon as the snow thaws. Flowering in northern Europe can be from early winter through to early spring, depending on the weather. To ensure plants flower for Christmas, they are often brought on in doors. Plants offered for sale often suffer from buds drying out even when cultivated properly. This is due to cuttings being consistently taken from the same parent plant which causes the quality to suffer. The Christmas rose can also be difficult to grow well in the garden.

The active substances in the plant are very similar to stinking hellebore so that the uses are also much the same (see *Helleborus foetidus*). A wider usage is similarly prevented by the extremely toxic nature of the plant.

Heracleum mantegazzianum, *giant hogweed.*

Helleborus niger, *Christmas rose.*

Heracleum mantegazzianum

GIANT HOGWEED, WILD PARSNIP, WILD RHUBARB

This species, which is related to our native hogweed or cow parsnip, originates from the Caucasus mountains. The plant has become widely naturalised through escape from cultivation. The flower umbels of this 100cm (39in) tall plant are as large in summer as an umbrella. Giant hogweed sets seed very readily in almost any type of soil and has become an invasive weed.

When getting rid of the plant it is important to avoid skin and eye contact with the sap. This contains furocoumarins which make the skin photosensitive or over-sensitive to sunlight. The extent of this sensitivity varies from one person to another but in some cases can result in serious burn blisters. Protect the skin immediately after any contact with the sap because the problem only occurs with exposure to light (especially strong sun) and wash the skin thoroughly before exposing yourself to the sun again. Warn children of the danger with this plant.

Heracleum sphondylium

HOGWEED, COW PARSNIP, KECK

The ordinary hogweed also contains substances which make the skin over-sensitive to sunlight (see *Heracleum mantegazzianum*). The native hog-

147

Heracleum mantegazzianum, *giant hogweed.*

weed can grow 200cm (79in) high but has more slender stems and smaller flower umbels. It grows in almost all of Europe, except the colder northern parts, in fertile, humus-rich, moisture-retaining soil.

Some people eat the young shoots of hogweed either raw or cooked. This is inadvisable because of the photo-sensitivity of substances in the plant and the ease with which the plant can be confused with other extremely poisonous umbelliferous plants.

Any medicinal use needs to be under strict medical

Heracleum sphondylium, *hogweed.*

supervision for safety. The herb is used to treat diarrhoea, to aid the digestion, as a stimulant, and to reduce blood pressure.

Herniaria glabra, *rupturewort.*

Herniaria glabra

RUPTUREWORT

Rupturewort does not cure hernias but does have beneficial properties for the stomach and intestines. Ruptures are often associated with intestinal disorders which can be treated with rupturewort. The medicinal effect is largely due to the diuretic properties of the saponins contained in the herb, which also relieve coughs, and help to free stubborn catarrh. Rupturewort helps to relive spasms and is used to this end to treat both bladder and kidney complaints. The herb should be used as fresh as possible.

Herniaria glabra is an annual or short-lived perennial which grows on moisture-retaining alkaline soil. The plant has thin, recumbent shoots with small leaves and tiny flowers.

Hesperis matronalis, *dame's violet.*

Hesperis matronalis, *dame's violet.*

Hesperis matronalis

DAME'S VIOLET, SWEET ROCKET

The dried leaves of dame's violet used to be taken aboard ships that were to make long voyages because they are rich in vitamin C and eating them could prevent scurvy.

These days the leaves are picked before the plant flowers in some parts of the world to add to salads. The taste is more pungent than cress or rocket so the herb needs to be used sparingly. In larger amounts, the herb can induce vomiting which is yet another reason to go easy on eating this plant.

The flowers give off their intense fragrance on early summer nights yet during the day no scent can be detected. The biennial to perennial plant originates from Italy but has become naturalised in other parts of Europe enjoying a mild climate and is found in gardens (preferring well-worked sandy soils). The plant grows 100–150cm (39–5ft) high and bears white or violet flowers in early summer.

Hibiscus rosa-sinensis

CHINESE HIBISCUS

The sap from the petals of the Chinese hibiscus is in particular used by the Chinese. It stems internal haemorrhages, reduces period pains, relieves

Hibiscus rosa-sinensis, *Chinese hibiscus.*

spasms, and cures sexual diseases. The sap can also be thickened to form a black dyestuff for addition to mascara and shoe polish. Harvesting of the sap from cultivated plants is inadvisable because these are usually treated to limit their growth and these chemicals used remain in the plant for a long time. The plants usually growth as a bush, reaching 200cm (79in) high but are usually sold in northern Europe as house plants that remain compact with many branches. They flower in summer and winter if kept at constant humidity and with a minimum temperature of 7°C (45°F).

Hieracium pilosella syn. *Pilosella officinarum*

MOUSE-EAR HAWKWEED

Mouse-ear hawkweed was once used to treat airway ailments such as asthma, bronchitis, and other bronchial infections. Infusions of the herb are drunk for 'flu, stomach and intestinal problems, diarrhoea, and liver ailments and used as an eye bath. The mild acting herb contains bitter substances and tannin. The plant, with its leaves covered with hairs, grows throughout Europe in dry, sunny places between low grasses. The solitary flowers are

Hieracium pilosella, *mouse-ear hawkweed.*

Hieracium pilosella, *mouse-ear hawkweed.*

borne on stems no longer than 30cm (12in) and appear in May to August.

Hippophae rhamnoides

SEA BUCKTHORN

The orange berries which ripen on the sea buckthorn in early autumn are rich in vitamins, in particular vitamin C. The berries are picked and turned into juice, syrup, or preserve for use against influenza and colds. The sap has a fresh taste and helps to cool feverish patients.

Hippophae rhamnoides, *sea buckthorn.*

Houttuynia cordata *'Plena', doku-dami.*

Sea buckthorn grows among sand dunes but also on shingle and sand banks alongside rivers in Europe. The bush grows about 50–200cm (39–79in) high and makes a useful decorative shrub for gardens with dry sandy soil. The branches have sharp thorns which the birds manage to evade in order to feast on the overripe berries in winter.

Hoheria populnea

LACE-BARK

Hoheria populnea grows into a tree 10m (30ft) high in New Zealand and gets its vernacular name because the pale brown bark peels on the trunks of older trees. The bark is used to make medicines for treating colds and tired eyes.

In Europe, lace-bark is cultivated as a container plant which bears clusters of white flowers between the leaves in late summer. Each little flower is about 2–3cm ($^3/_4$–$1^1/_4$in) across. The plant is kept to a bush by careful pruning. The plant is an evergreen and must over-winter where there is light but a minimum temperature of 5°C (41°F).

Hoheria populnea, *lace-bark.*

151

Houttuynia cordata *'Chameleon'*.

Houttuynia cordata, *doku-dami*.

Houttuynia cordata

DOKU-DAMI

Houttuynia can be increasingly found as a garden plant. The creeping roots grow especially quickly in moist soil. The best place for them is a bog garden on the edge of a pond where they can happily be immersed in up to 10cm (4in) of water. Two different cultivars are particularly popular for growing in gardens: the *Houttuynia cordata* 'Plena' with multiple flower bracts and *H. c.* 'Chameleon'

with colourful foliage of yellow, green, and red. In its countries of origin, in South-East Asia to the east of the Himalayas and in Japan the leaves of this marsh plant are used to garnish fish dishes because of the coriander taste. The plant is highly regarded medicinally for use as a diuretic, and for its antiseptic and fever abating properties.

Humulus lupulus

HOP

A yellow powder with a bitter taste is contained between the "scales" of hops which is used as a preservative and flavouring in brewing of beer. The bitter substances, including tannin, act as a stimulant and increase the appetite. New shoots from the plant can be eaten either raw or cooked. Hop is used medicinally in combination with other herbs. Together, these help to decrease nervous tension, improve night rest, and aid digestion. Dried hops in a small bag next to the pillow helps the user to sleep well. Hops are also widely used to flavour a variety of foods and are an important constituent in hair care products and are added to perfume. The flowering shoots can additionally be used to create a dyestuff than can be used to colour wool and other textiles sulphur yellow to dark brown.

The wild hop plant from milder parts of Europe and Asia has been cultivated for centuries. The selected cultivars grown for harvest have the most hop extract. This is only formed in the flowers of the female plants. Hop plants climb many meters or feet high up the supports in hop gardens or in nature up trees. The leaves are similar to those of vines. A popular and rapid-growing ornamental variety is *Humulus lupus* 'Aureus', which is has greenish gold foliage in the shade or golden yellow in the sun.

Humulus lupus, *hop*.

Humulus lupus *'Aureus'*, hop.

Hydrangea arborescens *'Annabelle'*, hydrangea.

Humulus lupus *'Aureus'*, hop.

The species from the eastern parts of North America is rarely cultivated in Europe but the cultivated form *Hydrangea arborescens* 'Annabelle' is a well-known decorative shrub in gardens. The shrub prefers moist soil and flowers mid-summer with large corymbs of sterile white florets which subsequently turn green. By cutting the shrub back almost to the ground, it will bear large rounded corymbs the following year on growth of about 100cm (39in). If the plant is not cut back, it will become unkempt, larger in size, but will bear small flower corymbs.

Hydrangea arborescens

WILD HYDRANGEA, SEVEN BARKS

The native North Americans had a treatment for kidney and bladder stones, bladder crystals, and infections of the bladder and urethra. They harvested the bark from the roots of the wild hydrangea and dissolved this in water. Medical science has subsequently confirmed the properties of this plant and extracts from the roots are now used to treat the ailments listed above.

Hyocyamus niger

HENBANE, HOGBEAN

When smeared with witches' brew a witch could fly on a broomstick. This may seem fantasy but in a manner of speaking, this was true. Witches' brew was made using henbane and deadly nightshade *(Atropa belladonna)*, herbs which contain hallucinogenic substances. These can be absorbed through the skin and induce a trance during which it is quite possible to imagine one is flying. The witchfinders used the same witches' brew for another purpose. They smeared the ointment on

153

Hyoscyamus niger, *henbane.*

Hyoscyamus niger grows as an annual or biennial in almost the whole of Europe and neighbouring parts of Asia and Africa. The plant needs to be placed in a sunny position on disturbed ground full of nutrients, such as rubbish tips. Populations in Britain are widely scattered.

℞ ✳

Hypericum perforatum

COMMON ST JOHN'S WORT, PERFORATE ST JOHN'S WORT

In the language of flowers, St John's wort stands for "superstition" and there are indeed all manner of rites associated with the plant. At the same time this is a herb of which the medicinal properties have been convincingly proven. It is not so long ago that it was discovered that some people suffer depression owing to absence of sunlight in the winter. Both additional light and St John's wort can help such patients.

The plant has long been popular as an anti-depressant with the major advantage that it can be used for months on end without problems. The only known

Hypericum perforatum, *St John's wort.*

the skin (especially the vagina) which caused the accused to have convulsions and hallucinate, "proving" them to be a witch.

Hyocyamus species have been in use for at least four thousand years, by the ancient Egyptians among others. The Greek priestesses of the oracle at Delphi were told to inhale the smoke from the seeds to induce a trance and create visions.

Today, henbane is mainly used to treat spasms, especially of the stomach and intestines, but also for treating Parkinson's disease. The herb is also applied externally for rheumatic and other pains. Use this herb only under medical supervision.

Hyoscyamus niger, *henbane.*

side-effect of the herb is that it makes the skin more sensitive to sunlight, so that users are advised to stay out of the strong sun. Grazing cattle often have major problems from this photosensitive property with blisters on exposed skin.

Hypericum is also valued in homeopathy (in addition to its use as anti-depressant) for the healing and antiseptic properties and of the herb and its ability to soften the skin.

Wool and textile dyers use the flowering shoots to dye fabrics yellow to orange, or any part of the herb to produce lemon yellow.

St John's wort is found widely as a wild plant throughout Europe in dry, sunny places, and also increasingly in all other parts of the world with a moderate climate. Translucent oil glands can be seen in the leaves of the plant, just as though there were perforations in the foliage (hence *perforatum*). The plants flower profusely from the longest day.

Hyssopus officinalis

HYSSOP

If used sparingly, hyssop is one of the most useful of kitchen herbs. A few finely sliced leaves are sufficient to put a kick in a salad. A little more of the

Hyssopus officinalis, *hyssop.*

bitter herb can be used in soups and sauces. With meat and game it is sufficient to rub the meat with hyssop to impart the sharp mint-like flavour. Hyssop aids digestion and helps to break down fat in meat and fish.

Hyssop is used medicinally for indigestion, stomach, and intestinal disorders, stimulation of the appetite, and increasing general resistance. The herb stimulates and purifies with the volatile oils having antiseptic properties that protect the user against infection. The fresh fragrance of hyssop is much sought after for perfume, pot-pourris, and once also as a herb to scatter on the floors of houses.

Hyssop officinalis originally grew in southern parts of Europe and into Asia as far s India. The herb has been cultivated elsewhere since the Middle Ages and has become naturalised even in northern climes where there is fairly dry, chalky soil, in sunny positions. The evergreen sub-shrub which grows about 50cm (20in) high is fully hardy. The plant bears blue, violet, pink or white flowers from the end of June to September and attracts hosts of bees.

Hyssopus officinalis, *hyssop.*

Courtesy The Kruidenhof, Buitenpost.

Inula helenium, *elecampane.*

Ilex aquifolium, *holly.*

Inula helenium, *elecampane.*

Ilex aquifolium

HOLLY

In southern lands, the cypress symbolises eternal life. In northern parts of Europe it is the holly which fulfils this role. The leathery leaves, often with sharp prickles around the edge, remain green summer and winter and bright red berries are born on female and male/female plants. Eventually, holly can grow into a tree of 20m (65ft) but they are usually kept to a shrub through pruning. Holly is fully hardy in western and southern parts of Europe. Tannin and other bitter substances are derived from the leaves which can be used to treat influenza, bronchitis, and rheumatic complaints. The symptoms of malaria can also be relived with the herb.

Inula helenium

ELECAMPANE, SCABWORT

Elecampane originates from Asia but has been cultivated since early times because of the known healing power of its roots. The herb has become naturalised in large parts of Europe and can be found close to places where it has been cultivated. The perennial is easily grown as a garden plant, which flowers from July with large yellow blooms and reaches about 50cm (20in) high. Chopped and dried pieces of root from older plants provide a bronchial dilating and expectorant substance used to treat asthma, coughs, emphysema, and bronchitis.

Indigofera heterantha syn. *I. gerardiana*

INDIGO

The leaves of *Indigofera heterantha* contain substances which can be used to dye clothing and wool blue. This is not easily done because the substances do not dissolve in water and dyer's of old had their own secret recipes for creating the indigo dye. The tropical *Indigofera* species were preferred for this purpose making them expensive in Europe because of the distances involved. Considerable sums of money were paid for this source of indigo dyestuff.

By the end of the sixteenth century other sources of indigo were discovered and *Indigofera* threatened to elbow aside the traditional blue woad *(Isatis tinctoria)*. It seemed as if the woad growers would lose their living but they were rescued in parts of Europe by a ban on the import of indigo.

Indigofera heterantha (sometimes also known as *I. h.* 'Gerardiana' or *I. gerardiana)* originates in the Himalayas and is fully hardy. The low, decidu-

Indigofera heterantha, *indigo.*

Indigofera heterantha, *indigo.*

ous shrub will eventually grow to 200cm (79in) high. It bears pink "butterfly" flowers in summer.

Ipomoea tricolor syn. *I. rubrocaerulea*

MORNING GLORY

The black seeds of morning glory contain a substance that is much like LSD, although with a less powerful action than lysergic acid diethylamide.

Ipomoea tricolor 'Heavenly Blue', morning glory.

Both are toxic substances which can cause hallucinations in quite low doses. Aztec shamans used the herb to induce trances in sick people. The finely ground seeds are used to make an infusion which is drunk by the patient. During the hallucinations the origins of the illness are said to be revealed so that it can be treated. Drug users in some developed countries have experimented with the seeds but this is deadly dangerous because of their high toxicity.

The morning glory is an annual climber which cannot be sown before May because the seedlings cannot withstand frost. They are very susceptible to being eaten by slugs. Once the shoots emerge, they quickly climb up any support and flower from July with large, funnel-shaped blue to purple blooms which last just for one day. On hot days, the flowers wilt by the early afternoon.

∗

Iris germanica

ORRIS

It is not entirely certain where orris originated. It naturalises easily on dry sunny slopes, especially in the Balkans and around the Mediterranean . Orris is a tough garden plant that will thrive in a sunny posi-

Iris germanica, *orris.*

Iris germanica, *orris.*

tion in dry soil. The plant grows to 100cm (39in) high but despite this cannot withstand competition from other plants. There are hundreds of varieties of the species with different colours and markings. The rhizomes of orris contain powerful substances with healing properties which act as an expectorant and are therefore useful for treating coughs. *Iris* is also used for catarrh, diarrhoea, and as a diuretic for treating gall bladder and spleen disorders. For other uses, see *Iris germanica* 'Florentina'.

🌱 🍶 ⚔ ☕

Iris germanica 'Florentina' syn. I. florentina

ORRIS ROOT

Orris root contains a volatile oil, partially consisting of irone, which smells of violets. The plant is grown on a large scale, above all in Italy, for the perfume and cosmetics industries. The aroma is also incorporated into liqueurs. After drying, the roots are chopped and finely ground. This powder can be used to clean teeth and teething children can be given a slice of the root to chew on. For medicinal use see *Iris germanica.*

Iris germanica *'Florentina', orris root.*

Iris pseudacorus, *yellow flag.*

Orris root grows a little taller than the species and the plant has white flowers tinged with lavender and a yellow "beard".

Iris pseudacorus

YELLOW FLAG

The rhizome of the yellow flag tastes extremely bitter and contains toxic substances. This was once used as a purgative to induce vomiting, with powered root also being used as snuff. Today much safer and better alternatives are available. The flowers provide a yellow dyestuff for colouring textiles including wool.

The yellow flag is a native plant of the waterside in standing fresh water or watercourses with little flow. The sword-like leaves grow 100–200cm (39–79in) high. The plant has yellow flowers in May. The seed case is filled with rows of brown disc-shaped seeds rather like miniature draught pieces. The plant will set seed in wet ground and the rhizomes spread to form a compact mat.

Iris pseudacorus 'Variegata' is a fine variegated form.

Iris pseudacorus *'Variegata'.*

Iris versicolor, *blue flag.*

Isatis tinctoria, *woad.*

Isatis tinctoria, *woad.*

Isatis tinctoria, *woad.*

Iris versicolor

BLUE FLAG, WILD IRIS

The native North Americans used the blue flag or wild iris to induce vomiting in the same way that the yellow flag was used in Europe. The medicinal action of both species has now been scientifically recognised. Pharmaceutical companies obtain iridine from the rhizome which is a strong laxative and also a diuretic. The fresh roots in particular contain sharp and bitter-tasting toxic substances so that the herb should only be used under expert supervision.

Iris versicolor grows in the moist wood and marshes of eastern and central parts of North America. Cultivate it in a bog garden, at the edge of a pond, or in moisture-retaining soil.

Isatis tinctoria

WOAD

Woad was one of the most important pigments and dyestuffs used by ancient Britons to paint their bodies and until replaced by indigo (see *Indigofera)* was the most important blue dye though with such a powerful smell its use was banned within eight kilometres (five miles) of her palaces by Queen Elizabeth I. The dyestuff indoxyl is colourless and has to be developed by a chemical process. The dyestuff is soaked with wool but the colour is not visible when the wool is removed from the bath. This only happens after exposure to oxygen. Woad was replaced as a blue dye by indigo from the end of the sixteenth century. It is a biennial to perennial plant that flowers in the second year. The 100cm (39in) high plants bears clusters of yellow flowers followed by winged seeds. Woad originates from western parts of Asia and eastern Europe but has become naturalised through escape from cultivation in western Europe. Historical accounts by Julius Caesar and others prove the plant was present in Britain before the birth of Christ.

J, K

Jasminum sambac, *Arabian jasmine.*

Jasminum sambac

ARABIAN JASMINE

Jasmine blossom is wonderfully scented. The blossoms have been gathered since ancient times for their powerful but sweet fragrance. The flowers are used in perfumes and cosmetics, and dried for use in pot-pourris and pomanders. Arabian jasmine is an important part of rituals in Hindu temples in India. The leaves are also used in that country to flavour tea. We can also buy jasmine tea.

Jasminum sambac probably originates from India but has been cultivated in other tropical lands. For those in less balmy climes, the plant makes a fine container and conservatory plant which flowers from spring until autumn with scented creamy-white blossoms. The woody climber is evergreen, requiring light in winter and a minimum temperature of 10°C (50°F).

Juglans regia

WALNUT

The walnut can grow 30m (100ft) high with a broad crown beneath which few other plants can survive because rainwater dripping to the ground contains juglon, that is released by the leaves, which prevents most other plants from growing. By this means, the walnut eliminates most of its competitors.

Juglon has fungicidal properties but is also used medicinally. Substances from walnut leaves are important for the treatment of diarrhoea, infections (especially of the mouth, throat, and eyes), and skin complaints such as eczema.

Juglans regia, *walnut.*

The fallen leaves of walnut can be used to form a beige to brown dyestuff for wool and other textiles, the shells surrounding the edible nuts provide a dark brown colour, while the bark enables various shades of brown.

Juniperus communis

COMMON JUNIPER

The black juniper berries stimulate the appetite and the oils contained are used to make spirit

Juniperus communis, *juniper.*

liquors such as gin, shortened from the Dutch *genever*. The berries themselves can be cooked and served in dishes such as game and sauerkraut. The berries are only born on the female bushes and only ripen after two or three years. The berries, which are borne between the needle-shaped leaves, are difficult to pick. Juniper bushes grow naturally on poor soil, in many parts of Europe and Asia, sometimes sandy and dry, or on limestone, elsewhere on moist acidic moorlands.

Juniper berries contain volatile oils and other substances which are diuretic and therefore used to relieve rheumatic complaints. Because of the irritating effect on the kidneys, juniper berries should not be used continuously over a period of time.

The berries can also provide a grey to dark green dyestuff for colouring wool and other textiles.

Juniperus sabina

SAVIN, EUROPEAN JUNIPER

The Sabine women used *Juniperus sabina* to induce abortions and the conifer was also taken internally for a number of other ailments although this has largely ceased outside homeopathy because of the high toxicity of the herb. The oils from the berries of savin bushes are used in ointments for use against warts and in promoting hair growth. The shrub grows naturally in central and southern parts of Europe and neighbouring Asia and is widely planted in gardens and public open space. The shrub grows without difficulty but rarely reaches more than 200cm (79in) high. Numerous cultivated varieties such as *Juniperus sabina* 'Hicksii' spread outwards more than upwards.

Kalmia latifolia

CALICO BUSH, MOUNTAIN LAUREL, IVYBUSH

Few garden enthusiasts are aware of the highly poisonous nature of this decorative shrub. Every part of this plant is extremely toxic, including nectar and

Juniperus sabina, *savin.*

Kalmia latifolia, *calico bush.*

game which eats the plant. The calico bush originates from eastern parts of North America. Clusters of bell-like flowers are born on the ends of twigs in spring. The shrub only thrives on acidic soil. In time, the shrub will grow to a height and spread of 200cm (79in) in a garden.

The leaf was once used to treat syphilis, fevers, diarrhoea, nerve pains, and skin complaints. Because of its high toxicity, *Kalmia* is rarely used in the present day.

Knautia arvensis syn. *Scabiosa arvensis*

FIELD SCABIOUS

The older botanical and common names for this species point to its use for treating scabies. The roots contain saponins which purify the blood and in the present day, field scabious is still regarded as a purifying herb for treatment of eczema and infections.

Field scabious grows throughout Europe and neighbouring parts of Asia in meadows and hedgerows. This perennial prefers alkaline soil. It flowers throughout summer with mauve blooms born on stems of 30–40cm (12–16in). The plant grows to 150cm (59in) high.

Knautia arvensis, *field scabious.*

L

Lamiastrum galeobdolon, *yellow archangel.*

Lamium galeobdolon syn. *Lamiastrum galeobdolon, Galeobdolon luteum*

YELLOW ARCHANGEL

In mild winters. yellow archangel retains its green foliage to benefit from the winter sunlight. In summer, the plant grows in the deep shade of broad-leafed trees in much of Europe, including Britain. This inhabitant of ancient woodland will also thrive in gardens and forms an entire patch. The plant is profusely covered with lip-form yellow flowers from late April to early June. Yellow archangel has similar properties to the white dead nettle (see *Lamium* album.)

Lamium maculatum

DEAD NETTLE

The pink dead nettle and white dead nettle are closely related. The flowers of *L. maculatum* are dark pink with a characteristic darker under lip. The plant spreads out with runners which root where they touch the ground. Variegated varieties with silvery-white patches in the central vein of the leaf are often grown in gardens. *Lamium maculatum* grows wild in many parts of Europe with a

Lamium maculatum, *dead nettle.*

northern reach just short of the English Channel although escape from cultivation means that the plant can be encountered north of this. *Lamium maculatum* can be used in the same way as white dead nettle (see *Lamium album*).

Lamium album

WHITE DEAD NETTLE, ARCHANGEL

The flowers of the white dead nettle produce so much nectar that we can suck it from them. Pluck a flower from its stem and suck the back of the flower and nectar will coat your tongue. The insects which congregate in large numbers on the plant will not miss one or two flowers. The plant flowers from May until December and is widely found in almost any hedgerow, verge, or patch of waste ground.

The white flowers can easily be plucked from the stem and are then carefully and thoroughly dried to make a delicious herbal tea on its own or added to other tea mixtures. The tea is soothing and helps promote good sleep, purifies the blood, has expectorant properties, and reduces infections (especially in the urethra and prostrate gland). The tea, taken internally or as douche also helps with white discharge that can affect young women. A widely cultivated white dead nettle is sold as *Lamium maculatum* 'Album'.

Lamium album, *white dead nettle.*

Lantana camara.

Laurus nobilis, *bay*.

Lantana camara.

Lantana camara

People could be seen in Paris in the nineteenth century wandering about the city with purple hair. It is certain that they had bathed in water to which *Lantana camara* had been added. It suddenly became fashionable to add an extract from the flowers to bath water. The herb was reputed to purify the body but those with fair or grey hair which came into contact with the water had to endure with purple hair for a time.

Lantana camara has other colourful tricks to play. The flowers change colour like a crystal ball from orange to dark red or from yellow to pink. In South America, where the plant is native, it is regarded as a talisman for good luck, preventing misfortune.

The plant is easily grown as a container plant. The plant grows rapidly and has an abundance of white, yellow, orange, red, pink, to lilac flowers. Protect the plant from frost.

Laurus nobilis

BAY, BAY LAUREL, SWEET BAY

Large parts of Europe were once covered with forests of bay trees but these were lost during the

Laurus nobilis, *bay*.

164

Ice Ages except on certain islands in North Africa. The shrub-like tree made its return as a kitchen herb, medicinal plant, and symbol of victory. The Roman's crowned victors of their tournaments with wreaths of laurel (awarding them their laurels).

Bay is an evergreen plant whose leaves can be harvested at all times of the year. The leaves are dried and the volatile oils they contain impart a taste all their own to savoury dishes, soups, and casseroles to which they are added. The berries of the plant contain oil which is used as flavouring in liqueurs and as aromatic for perfumes.

The crushed leaves are astringent and can be placed on burns and bruises to speed healing.

The bay tree can only be grown in northern Europe as a container plant because it can withstand little frost. Place the plant during winter where there is ample light but not too much warmth. Place outside in summer in either partial shade or the full sun.

Lavandula augustfolia syn. *L. officinalis, L. spica, L. vera*

COMMON LAVENDER, ENGLISH LAVENDER

No other herb is as well-known for its scent as lavender. The botanical name comes from the

Lavandula angustifolia, *common lavender.*

Lavandula angustifolia *'Hidcote'.*

Latin for washing: *lavare.* Before soap was discovered, people washed with lavender water. This was not such a bad idea, for soap makes the skin alkaline and this is precisely the right conditions for bacteria (which cause body odour) to develop rapidly. Lavender is neither alkaline or acidic and by adding lavender to washing water or flannel or rubbing lavender oil on the skin the fresh scent is imparted. Lavender in bath water not only smells nice, it also helps you to relax.

The volatile oils which spread the fragrance are particularly contained in the flowers. The flowering stems are picked when they begin to bloom and then dried in small bunches or the flowers removed from the stems and dried. Once lavender flowers were strewn on the floors of houses to make them smell sweeter, and to drive away insects. Later, lavender bags, pot-pourris, and pomanders became popular. Many linen cupboards and chests still have lavender bags, and those who use them know the fresh-smelling result. Currently, lavender oil is widely used in oil burners which evaporate the oil. Lavender is widely used in the perfume industry and the plant is cultivated on a large scale for adding to soap and other cosmetic products.

Those who really like lavender can also add the leaves to casseroles and fish dishes, as is widely done in France. Most will find the taste of the herb is too bitter.

Medicinally, lavender is renowned for its soothing relaxation. The dried flowers are used to make a relaxing tea or tincture. Lavender oil added to bath water promotes rest and relaxation. A lavender bag close to the pillow is beneficial for night rest. Lavender spirit is used to massage rheumatic joints to relieve pain, tension headaches, and muscle pains. Pregnant women should not use lavender as medicine.

The lavender species originate from the countries around the Mediterranean and surroundings parts of Asia to India. They grow as low shrubs on dry, sunny places, often on chalky soil. Try to imitate these circumstances as closely as possible and you will derive a great deal of pleasure from the many

Lavandula angustifolia *'Munstead'*.

Lavandula dentata, *lavender*.

forms of *Lavandula angustifolia* and *Lavandula x intermedia* which can withstand temperatures of minus 15–20°C (5°F to -4°F). Frost damaged branches can be removed by pruning in the spring. In any event it is important to prune lavender bushes back thoroughly each year to prevent them becoming straggly. Do not cut back too far because woody growth without foliage will not produce new shoots.

Lavender bushes combine superbly with roses and provide a grey accent in ornamental gardens. They are ideal for making low hedges. The flowers appear in late summer.

Lavandula augustifolia 'Hidcote' forms a compact bush of about 30cm (12in) with tight, erect flower stems. Another popular cultivar is *Lavandula augustifolia* 'Munstead', that grows about 45cm (18in) high with fairly large lilac flowers.

Lavandula dentata

LAVENDER

The leaves of *L. dentata* are scalloped. This species originates from the Atlantic islands, western Mediterranean – on the Iberian Peninsula and coast of North Africa, and the Arabian Peninsula.

The shrub is not fully hardy and will only survive harsh winters near coasts. Plant them in a sheltered position or in a pot which should then be over-wintered in a frost free place with plenty of light. See *Lavandula augustifolia* for use and further care information.

Lavandula latifolia

SPIKE LAVENDER

Spike lavender contains less volatile oils than the common lavender yet it is a hybrid of these two species that is grown commercially: *Lavendula x intermedia* (English lavender). These shrubs can be seen in Provence in France growing in long rows, winding like purple snakes through the hills. The flowers are born on long stems which are easily harvested by machine.

The almost spoon-shaped leaves of spike lavender are fairly wide and attractively covered with white felt-like hairs. This hybrid can withstand temperatures down to about minus 10°C (14°F). See *Lavandula augustifolia* for use and further care information.

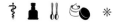

Lavandula latifolia, *spike lavender.*

Lavandula stoechas, *French lavender.*

Lavandula stoechas

FRENCH LAVENDER

French lavender has ovoid-oblong spikes with linear leaves. The calyx stands up like a quiff above the flower. Although the flowers of this lavender are more highly scented than common lavender, they are more difficult to harvest.

French lavender is an extremely variable species from the Mediterranean yet is more hardy than *L. dentata*, although it can only withstand frosts to minus 15°C (5°F). See *Lavandula augustifolia* for use and further care information.

Lavandula latifolia, *spike lavender.*

Lavandula stoechas var. *leucantha.*

167

Lavandula stoechas var. *leucantha*.

Leonurus cardiaca, *motherwort*.

Leonurus cardiaca, *motherwort*.

Lavandula stoechas var. *leucantha*

This variety of French lavender was discovered in the eastern Pyrenees in 1925. The flowers are white with a white to green calyx at the top of the flower forms. The leaves are slightly less grey than the species but otherwise they are much the same.

Leonurus cardiaca

MOTHERWORT

The species name *cardiaca* points to the medicinal use of this herb for heart complaints and thrombosis, the common name to its former use to treat anxiety in pregnant women. The plant originates from Asia. The plant was collected and cultivated in European monastery and university botanical gardens from the Middle Ages. It escaped from cultivation and has now become widely naturalised although because it has a preference for the same setting as stinging nettles, which are much stronger, it is becoming increasingly rare.

Motherwort is still used to calm the heart and reduce thrombosis. The glycosides contained are particularly beneficial for palpitations and flushes. Despite the use in ancient Greece from which it gets its name, the herb should not be used by pregnant women.

Lepidium sativum

CRESS

Most people know cress as a mat of green in a punnet from the greengrocer. If cress is allowed to continue growing it will reach 40cm (16in) and bear white flowers. This annual plant has been cultivated for its pungent taste since ancient times. The newly emerged shoots taste wonderful in salads or sandwiches. They can also be added to soups, sauces, and omelettes, just before serving. Most children do not like the pungent taste but the spicy taste can be modified with a little lemon juice and sugar. Cultivation of cress is child's play. Sow the seeds close together on moist soil or wet cotton wool, absorbent paper or such like. The shoots appear in a few days and within a week there will be a dense mat of shoots which can be used. By waiting another week, the volume will be increased and if then only the tips of the plants are cut, a second (or even third) harvest is possible. Cress can be grown indoors the year round but out of doors from March.

Leucanthemum vulgare syn. *Chrysanthemum leucanthemum*

OX-EYE DAISY, MARGUERITE

Ox-eye daisies are a native wild flower throughout most of Europe, growing on open soils, predominantly clay, chalk, or loam, and moderately fertile soils. The plant is becoming less common in arable land through extensive application of fertiliser, but

Lepidium sativum, *cress.*

Lepidium sativum, *cress.*

Leucanthemum vulgare, *ox-eye daisy.*

Leucanthemum vulgare, *ox-eye daisy.*

this perennial can easily be grown in verges, gardens, and parks.

The entire plant is used as a dyestuff for wool and other textiles, creating yellow, orange, or brown, depending on the treatment given.

Levisticum officinale

LOVAGE

A cheese sandwich with a few slices of lovage taste wonderful. Grown in fertile, moisture-retaining, lovage will mature into a sturdy perennial of about 200cm (79in) high. Clusters of green-yellow flowers appear in early summer which change into ribbed seeds which sow themselves so that new plants will constantly appear. One plant is adequate for its herbal use because only a little is needed to flavour soups and sauces. The seeds have the same taste but are sweeter. The seeds are used for their flavour in liqueurs and as basic ingredients for the perfume industry. In the kitchen they are used to spice up salads and mashed potato. Leaves that have been steamed until tender can be eaten as a vegetable, the stems can be candied, and the roots can be peeled and cooked as a vegetable too.

Levisticum officinale, *lovage.*

Infusion of the seeds, leaves, but particularly the roots, can be used as a diuretic to ease rheumatic complaints and aid trouble-free urination. Lovage stimulates the appetite, aids digestion, and prevents wind. Pregnant women should not use the herb.

Ligustrum licidum

GLOSSY PRIVET, CHINESE PRIVET

The people of Asia recognize the oval blue-black fruits of Chinese privet as of great importance. They prepare medicine from the berries that kill bacteria, reduce tumours, and stimulate the action of the kidneys and liver. The purifying and diuretic herb can be used for a range of ailments such as rheumatism, cataract, and sleeplessness. Decoctions from the berries should only be taken under medical supervision because of their toxicity. Chinese privet is insufficiently hardy to be grown out of doors all year round in northern Europe so it needs to be grown as a pot plant which should over-winter in a cool, well-lit place.

Ligustrum licidum, *Chinese privet.*

Ligustrum vulgare, *common privet.*

Lilium candidum, *madonna lily.*

Ligustrum vulgare

COMMON PRIVET

Privet grows widely throughout low-lying parts of Europe, preferring alkaline soil so that it is often found on chalk or sandy soils such as dunes. The shrub grows to about 5m (16ft) high but remains much lower in exposed places, often being formed by the wind into a low rounded form. The plumes of white flowers with their sweet scent in summer attract hordes of insects.

Privet is no longer used medicinally but is still suitable for use to create dyestuffs for colouring wool and other textiles. The leaves provide yellow and green, while the poisonous black berries provide blue to blue-grey.

Lilium candidum

MADONNA LILY

The madonna lily is named after the Virgin Mary, mother of Christ. Given this, the former uses of this herb are remarkable: substances from the scales of the corm were used to treat severe period pains and also as a diuretic. The herb was especially used for difficult labour. Externally, madonna lily was used to treat burns, bruises, and skin ailments but is rarely used these days because of the plant's scarcity.

The plant grows wild in the Balkans and the countries of the eastern Mediterranean but had been cultivated in monastery herb gardens in other countries from the Middle Ages for its medicinal properties. It is now a much prized but difficult to grow garden plant which prefers a sunny position on fertile and alkaline soil that is both moisture-retaining yet well drained.

Lilium martagon, *common turkscap lily.*

Lilium martagon *var.* album, *white turkscap lily.*

Linaria vulgaris, *common toadflax.*

Linaria vulgaris, *common toadflax.*

Lilium martagon

COMMON TURKSCAP LILY

The petals of the turkscap lily bend right back on themselves to resemble a turban. These flowers are born on stems of up to 150cm (59in) long. The species has purple or mauve flowers with darker flecks. A white-flowered cultivar, *Lilium martagon* var. *album* is often planted in gardens for its striking white blooms. For care see *Lilium candidum,* with the exception that *L. martagon* is a woodland plant that will grow in partial shade.
The turkscap lily is also used for female complaints as the madonna lily, such as menstruation problems and stretching of the womb. The plant is virtually unused for these purposes these days.

Linaria vulgaris

COMMON TOADFLAX

The common toadflax can be seen flowering from July along field borders, country roads, and waste land. This perennial has a preference for a sunny position on open stony or sandy soil. It is a native plant of much of Europe and western parts of Asia but has become naturalised in other parts of the world where it has been taken because of its attractive flowers. The roots rapidly spread in favourable sites and the plant also readily self seeds. It is an attractive decorative plant for a wild flower garden. Although little is known about the active substances in this plant, toadflax has a long history of medicinal use for jaundice, skin and intestinal infections, oedema, and gall bladder disorders. Today the herb is also used in salves for treating blood vessel problems such as haemorrhoid.

The flowers provide a yellow dyestuff which can be used to colour wool and other textiles yellow, orange, green, or brown.

ϡ /

Linum usitatissimum

FLAX, LINSEED, FLAXSEED

Few plants are as useful as flax or linseed. The fibres, or flax make linen, while the seeds are rich in linoleic and linolenic acids. The husks of the seeds after pressing are made into linseed cake which cattle enjoy eating. The oil is not just used in food for human consumption but also incorporated in paints, fillers, and glues.

In addition to the 30 per cent linseed oil in the seeds, they also contain mucilaginous substances which are used to treat bronchitis, sore throat, coughs, and infections of the throat and mouth. The best known use of linseed is as a laxative. The intestines are not overly irritated by the use of the herb so that it is possible to use linseed over a period of time without ill effects. The seeds are milled or crushed and are often then soaked in water but the best results are achieved by mixing the crushed seeds in salads or other cold food to be eaten raw. The seeds then swell up in the stomach and stimulate the function of the digestive system. The small amount of prussic acid contained within the seeds is not harmful when taken in normal doses.

Linum usitatissimum, *flax or linseed.*

Linum usitatissimum, *flax or linseed.*

Courtesy The Kruidenhof, Buitenpost.

Flax is an annual plant which man has cultivated since the Stone Age. Its origins were then unknown and it readily self-seeded itself from arable land into surrounding land. By selection, sturdy varieties were found that were better for production of flax for linen while shorter varieties which flowered profusely were found to contain more oil. The decoratively arching stems are filled in July and August with a succession of fine blue (sometimes white) flowers, making flax an excellent decorative garden plant. It grows best in a sunny position of well-drained soil.

ϡ ⏦ ✳

Lithospermum erthrorhizon syn. L. officinale

GROMWELL

The fruits of gromwell are smooth and shiny so that they sparkle like pearls in the leaf axils. This perennial grows about 50cm (20in) high and bears white to green flowers in June–July. It is a native plant of much of Europe, although in Britain the purple gromwell *(L. purpureocaeruleum)* is native.

A violet dyestuff can be won from the roots of the plant but the plant also has medicinal properties.

Lithospermum erythrorhizon, *gromwell.*

Lobelia siphilitica, *great lobelia.*

Lobelia siphilitica, *great lobelia.*

The entire plant can be dried for use in infusions for herbal tea to treat kidney and liver complaints, measles, and jaundice. Those who want children can best avoid the herb because the native American Shoshoni used a closely related species *(Lithospermum ruderale)* as a contraceptive which causes permanent infertility if used for a long period of time.

Lobelia siphilitica

GREAT LOBELIA

This lobelia gets its name from the venereal disease syphilis, which its roots were used to treat. The roots contain substances that have beneficial properties for oedema, diarrhoea, and dysentery. In common with the better known pharmaceutical herb *Lobelia inflata* (Indian tobacco, asthma weed, or pukeweed), the great lobelia also helps with bronchial asthma and spasms.

This species originates from the moist woods and marshes of eastern USA. It is cultivated in gardens as an ornamental plant which reaches 100cm (39in) high during flowering in the summer. The blue to purple flowers readily set seed in the northern European climate in moist ground, especially in bog gardens at the edges of ponds where the plant is most at home.

Lonicera periclymenum

COMMON HONEYSUCKLE

Many a girl may have once smuggled a sprig of honeysuckle into her room because her parents forbade it, because such things did not belong in the house. According to the thoughts of the times, honeysuckle could conjure up erotic dreams. Certainly honeysuckle has long been associated with love in literature, for as long as man has written, no doubt because of its sweet night-time fragrance. It is not surprising that this "mid-summer-night's fragrance" is so popular with the makers of soap and perfume.

The plant hopes to attract moths to it with that night-time fragrance to pollinate its flowers. Wild honeysuckle often grows in shade within a wood but always flowers more profusely when it grows on the edge of the wood where it has more sunlight. The stems wind themselves around branches of trees and other supports so that the plant can climb many meters or feet high. The flowers grow at the end of the stems and they are followed by red berries which are eaten by birds. Honeysuckle has a long history as a medicinal plant. Dried flowers and leaves are antiseptic and diuretic. Herbal tea made with the flower buds helps against catarrh and is useful for heavy coughs and asthma. Infusions are also used to make a cough syrup. Crushed leaves are antiseptic and can be used to treat skin infections. Homeopaths prescribe decoctions from the leaf for people who get worked up and are quick to anger. Never use the berries because their are moderately poisonous.

Lonicera periclymenum, *common honeysuckle.*

Lophophora williamsii, *dumpling cactus.*

Lophophora williamsii syn. *L. echinata, L. lutea*

DUMPLING CACTUS

The men of the Huichol tribe in Mexico make a 300km (187 miles) trek on foot every year to the place where the most remarkable cactus on earth grows. They call it peyote. When they arrive in the Sierra Madre they shoot the first of the plant's they find with bow and arrow for this is the cactus of the deer. After eating the plant they first experience unpleasant symptoms such as sickness, pressure in the head, and extreme sensitivity to light. After two hours these experiences are replaced by very colourful and crystal clear visions accompanied by wonderful music. In these trances, the native Mexicans make contact with their ancestors.

The dumpling cactus has developed chemical substances to deter animals from eating it. The most important of these is mescaline from which its local name is derived. In Mexico, the plants contain 1.4 per cent of mescaline but when cultivated in Europe this drops by about half. The dumpling cactus is a slow-growing plant with a deep tap root so it requires a very deep pot with very open soil, preferably with some clay. Only water in summer when the weather is hot and then allow to dry out fully before watering again.

Use of the plant as an hallucinogenic is not without risk. Both overdoses and long-term use can be damaging for health. Additionally, cultivated plants have often been treated with a systemic toxic chemicals which is absorbed in the plant.

The plant can have beneficial medicinal uses under strict medical supervision for angina and nerve pains. In homeopathic medicine, extracts from the herb are used for treating hallucinations and co-ordination problems.

Lotus corniculatus, *common bird's-foot-trefoil.*

Lycopus europaeus, *gypsywort.*

Lotus corniculatus, *common bird's-foot-trefoil.*

and is also beneficial for some of the unhealthy side-effects. The above ground parts of the plant can be used to make an infusion. There are preparations in which gypsywort and motherwort are combined, or homeopathic medicines are used.

Gypsywort is found widely in moist and boggy places. It grows to 100cm (39in) high, flowering from June to September with small flowers in the leaf axils.

℞

Lycopus europaeus, *gypsywort.*

Lotus corniculatus

COMMON BIRD'S-FOOT-TREFOIL

Common bird's-foot-trefoil protects itself against being eaten by animals with prussic acid. The amount is very low so that only animals which each a great deal of the plant will suffer the consequences. Below the harmful dose, common bird's-foot-trefoil can have beneficial effects. Milk from cattle fed with some of the herb is of better quality. The plant is common to grazed and mown pasture throughout Europe and this perennial will grow on all manner of different soil types.

✳

Lycopus europaeus

GYPSYWORT, BUGLEWEED

Nervous people appear to burn off their food intake more rapidly than others because of their anxiety state. They can often eat quite normally and yet remain thin. Cause and effect can often be confused in this situation. An overactive thyroid gland raises the metabolism so that food is rapidly converted into energy. It is the overactive thyroid which is the cause of the nervousness, which can also result in palpitations. Gypsywort or bugleweed helps to reduce the activity of the thyroid

Lysimachia nummularia, *creeping jenny.*

Lysimachia nummularia

CREEPING JENNY

Creeping jenny has a long history of use in herbal folk medicine. A compress with an infusion is placed on wounds that are slow to heal. Drinking the herbal tea from the plant heals internal haemorrhages and is also useful as cough mixture. Although the modern pharmacy has no further use for creeping jenny, it is useful for treating coughs. The herb is added to dried leaves of butterbur to make a herbal tea.

Creeping jenny occurs naturally in the wild in moist soil, often in pasture land beside water. It is a perennial with creeping shoots. Where the runners touch the ground, they root. The plant is covered with yellow flowers from June to August, making it an excellent ground cover plant for the ornamental garden. The plant can become rampant on moist soil.

Lysimachia vulgaris

COMMON LOOSESTRIFE

Common loosestrife can stem bleeding (especially in the nose and mouth) and is also used to treat diarrhoea. Ointments using the herb help to heal wounds and to disinfect boils. Although the plant contains substances which have these beneficial

Lysimachia vulgaris, *common loosestrife.*

177

effects, its has fallen into disuse as a herbal medicine.

The common loosestrife grows in low-lying water meadows, along the banks of rivers, and in lowland areas throughout northern and western Europe and adjoining parts of Asia. The perennial, which grows to about 50cm (20in) high spreads through creeping roots and can become rampant in moist soil. The plant is ideal for use in moist parts of a "natural" garden where it will flower abundantly between June and August.

Lythrum salicaria

PURPLE LOOSESTRIFE

Purple loosestrife is often found growing in combination with common loosestrife on the banks of streams and ponds. Purple loosestrife is especially found of water and is often found at the water's edge. The plant is a pioneer which disappears once the bank dries out when it is elbowed aside by other plants. Provide it is protected in a garden from competition with other plants, purple loosestrife can grow in dry places. It reaches 150cm (5ft) high and blooms with ear-shaped carmine to purple flowers from June to August.

Purple loosestrife contains tannin and was therefore once used in the leather tanning industry. This same substance helps to stem bleeding and for this reason, purple loosestrife was for centuries known as a wound-healing herb which also disinfects. The herb is also useful for diarrhoea, inflammation of the

Lythrum salicaria, *purple loosestrife.*

stomach lining, and is often used to treat typhoid and dysentery. The sap from the roots provides a red dyestuff for wool and other textiles.

Herb garden of Els de Boer in Warffum, Holland.

178

ℳ

Macleaya cordata, *plume poppy.*

Mahonia aquifolium *'Apollo', Oregon grape.*

Macleaya cordata syn. *Bocconia cordata*

PLUME POPPY

The plume poppy originates from Japan and eastern China but has found its place in European ornamental gardens. The plant has attractive foliage with lobed leaves and it bears plumes of white to copper flowers in later summer. By that time the plant has grown to 200cm (79in). Only the roots and underground runners remain of this perennial during winter but these can become rampant and creep great distances under paving. If the roots are pulled out it will soon become apparent what use the plant has: as a dyestuff. The roots contain a very difficult to remove orange dye. The above ground parts of the plant are used to dye wool and other textiles orange-yellow.

/

Mahonia aquifolium

OREGON GRAPE, MOUNTAIN GRAPE

Mahonia are part of the *Berberis* family and the chemistry of *M. aquifolium* is similar to *Berberis vulgaris,* containing berberine, although the Oregon grape contains less of the antiseptic substance, so that it is used in a different way. The active ingredients from the roots are used in homeopathic medicine for psoriasis. The astringent herb is mainly used in herbal medicine to treat infections of the stomach lining and diarrhoea.

Mahonia aquifolium *'Green Ripple', Oregon grape.*

Dyestuff for colouring wool and other textiles green-yellow, orange, and pink can be created from the roots, branches, and leaves of the plant.

The natural habitat of these plants in the north-western parts of North America. The plant is widely found in Europe in both gardens and public open space. It is almost indestructible, has prickly leaves, and remains fairly low at a maximum of 200cm (79in) high. The shrub flowers early in spring and even sometimes at the end of winter. The sweet scented yellow flowers attract many insects.

Malva moschata

MUSK MALLOW

Although musk mallow originates in southern Europe and north-west Africa, it also now grows wild in northern and central Europe. The decorative value of the approx. 70cm (28in) tall perennial was appreciated long ago. It flowers from June to September with pink or white flowers which are arranged at the top of the plant. The plant is easily cultivated in gardens.

For the medicinal use see *Malva sylvestris*. The properties of musk mallow are less potent than common mallow.

Malva neglecta, *dwarf mallow.*

Courtesy The Kruidenhof, Buitenpost.

Malva neglecta

DWARF MALLOW

The stems of dwarf mallow grow almost totally recumbent and only grow upwards about 50cm (20in). This annual grows wild throughout Europe and adjoining parts of Africa and south-west Asia. The leaf axils are decorated from June to September with little mauve to pink flowers.

For medicinal use see *Malva sylvestris*.

Malva sylvestris

COMMON MALLOW, BLUE MALLOW, HIGH MALLOW

Common mallow was one of the most important medicinal herbs for a very long time. It was regarded as a panacea for all manner of ills. *Malva sylvestris* is indeed a beneficent herb even though the phenomenal powers it was accorded are no longer recognized. The plant contains mucilaginous substances that soothe irritated tissues. The dried flowers from common mallow are therefore often added to herbal tea mixtures for coughs and other respiratory problems such as bronchitis,

Malva sylvestris, *common mallow.*

Malva moschata, *musk mallow.*

Malva sylvestris *'Primley Blue', common mallow cultivar.*

Malva verticillata *'Crispa'.*

asthma, and emphysema. The tea can be used as a gargle for throat infections and can also help with diarrhoea and stomach complaints.

Malva sylvestris prefers fertile disturbed soil and grows readily on rubbish tips, ruins, and close to rivers. This 50cm (20in) tall perennial also thrives on arable land. It flowers from June to September with pink-purple blooms. There are some fine garden cultivars, such as *Malva sylvestris* 'Primley Blue', which grows outwards rather than upwards and which has blue-purple flowers.

Malva verticillata 'Crispa'

FARMER'S TOBACCO

The lowest leaves of this type of mallow are large enough to serve a dessert on. A confection of fruit or fruit salad looks particularly good with the leave as garnish, not to be eaten.

Malva verticillata originates in southern Europe and Asia. The annual (occasionally biennial) grows as tall as a man but the somewhat smaller cultivar 'Crispa' is often grown in gardens with seeds sometimes escaping from cultivation. The white to lavender flowers are borne in tight clusters in the leaf axils and at the top of stems. The plant flowers from mid summer into autumn.

Malus domestica

APPLE

The apple is not just a tasty fruit but also a good medicine. "An apple a day keeps the doctor at bay," goes the saying and indeed moderate consumption of apples is good for the health, although excess is harmful. Eating too many apples causes excess acid in the stomach.

An apple is ideal for a morning purifying fruit diet in combination with other less acidic fruits. Apples are both laxative yet surprisingly help combat diarrhoea. Apple sauce in particular is good for stopping diarrhoea and dysentery and reduces inflammation of the lining of the stomach and colon. Apple sauce can be eaten without problem for stomach ulcers or colitis.

Infusion of apple peel (approx. 5 gram dried peel per cup) can be used for inflammation with a fever. Only use organically grown apples which have never been sprayed with any chemicals.

The bark from branches can be used to create a dyestuff to colour wool and other textiles beige.

The apple is a native shrub to small tree which is extremely rare in its original form. Attempts are being made to find an example of the original wild species in order to propagate it. Domesticated offspring from the original wild species are found in orchards and gardens, from which many thousands of cultivars have been selected, each with its own combination of characteristics so far as the shape, colour, taste of the fruit, storing properties, and resistance to disease are concerned. The cultivars are almost always grafted onto other root stock. The root stock has a great influence over the growing form of the tree. An expert in apple trees

Malus domestica *'Court Pendu', apple.*

Marrubium vulgare, *horehound.*

will advise on selection. Apple trees will grow on almost any soil that is not too acidic but they prefer alkaline clay soil. Apple trees are very susceptible to stagnant water around their roots.

🜚 ╱ ⚕

Marrubium vulgare

HOREHOUND, HOARHOUND, WHITE HOREHOUND

The small white flowers of horehound flock with bees during their bloom from June to October. This perennial grows to about 40cm (16in) and has a preference for a sunny position in well-worked, and ideally alkaline, soil. The natural area for this plant is around the Mediterranean. The plant can be found naturalised further north. Horehound is popular for ornamental gardens because of its grey-haired green foliage.

Horehound has been used for thousands of years. The ancient Egyptians and Greeks knew it as a cough remedy. In subsequent times the bitter tasting plant, which smells of apple, was used for a wide range of uses: to stimulate the appetite, and to stimulate gall bladder function in people with digestive disorders, for diarrhoea, as an antiseptic, as an addition to relaxing herbal teas, but most of

all for coughs. *Marrubium* has an expectorant action but also soothes and it is therefore incorporated in cough lozenges, cough mixture, and also used for infusions or stronger decoctions.

🜚

Matricaria recutita syn. M. chamomilla, Chamomilla recutita

GERMAN CHAMOMILE, SCENTED MAYWEED

In continental Europe, where white sand is widely used for road building and in the foundations of buildings, it will often be covered in summer by the

Matricaria recutita, *German chamomile.*

yellow and white of German chamomile. The wild plant grows otherwise on disturbed clay and loam such as ploughed fields but always in the sun. *Matricaria recutita* is a summer-flowering annual which can be seen in bloom from June to August. The daisy-like flowers can be told apart from other chamomiles by the hollow elongated cap (the other types only have hollow caps when they have been eaten by larvae).

The blooms are harvested during flowering. This is easily done by puling them off with a fork. They are then dried in the shade because flowers dried in the sun will fall apart. Once dry, the famous chamomile tea can be made which tastes delicious and has a sedative effect which is useful for stress, sleeplessness, and nervous indigestion. The tea also helps stomach complaints, including ulcers and inflammation of the lining. The herb eases inflammation and is therefore very suitable for bathing (for skin inflammation), vaginal douches, or in a compress for inflamed or slow to heal wounds.

Inhalation of the wonderful aroma of chamomile (in a bowl of almost boiling water) is useful for colds and inflamed nose, throat, and sinuses.

Some people are allergic to the herb so it is best to try with a low dose initially. The oil from the flowerheads is important in the cosmetic industry and widely used in soap and shampoo.

Medicago sativa ssp. sativa

LUCERNE, ALFALFA

Lucerne is one of the most important fodder crops there is. In parts of Asia and Africa where the soil is poor, lucerne offers a solution to small-scale farmers who are able to harvest the crop five times in a year. The plant has widespread and deep roots and recovers quickly from mowing. The root balls derive nitrogen from the air, making cultivation on poor soil possible. In Europe's intensive agriculture, the plant is mainly grown as a green manure or in association with beekeeping. Lucerne is a hardy perennial which originates from south-west Asia but is now cultivated throughout much of the world.

It is even possible to grow lucerne as a house plant. The seeds germinate within a few days provided they are kept moist. The new shoots are sold

Medicago sativa *ssp.* sativa, *lucerne.*

Matricaria recutita, *German chamomile.*

Arabic women tend lucerne.

Medicago sativa *ssp.* sativa, *alfalfa.*

Melilotus officinalis syn. *M. arvensis*

AYELLOW MELILOT, RIBBED MELILOT, YELLOW SWEET CLOVER

Without knowing it, you may eat yellow melilot when you eat certain cheese (such as Gruyère) or drink some beers or herbal bitters. The herb is added to these to impart flavour. The leaves can also be added to casseroles and stews. This should keep the moths away from your table because dried melilot leaves are an age-old proven moth deterrent. People however like the aroma from the leaves so that they are added to pot-pourris. Yellow melilot is used for a wide range of ailments and among the homeopathic uses are for nerve pain, headaches, and migraine. The best-known use is to bring down inflammation in wounds by adding it to plasters and for ointments to guard against thrombosis. The blood thinning properties of the herb make it unsuitable for use by people whose blood does not clot readily. *Melilotus officinalis* grows virtually throughout Europe, in particular in a sunny position on disturbed soil, such as railway yards, newly created embankments, and sandy verges. The biennial flowers from June to September with scented lemon yellow blooms which attract many bees. Depending on soil conditions and location, yellow melilot grows 100–200cm (39–59in) high.

Melilotus officinalis, *yellow melilot.*

under the Arabic name of alfalfa. The Arabic literally means "father of all food." Alfalfa shoots have a pleasant woodland smell and taste slightly of cress. They are delicious on bread with cheese and tomato or added to salads or as flavouring in sauces. They can also be strewn as garnish on hot dishes such as omelettes.

Lucerne provides a tonic, especially for anaemic people, women suffering from pre-menstrual syndrome, and diabetics. The herb is rich in protein, minerals, and vitamins and helps to reduce cholesterol levels.

Melissa officinalis

LEMON BALM, BALM, MELISSA

Lemon balm is regarded as an elixir of life for body and soul, driving out depression and reinvigorating the body. This was known long before the arrival of aromatherapy. The volatile oils with their pronounced aroma of lemon both relax and provide new vigour. The dried leaves provide a fresh fragrance in the house which helps to keep midges at bay. The dried herb is often added to pot-pourris. A few drops of the oil in bath water makes for a wonderful relaxing bath.

The relaxing properties of the herb are at the forefront of uses in folk medicine. Tea made with the leaves, sweetened with honey, is a well-proven night-cap, particularly for people who suffer nervous tension and heart spasms. These same people often suffer from nervous tummy and gut problems which can be eased by lemon balm's ability to relieve spasms.

Lemon balm is available in a number of forms: as oil (for bath and massage), ointment (to deter insects and treat bites), in the form of Carmelite water (with other herbs dissolved in alcohol), tincture (dissolved in a mixture of water and alcohol), and dried leaves for making lemon balm tea. The fresh leaves of lemon balm have a taste between lemon and mint. These are ideal in refreshing fruit drinks on a hot day, as flavouring in liqueurs, and to add flavour to salads. A little finely chopped lemon balm gives a special taste to marinades for lamb, fish, and egg dishes. Do not cook lemon balm with dishes because it loses its flavour and aroma.

Melissa officinalis probably originated from Asia but has grown around the Mediterranean for several thousand years. It is a perennial with creeping roots which grows to between 50cm (20in) and 100cm (39in) tall. The leaves which smell like lemons are picked before the plant flowers. It does so from June to September with small pale flowers. Lemon balm thrives in most gardens and can become rampant (from seed and creeping roots). But it is almost impossible to have too much of such a useful herb.

Melissa officinalis 'Aurea' is a golden variegated form of lemon balm which has the same properties and uses as the species.

Melittis melissophyllum

BASTARD BALM

Bastard balm contains cumarin, a substance which is added to liqueurs and white wines as an aromat-

Melittis melissophyllum, *bastard balm.*

Melissa officinalis, *lemon balm.*

Melissa officinalis *'Aurea', lemon balm.*

185

ic. Cumarin exudes the scent of fresh hay. The substance also relieves spasms and is therefore used (in a limited way) as a medicine (see *Galium odoratum)*.

Bastard balm is an attractive, low habit ornamental plant. The white, pink, or purple flowers (often two colours) are fairly large for a 50cm (20in) high plant. This perennial gets its botanical name from the typical honey aroma which the plant exudes. Bees are eager visitors to the herb.

♀ ▲ ⬯ ✳

Mentha aquatica syn. *M. hirsata*

WATERMINT

Water mint is a native throughout Europe, growing in moist to marshy ground. It thrives well in a bog garden and can grow to 50cm (20in). If the surface creeping rhizomes reach the water's edge it will grow half submerged with flabbier and lighter green growth. Watermint flowers between July and September with terminal flowerheads of lilac on the ends of shoots and smaller clusters in the leaf axils.

The scent of watermint can be readily detected at the waterside without treading on it. It exudes a characteristic mint aroma but with a definite undertone of ditch soil. Because of this it is less popular than other culinary mints, with the exception of more pungent mint sauces.

Medicinally, watermint stimulates gall bladder function, aids the digestion, and eases spasms. Diarrhoea and stomach 'flu are also helped by the herb (also see gingermint).

Mentha x gentilis syn. *M. cardiaca*, *M. x gentilis*

GINGERMINT

Spearmint *(Mentha spicata)* originates in southern Europe but was brought north for cultivation in herb gardens where it crossed with the native corn or field mint *(Mentha arvensis)* which is virtually never used as a culinary herb. The resulting hybrid is *Mentha* x *gracilis*, gingermint or redmint. This hybrid escaped from cultivation and can be found naturalised in much of northern Europe. The variegated form of gingermint *Mentha* x *gracilis* 'Variegata' is very like the ordinary gingermint and shares its common name and slight ginger aromatic smell from its leaves. Tomato and fruit salads taste better for a little gingermint. The herb aids digestion and the aromatic oils from the plant are used as flavouring in food production.

The medical properties of gingermint are identical to peppermint (see *Mentha* x *piperata)*.

♀ ▲ ⬯

Mentha x gracilis *'Variegata', gingermint.*

Mentha aquatica, *watermint.*

Mentha longifolia syn. M. sylvestris, M. incana

HORSEMINT

Horsemint not only has elongated grey-green leaves but also bears 10cm (4in) long tapering flowering spikes of pink in July to September. The almost 100cm (39in) high perennial has become naturalised in much of continental Europe. The most obvious difference between it and Egyptian mint *(M. x niliaca)* is Egyptian mint's wrinkled leaves compared with the smooth veins of

Mentha longifolia *'Buddleja', Boodle mint.*

Mentha longifolia, *horsemint.*

Mentha longifolia *'Buddleja', Boodle mint.*

horsemint. Horsemint has virtually identical properties to peppermint (see *Mentha* x *piperata*) but is less widely used as a herb. Most people regard this as a plant for the ornamental garden yet the leaves are ideal for preserving and can be added to chutney for oriental cooking. The oil serves as a flavouring for sweets and cakes.

A favourite ornamental garden cultivar is *Mentha longifolia* 'Buddleja' or 'Buddleia' sometimes known as Buddleia mint. It flowers in late summer with long drooping spikes rather like the flower plumes of *Buddleja*. Just like the plants from which it gets its name, it attracts scores of butterflies.

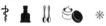

Mentha x niliaca

EGYPTIAN MINT

Egyptian mint is a cross between pineapple mint and horsemint. The plant has smaller leaves than horsemint that are cleared wrinkled. This perennial grows 100cm (39in) high and has pale pink terminal flower spikes between July and September. The plant readily becomes rampant through creeping roots and often escapes from cultivation when gardeners discard surplus plants.

187

Mentha *x* niliaca, *Egyptian mint.*

Mentha *x* niliaca, *Egyptian mint.*

Egyptian mint is less highly regarded as a culinary herb than peppermint but has similar uses (see *Mentha* x *piperata*). Mint tea can be made for rinsing the mouth to treat inflamed gums.

☤ 🜍 ✂ ☕ ✳

Mentha *x* piperata, *peppermint.*

Mentha x *piperata* syn. *M. nigricans*

PEPPERMINT

Spearmint *(Mentha spicata)* is a wild plant from southern Europe that was brought north. A crossing between this species and watermint *(M. aquatica)* was noted in England in 1696, forming the hybrid peppermint, which is the most important of all the mints, with the purest mint aroma of them all. The leaves are fairly long and often have a metallic sheen on their upper sides. The flower clusters appear in July and August as long terminal spikes, often with small clusters at the next pair of leaves on the stem. Peppermint is easily grown in gardens and naturalises readily. The cultivar *Mentha* x *piperata* 'Crispa' is often grown in gardens. It has noticeably wrinkled leaves with pointed teeth but can be used in precisely the same way as peppermint.

Peppermint is one of the most important herbs. The dried leaves provide a refreshing mint tea for hot days and the fresh leaves can be (sparingly) added to salads and are ideal with fish, cheese, and quark (low-fat curd cheese). It forms the basis for mint sauces and is also used as an edible garnish on dishes, especially ice-cream and chocolate desserts. Peppermint is also widely used in potpourris, liqueurs, medicines, tobacco, and ice creams.

The herb is prescribed medicinally for queasiness, vomiting, diarrhoea, stomach 'flu, under-active gall bladder, colds, influenza, stomach ulcers, intestinal spasms, colic, nerve pains, and rheumatism. Some people react adversely to peppermint. Do not give the herb to children (especially not in

Mentha *x* piperata *'Crispa'*.

Mentha pulegium, *pennyroyal*.

concentrated decoctions). The volatile oils contain 60 per cent menthol. Some adults are also allergic to the oil. A few drops of the oil in water on an oil burner will spread the aroma of menthol and keep midges away.

℞ ⚗ ✂ ⊙ ✳

Mentha pulegium, *pennyroyal*.

Mentha pulegium

PENNYROYAL

At first pennyroyal forms a small plant which exudes a strong aroma of mint. During the course of the summer, the stems grow erect to about 50cm (20in) and the top pair of leaves are surrounded by whorls of pink to lilac florets. The original range of pennyroyal, which rarely becomes rampant, was south-west and central Europe but it holds its own as a garden plant in all but the coldest parts of Europe. The plant has a clear preference for moist, acidic sandy soil.

The strongly aromatic herb can be added with moderation to salads, soups, and sauces. The herb was once especially used medicinally to aid digestion. In addition to indigestion and colic, the herb also relieves cramp and can be used to reduce period pains. Pregnant women should not use pennyroyal.

Pennyroyal oil is incorporated in ointments to improve circulation to the skin and prevent fleas. A little of the dried leaves in a pillow (or in a pet's basket) keeps fleas away.

℞ ✂ ✳

Mentha spicata, *spearmint.*

Mentha spicata *'Crispa', curly spearmint.*

Courtesy The Kruidenhof, Buitenpost.

Mentha spicata syn. *M. crispa, M. viridis*

SPEARMINT

Spearmint resemble Egyptian mint but does not have the woolly hairs on its stems and also has greener and more pointed leaves that are sweetly aromatic. The flower spikes are usually less branched than in the illustration so that the name spearmint is more appropriate. The plant usually starts blooming in August, making it useful for the autumn garden. The plant spreads rapidly through creeping roots and is therefore often thrown away by gardeners and escapes into the wild. It will happily grow in moist places and more than hold its own. This is the main constituent of mint sauce and jelly served with lamb but the oils are also widely used as a commercial flavouring for all manner of processed foods and sweets. For other uses, see *Mentha* x *piperata.*

Mentha spicata 'Crispa'

CURLY SPEARMINT

There is also a curly-leaf variant of spearmint which is widely cultivated for the production of

mint oil. The oil is mild in nature yet has a strong aroma of mint which makes this cultivar ideal for adding as aromatic to processed food and sweets. This version can be used in the same ways as peppermint (see *Mentha* x *piperata),* Mint tea with this mint has a superb taste but if you do not like it then pour it over your head because it is ideal for treating dandruff.

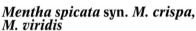

Mentha spicata 'Nana' syn. *M. s.* 'Moroccan'

MOROCCAN SPEARMINT

There is great confusion in the naming of mints because there are so few pure plants since the species readily cross with each other. Provided the species are grown well apart from each other this is not a problem but once they are placed close to each other all manner of hybrids are created. Most mint planted in gardens is no longer true to species so that the names give a mere indication of the characteristics of the plant. This is equally true of Moroccan mint which is known by both the botanical names indicated above.

Mentha spicata *'Nana', Moroccan mint.*

Mentha suaveolens, *applemint.*

hairs will be unpleasant in the mouth. This makes applemint less suitable for garnishing food. Other than this, the uses are the same as peppermint (see *Mentha spicata* x *piperata*).

The leaves have a delicate flavour and fragrance and make a wonderful mint tea which is mild and refreshing. I find no mint tea tastier than Moroccan mint.

The plant has the same potential uses as peppermint (see *Mentha* x *piperata*).

Mentha suaveolens syn. *M. insularis, M. macrostachya*

APPLEMINT, WOOLLY MINT

Applemint is a native in Britain and parts of Europe. Elsewhere it has become naturalised through escape from cultivation. The rampant creeping roots spread out in all directions, even appearing between paving. The shoots grow upwards to about 100cm (39in) and are covered with downy hairs, as are the ovoid leaves. The terminal pink flower spikes catch the eye between July and September.

Apple mint is renowned for fruity aroma of its leaves from which the name applemint is derived. The taste combines well with sweet dishes. Cook the leaves with the dish because otherwise the leaf

Mentha suaveolens 'Variegata'

PINEAPPLE MINT

A variegated form of applemint is often grown in ornamental gardens for its attractive foliage.

Mentha suaveolens *'Variegata', pineapple mint.*

Courtesy The Kruidenhof, Buitenpost.

Mentha suaveolens 'Variegata', pineapple mint.

Mentha x villosa, *Bowles' mint.*

Menyanthes trifoliata

BOG BEAN, BUCKBEAN, MARSH TREFOIL

The thick creeping roots of bog bean are usually under water in shallow water or on the surface in marshes with trifoliate leaves above water. In May to June, beautiful white to pale pink flowers with fringes appear on the plant. In poor soil the plant may not flower. Bogbean grows wild in wetlands throughout Europe but has become less widespread with drainage of its habitat. The plant is easily cultivated in a bog garden or pond. The leaves can be dried and used to make an infusion for treating all manner of stomach and intestinal disorders. The tannin helps with diarrhoea and together with other bitter substances they help stimulate the appetite, and stimulate the production of gastric juices. The plant was commonly prescribed as a tonic for patients recuperating from serious illnesses or operations. The herb is used homoeopathically for treating nerve pains, particularly facial neuralgia.

⚕

This mint is grey-green with irregular white to creamy patches along the leaf margins. Touching the leaves released a sweet fruit aroma, which for me has nothing of pineapple but which others deem resembles that fruit. Variegated varieties are usually less robust than the original plain green species but pineapple mint is the exception to this rule. It grows trouble free and is extremely hardy. Its uses are the same as peppermint (see *Mentha* x *piperata*) but it has more of a fruity than menthol taste.

⚕ 🜀 ⚖ 🝉 ✳

Mentha x *villosa*

BOWLES' MINT

This cross between spearmint and applemint is an extremely variable hybrid which has characteristics between both parents: the leaves are rounder than spearmint and less hairy than applemint. Bowles' mint is sterile, producing no seed, reproducing solely by creeping root runners. Bowles' mint has similar uses as peppermint (see *Mentha* x *piperata*). The variety *Mentha* x *villosa* var. *alopecuroides* is widely grown in gardens.

⚕ 🜀 ⚖ 🝉 ✳

Menyanthes trifoliata, *bog bean.*

Monarda didyama, *bergamot.*

Monarda didyama, *bergamot.*

Monarda didyama *'Croftway Pink', bergamot.*

Monarda didyama

BERGAMOT, BEE BALM, OSWEGO TEA

The flowers of bergamot can be used to make a relaxing herbal tea. Add a few flowers to normal tea for an especially tasty drink or mix them into a salad to add flavour and colour. The flowers are also frequently used in pot-pourris for their characteristic fragrance.

When the Europeans arrived in America, the native Americans used the plant as a medicinal herb. Herbal tea is useful for colds and is placed on wounds to aid healing. Today the various cultivars of bergamot are mainly grown for their looks in ornamental gardens. They make an attractive clump of between 100–150cm (39–5ft) high, flowering in late summer with white, pink, red, or purple blooms. Plant this North American native in fertile and moisture-retaining soil, either in the sun or partial shade.

Monarda didyama 'Croftway Pink' grows to about 100cm (39in) high and has pink flowers.

193

Morus nigra, *black mulberry.*

Morus nigra

BLACK MULBERRY

Black mulberries are never found in a shop because they are too delicate to be transported. When picked, they leave reddish-black juice on your fingers. The fruit are tasty when ripe, resembling raspberries in appearance but with smaller sap cells. The best use of them is for either juice or jam. Eaten raw they have a sweet taste with an acidic aftertaste but are a trifle insipid. The leaf, fruit, twigs, and bark of the roots have been used medicinally in China for thousands of years.

Morus nigra, *black mulberry.*

The fruits are mildly laxative, a tonic, and help with ringing in the ears. The leaves are bactericidal and are placed on infected wounds or to make infusions to treat colds. A decoction of the twigs reduces blood pressure and is useful for rheumatism. The water used to cook the outer bark of the roots is diuretic and helps with asthma. The autumn leaves can be used to form a yellow dyestuff for wool and other textiles.

The black mulberry will eventually grow into a tree of 15m (50ft) although there are grafted forms for gardens with weeping branches that look like green columns in summer and make it easier to reach the fruit. The trees are hardy but the leaves do not emerge until late spring.

♀ ∕ ⚌

Morus alba syn. *M. bombycis*

WHITE MULBERRY

The leaves of the white mulberry are of incalculable value for the silk worm, Without this tree they would not spin their silk threads. The white mulberry contains the same chemical compounds as the black mulberry and can therefore be used to treat the same ailments (see *Albus nigra*).

The white mulberry will eventually grow to 15m (50ft) and is less hardy than its black counterpart, so that it is more widely grown in southern Europe. There are weeping forms such as *Morus alba* 'Pendula' which is more compact in height (3m/10ft) but will eventually have a broad span (5m/15ft).

♀ ⚌ ✳

Myosotis arvensis

FIELD FORGET-ME-NOT

The field forget-me-not has been used as herbal medicine since Medieval times. Its beneficial prop-

Morus alba *'Pendula', weeping white mulberry.*

Myosotis arvensis, *field forget-me-not.*

Myrica gale, *sweet gale.*

away and are therefore placed in linen chests and cupboards and also deter flies. The strong tasting aromatic herbal tea from the plant is taken for diarrhoea.

Myricaria germanica

GERMAN TAMARISK

Myricaria germanica rarely appears in English plant books and has no recognised common name. It is of the same family as tamarisks but in a genus

Myricaria germanica, *German tamarisk.*

erties in treating tuberculosis have been scientifically verified. The herb is little used today because the disease has more or less disappeared in Europe and in the outbreaks which occur from time to time, the sufferers receive intensive treatment.
Myosotis arvensis grows throughout Europe as a weed in arable land, in pasture land, and in the scrub at field edges. This annual (occasionally biennial) readily self seeds itself in gardens.

Myrica gale

SWEET GALE, BOG MYRTLE

The sweet gale or bog myrtle spreads a wonderful balsamic fragrance from its clumps in summer. This native shrub grows best in peaty soils close to water where they reach about 100–150cm (39–59in) high. The branches are covered in spring with elongated brown catkins which are replaced by tiny yellow-brown fruits which are covered in resin. Sweet gale bushes are ideal for a natural-look garden where they should be planted in moist acidic peat or sandy soil.
The resin from the plant can be used for candles which exude a balsamic aroma while they burn. Dried twigs not only smell sweet, they keep moths

of its own. The shrub grows to between 100–200cm (39–59in) in the higher parts of Europe, in gravel beds of rivers and rocky uplands. The grey-green leaves overlap each other on the slender erect stems like roofing tiles. Spikes of pale pink to reddish flowers at the ends of stems from May to August.

Myricaria germanica has been used as a herbal medicine since ancient times. Hippocrates reported the beneficial effect of the leaves on white secretions in young women, while the seeds were said to aid infertility. The use of the herb for treating jaundice and spleen disorders were discovered by herbalists somewhat later. The herb has fallen into disuse, perhaps because it contains toxic substances and should therefore only be used under medical supervision.

Myristica fragrans

NUTMEG, JATIPHALA

Those who grate nutmeg over a rice pudding need not worry that the spice was once used to induce miscarriages or that the women who ingested large quantities to this end went quite literally off their head. Nutmeg contains an hallucinogen, which is also toxic.

Nutmeg is a tropical tree from eastern Indo-China discovered by Arab traders before the time of Christ but not discovered by the west until about 1500. The female trees bear fleshy golden fruits, inside which is a reddish-orange aril (from which mace is derived) surrounding the nut in a woody brown shell. Both mace and nutmeg are rich in volatile oils which contain high concentrations of safrole and myristicin. The dried nuts are grated as a spice and mace is usually dried and ground as a powder for similar uses but with less pungency.

Grated nutmeg is used in addition to rice pudding, to flavour bakery products, puddings, drinks, meat dishes, vegetables (such as spinach and mushrooms), cheese dishes, sauces (such as onion, bread, and *béchamel)*, and pasta fillings. Mace has

Myristica fragrans, *nutmeg.*

Myristica fragrans, *mace.*

a milder flavour and is often added during cooking to soups, fish, and chicken dishes.

The former medicinal uses of nutmeg are now less important than those of culinary spice. Previously it was highly regarded for treating early morning diarrhoea, queasiness, indigestion, or stomach problems caused by influenza or food poisoning. The oil can be rubbed on gums for toothache and there are also massage oils incorporating mace for treating rheumatism and muscular aches.

A fatty oil known as "nutmeg butter" is incorporated in soap, ointments, candles, and perfume for an intense fragrance.

Myrrhis odorata

SWEET CICELY, SWEET CHERVIL, GARDEN MYRRH

When the leaves of sweet cicely emerge they appear like a fern emerging. The leaf is very attractively formed like a fern and popular with those who press plants for mounting on paper. This is a wild perennial from the mountains of Europe where it grows beside streams and the edges of moist woodland. In gardens the leaves emerge in March followed by the flower umbels in May to June.

Myrrhis odorata, *sweet cicely.*

Myrtus communis *'Variegata', myrtle.*

The plant is decorated after flowering by the erect seeds. While these are still green they can be eaten or added to salads and fruit salads. They have a sweet aniseed flavour. The ripe seeds can be ground and used as furniture wax.

When the leaves are crushed, they smell of liquorice. These can be added to salads, soups, and sauces or cooked with sharp-tasting dishes, such as rhubarb, as a natural sweetener so that less sugar is needed. The oil from the herb is used to flavour liqueurs and tobacco.

Sweet cicely is mildly laxative, aids digestion, acts as a tonic, and is useful for anaemia and coughs.

The leaf stalks can be used to dye wool or other textiles green or orange-brown.

This perennial grows best in moisture-retaining soil that is both fertile and rich in humus. It reaches about 150cm (5ft), is hardy, and readily self-seeds itself.

⚕ / ‖ ☕ ✳

Myrtus communis

MYRTLE

Myrtle was linked in Greek mythology with beauty and love. The wonderfully fragrant flowers certainly lend themselves to both. Indeed after eating the plant even the urine smells of violets. The flowers or buds (without the green parts) can be added to salads and fruit salads, twigs can be cooked with

Myrtus communis, *myrtle.*

meat dishes, and the berries are widely used in the Middle East as a spice. The taste is somewhat similar but milder than juniper berries.

Dried leaves and flowers exude their fragrance for a long time and are therefore incorporated in pot-pourris and pomanders. Oil of myrtle is a constituent of perfume, soap, ointments, and shampoo and is used externally to treat acne and gum disease. Crushed leaves heal grazes and are also used to treat psoriasis. Drinking an infusion of the leaves helps with sinusitis and coughs.

Myrtus communis occurs naturally in the scrub or *masqui* around the Mediterranean shores. This evergreen bush can withstand about minus 10°C (14°F) grown in the ground so it is usually cultivated in northern latitudes as a container plant. Place it in a sunny position in soil that contains no lime and water with either rainwater or boiled water. The pot must never be so over-watered that water stands on the surface. Over-winter in a cool place (2–12°C/35–53°F) with ample light. If well cared for, container-grown plants can reach 200cm (79in) in height and breadth but can be kept smaller by pruning.

Myrtus communis 'Variegata' is a variegated form with yellow leaf margins.

⚕ 🍶 ‖ ☕ ✳

197

fairly poisonous, so that cattle usually leave it alone. Where the soil is poor, and this is precisely where bog asphodel grows, sheep and cattle may well graze the plant and then become oversensitive to sunlight. This can result in blisters on unprotected skin. The Latin name *ossifragum* or "bone break" was given because farmers thought the herb was responsible for injuring the legs of their sheep but it is now realized that this is due to the poor nature of the pasture, low in calcium, in which the plant is found.

Lovely yellow flowers appear in July on stems of about 15cm (6in) long and these are followed in autumn by dark orange fruits. It grows on wet heaths, moorlands, wetlands and mountainous regions particularly in western and northern Britain, although lowland colonies are rare due to drainage of its habitat.

Narcissus 'Thalia', daffodil.

Narcissus 'Thalia'

DAFFODIL, NARCISSUS

It is often the case that plants with medicinal properties are also poisonous and this is equally true of the daffodil, of which the bulbs are toxic. The flowers, especially those of poet's narcissus, have a stupor-inducing fragrance if too many are placed indoors. The name *Narcissus* is probably derived from the narcotic effect of the plants and the Greek *narcao*, meaning stupefying.

Daffodils have been used since early times as a medicinal herb. Recently it was discovered that they contain galanthamin which can treat dementia. A Scottish company is researching whether galanthamin can be commercially produced to treat Alzheimer's disease. To mark this, a daffodil has been named after the discoverer of this ailment. The plant is named *Narcissus* 'Alois Alzheimer'.

Daffodil bulbs are best planted in September to give them a chance to root in the autumn. This increases the chances of early spring flowering. Most daffodils originate from southern Europe but grow without difficulty further north, especially when planted in fertile, moisture-retaining soil where they will flower year-after-year and propagate themselves mainly by division of the bulb.

Narthecium ossifragum

BOG ASPHODEL

It is known that bog asphodel is a natural antibiotic but not yet known how the plant combats infection. That is the positive side of the plant which is

Nasturtium officinale syn. Rorippa nasturtium-aquaticum

WATERCRESS

Spring is time for the big spring clean and the same is true for the body. Watercress is ideal for this purpose because it is diuretic, stimulates gall, liver,

Narthecium ossifraga, *bog asphodel.*

and kidney function, and aid digestion. An additional benefit of these properties is that it thereby also helps to treat rheumatism, gout, and eczema.

Watercress is extremely rich in vitamins A, C, and D and contains other important nutritional elements such as iron and potassium. Quite apart from the health-giving properties of watercress, its spicy taste is much appreciated by many, who add the uncooked leaves to salads or make watercress soup.

Once watercress only grew in those parts of Europe and Asia with a moderate climate but this edible plant is now cultivated anywhere with a moderate climate and can also be found growing wild. Before harvesting the plant from the wild it is essential to know that the water is pure in which it grows. Water infected by cattle or run-off from sewerage systems can cause liver fluke infestation, a parasite which can seriously damage the liver.

Some continental European countries grow a smaller-leafed version *(N. microphyllum)* which is hardier, being able to withstand temperatures down to minus 15°C (5°F), whereas watercress suffers leaf damage and cannot be sold. Consequently hybrids of the two are often grown commercially.

Both species grow in clean, preferably flowing water, in stream beds or areas with ground water. Watercress prefers chalk streams or other alkaline sources, while the small-leafed form is less fussy. Both types can only be cultivated with flowing, cool water, or in a pot standing in a tray or saucer of water, which must be replaced daily.

♀ ♊

Nelumbo nucifera syn. *Nelumbium speciosum*

SACRED LOTUS, PADMA

In southern Asia, the lotus is a sacred flower which is associated with the sun's rebirth every new dawn. This shows a similarity with the ancient Egyptians belief that a water lily gave birth to the sun in the form of a scarab (dung) beetle.

In the Far East, the leaves, flowers, and roots of the lotus have been used medicinally for at least 1,500 years, especially to stem bleeding but also to strengthen the heart. The dried root provides an edible flour that is known as Chinese arrowroot.

Sacred lotus only grows in tropical climates, with

Nelumbo nucifera, *sacred lotus*.

its roots in still water and the leaves and flowers above. The base of dried lotus flowers are widely used in flower arranging.

☫ ‖ ✳

Nepeta cataria

CATNIP, CATMINT

Catnip has a sedative effect on humans but it excites cats to a frenzy. They can react so strongly to the herb that the plant is wrecked by them but at others they may eat from the plant and then lay down in the midst of the plant. Humans experience the fragrance of catnip as a mixture of mint with lemon. Under the right circumstances, the fragrance can be detected some way off from the plant.

Before real tea arrived from the east, catnip was much more widely used. Herbal tea was made from the leaves and at the same time the healing properties were enjoyed: treatment for sore throats, colds, bronchitis, asthma, and relief for spasms, thereby helping with painful menstruation and stomach or intestinal cramp. The herb was especially given to babies and small children who were restless as a result of colic. Catnip helps restless people to sleep and an infusion or decoction can help with tense headaches.

The fresh leaves can be added in moderation to flavour salads. The entire plant is suitable for use to dye wool and other textiles.

Catnip probably originated in eastern Europe but has grown wild since before anyone can remember in other parts of Europe. Depending on its growing circumstances, the plant reaches either about 30cm (12in) or up to 100cm (39in) high and has a strong preference for lime-rich and fertile soil, so

Nepeta cataria, *catnip*.

Nepeta cataria *'Citriodora', catnip*.

that it grows well on chalk The leaves resemble a large stinging nettle so that the plant tends only to be noticed while flowering. The white flowers with purple streaks form spikes on the stems.

Nepeta cataria 'Citriodora'

CATNIP, CATMINT

This cultivar of catnip is often preferred for herbal tea because of the pronounced lemon fragrance of the leaves which make the tea taste delicious. The flowers of this cultivar are the same colour as the species but are also available in darker colours, as illustrated.

For uses see *Nepeta Cataria*.

Nerium oleander

OLEANDER, ROSE BAY

All parts of oleander or rose bay are so poisonous that even small doses can be fatal. Soldiers have died from eating meat cooked over a fire on an oleander branch. The plant contains heart glycosides which in the correct dosage can be beneficial for heart patients, especially for irregular or weak heart beats. Self-medication with this extremely toxic plant is absolutely out of the question. Oleander is also used in homeopathic form for heart problems.

Nerium oleander grows wild in a narrow ring of countries around the Mediterranean, in eastern parts of Asia Minor, and on the southern fringes of the Himalayas to western China. The oleander gives the appearance of growing in dry conditions but they are often to be found in the beds of dried-up rivers and other places where the roots can reach ground water. If grown as a container plant water and feed them copiously while they are growing. Keep them drier and free from frost (but

Nerium oleander *'Papa Gambetta', oleander.*

Nerium oleander *'Angiolo Pucci', oleander.*

not warmer than 15°C (59°F) during winter. The oleander will only flower if it has had plenty of light during the winter. The flowers are usually deep pink but cultivars have a range of colours: white, pale yellow (as *Nerium oleander* 'Angiolo Pucci), yellow, apricot, salmon pink (as *Nerium oleander* 'Papa Gambetta'), dark red, or purple.

Nicotiana rustica

WILD TOBACCO

Wild tobacco is also cultivated for one of the most powerful insecticides: nicotine. This substance is so poisonous that its use for pest control is banned in many countries while its use as a drug derived from tobacco continues to be tolerated, although most governments try to deter people from smoking.

Nicotiana rustica mainly grows in the lower mountains of South and Central America. When the white man first landed there, they saw with surprise that smoke came from the mouths of the indigenous people. They took the tobacco leaves with them to Europe where smoke soon begin to

Nicotiana rustica, *wild tobacco.*

issue from the European's mouths too. Once the main tobacco plant was discovered, wild tobacco was relegated.

Nicotiana rustica is an annual which can grow to 150cm (5ft) high. The leaves themselves can grow to 30cm (12in) long. The flower bears yellow-green flowers in late summer which remain open through the day. The plant is easily grown from seed for the garden.

✳

Nicotiana tabacum

TOBACCO

Tobacco originated from the borders of Argentina and Bolivia, where it was discovered by the white man after the original encounters with wild tobacco. The native people in the region knew the plant as both a stimulating and relaxing source of enjoyment. The quality of *Nicotiana tabacum* is superior to wild tobacco and today numerous cultivars are grown.

This tobacco also contains toxic substances, including nicotine, although these days nicotine is also used to help wean smokers off their addiction in the form of nicotine patches. Nicotine was once used to treat all manner of ailments but the inter-

Nicotiana tabacum, *tobacco.*

Nicotiana rustica, *wild tobacco.*

Nicotiana tabacum, *drying tobacco leaf.*

Nicotiana tabacum, *tobacco dealer in Arabia.*

nal consumption of this toxin is now regarded as too dangerous.

Tobacco is mainly grown in hot climates but it can also be grown in Europe. The biggest problem is curing the leaves. Special wooden sheds are built for this purpose. In Arab countries, the whole dried leaf is sold and the customer cuts or crumbles the tobacco and then adds syrup to it for smoking through water in a hookah pipe. It is possible to grow tobacco in Europe as an annual which grows about 100cm (39in) high, bearing green-white to pinkish-red flowers in late summer which remain open during the day.

Nigella damascena

LOVE-IN-THE-MIST, DEVIL-IN-A-BUSH

Love-in-the-mist, which originated from southern Europe and North Africa, is one of the most popular annuals for ornamental gardens. The up to 50cm (20in) high plant bears blue, white, or pink flowers from July. After flowering, horn-like swollen fruits appear amidst the pastoral branched foliage.

The seeds of *Nigella damascena* contain oils that are used in the cosmetic and perfume industries. Medical properties are sometimes claimed for the

Nigella damascena, *love-in-the-mist.*

herb but this is through confusion with *Nigella sativa*.

Nigella sativa

BLACK CUMIN, NUTMEG FLOWER, ROMAN CORIANDER

When pepper was unknown in Europe, food was spiced with black cumin, which are the seeds of *Nigella sativa*. This annual originated from southwestern parts of Asia and was being widely cultivated in Europe during the reign of Charlemagne (742–814 AD). The plant grows to about 30cm (12in) high and has pale yellow flowers in July that can be tinged with blue. After flowering, pointed fruits with eight segments are formed containing the seeds. These contain a fragrant oil which is used, among other uses, for making perfume.

Black cumin is beneficial for gall function and stomach juices so that it aids digestion. Substances within the herb relieve spasms and are useful for diarrhoea, wind, period pains, and following labour. They may also be beneficial for the respiratory system, providing relief for asthma sufferers.

Nymphaea alba

WHITE WATER LILY

Perhaps it is because the white water lily was associated with purity and virginity that the plant was once a popular medicine for treating disorders of the sexual organs, including vaginal problems, gonorrhoea, and period pains. The roots were dried and powdered and used to reduce sexual desire. Water lily is still used in homeopathic medicine for this latter purpose, as well as for incontinence, and back problems. Otherwise, *Nymphaea* is virtually unused in medicine.

Water lilies grow in still or almost still water of 50cm–100cm (20in–39in) deep. The leaves and flowers appear on the surface of the water from early summer but can stick out above water if the level falls. The creeping roots grow rampantly.

Nigella sativa, *black cumin.*

Nymphaea alba, *white water lily.*

Nymphaea alba, *white water lily.*

O

Ocimum basilicum, *basil.*

Ocimum basilicum, *basil.*

Ocimum basilicum

BASIL, SWEET BASIL

Nothing can beat a sandwich with ripe tomatoes and a few leaves of basil on a sunny summer's day. The herb has an indescribable aroma that once experienced is never forgotten. The herb was considered the "king of herbs" as long ago as ancient Greece. The Greek basileus means "king".

Basil plays an important role during courting on the island of Malta. Marriageable women place a pot of basil in specially designed recesses on either side of their window to signify that they are available to marry.

The herb originates from India but has been popular in southern Europe for a very long time. Basil features extensively in Italian cooking. Chopped basil is sprinkled over pasta sauce when it has been cooked, while tomato and egg dishes are rarely served without basil. The herb helps to digest "heavy" meals and is therefore often added to oily fish. Dried basil loses its flavour but the plant can be harvested and kept in the deep freeze. In northern Europe, basil was mainly used with meat dishes and sausages but was unrecognisable because it was added during cooking. This causes basil to lose most of its characteristic aroma and flavour.

The plant contains a great deal of volatile oil which is used in making perfume. Not everything finds the fragrance pleasant for a pot of basil near a window wards off insects.

Drinking infusions of basil aids digestion, and helps prevent wind, and nervous stomach and gut spasms. The herb helps to induce calm, aids sleeping, and can mitigate a migraine.

Unfortunately, this wonder herb, that has so many useful properties, is difficult to cultivate. The annual cannot be sown outside until May and then only in a sunny, sheltered position. Growing basil as a pot plant behind glass is recommended for northern Europe because the plant will yield to fungal disease after long periods of wet weather. If well cared for, the plant can grow to 50cm (20in) high. By clipping off flowering shoots, the plant will produce more shoots and increase the harvest of leaves.

⚕ 🍶 ⚔ ✳

Ocimum basilicum *'Citriodorum', lemon basil.*

Ocimum basilicum *'HORAPHA', aniseed basil.*

Ocimum basilicum 'Citriodorum' syn. *O. citriodorum*

LEMON BASIL

The leaves of this cultivar have a pronounced lemon aroma. The taste is ideal with fish but less suitable for tomato and egg. The shoots are ideal for making herb vinegar. This small-leafed cultivar is easier to grow in northern climates than the large-leafed forms. For uses see *Ocimum basilicum.*

Ocimum basilicum 'HORAPHA'

ANISEED BASIL

There are countless forms of aniseed basil with a different flavour. These are often sold without the correct botanical name, such as 'HORAPHA' which has a taste similar to other cultivars which have names such as *O. basilicum* 'Anise', and *O. basilicum* 'Licorice' (which are the same cultivar). For use and cultivation, see *Ocimum basilicum.*

Oenothera biennis, *common evening primrose.*

Oenothera biennis

COMMON EVENING PRIMROSE

Towards the evening, the flowers of evening primrose suddenly open. The buds open within a minute to reveal large yellow flowers which are mainly pollinated by moths. The flowers close up again during the following morning but open once more that evening. In this way the evening primrose flowers throughout the summer months on one stem while the stem grows steadily longer. The elongated downy seed pods also ripen from bottom to top and release a great deal of seed a little at a time from late summer until winter. This germinates readily on sandy soil.

The following year the plant forms a leaf rosette but does not flower. *Oenothera biennis* is a biennial that was discovered in America in the seventeenth century and brought to Europe where is has become widely naturalised, especially in sunny positions on sandy soil. The roots of the plant were eaten in America and this was copied in Europe. The taste is akin to black salsify (oyster or oyster plant). The seeds are pressed for their oil which is incorporated in cosmetics and skin creams. The active substance is the unsaturated fatty acid gamma-linoleic acid which helps rectify hormonal problems (such as pre-menstrual tension). Evening primrose is also used to treat eczema, rheumatoid arthritis, burns, acne, brittle nails, dry eyes and skin, high blood pressure, liver complaints. There are also capsules with extract of evening primrose for hangovers. The flowering tips of the plants were formerly used to make herbal tea to treat coughs, and stomach and gut spasms.

Oenothera biennis, *common evening primrose.*

Olea europaea, *olive.*

Olea europaea

OLIVE

Two olive branches flank the letters "UN" in the emblem of the United Nations. Olive branches have long been associated with peace, wisdom, and prosperity. This is not so strange, since the olive tree grows extremely slowly and it is a long time before it delivers an abundant harvest of olives. *Olea* can only spread her benefaction when society is stable and at peace. The slightly elongated fruits are pressed to produce the finest of edible oils. The best olive oil comes from the first, cold pressing. The remains of the fruit are pressed once more and then often heated for a third pressing. The best extra virgin olive oil will usually bear "first, cold pressing" on the label.

Olive oil is widely used for cooking. It not only gives a wonderful taste to the dishes (which not everyone can appreciate) but is also extremely healthy. The cholesterol level in the blood is reduced by replacing animal fat with olive oil, reducing the risk of heart disease and thrombosis. The purest olive oil taste is best enjoyed by adding olive oil as dressing to salad (with vinegar if preferred).

Olea europaea, *olive.*

Ononis spinosa, *spring restharrow.*

The olives themselves are added to many dishes, especially salads and pizza. The green olives in particular are often stuffed (with the stone removed) with fish or other savoury filling. Olive oil is used in the production of cosmetics such as soap, creams, anti-dandruff shampoo, and emulsions.

The olive leaves were once used to treat high blood pressure and grazes but are little used these days. Olives have a powerful yet mild laxative effect.

Ononis spinosa

SPRING RESTHARROW

Spring restharrow grows in western and central Europe along the coasts and rivers, on arable and grass land. The plant prefers a sunny position and

Ononis spinosa, *spring restharrow.*

Courtesy The Kruidenhof, Buitenpost.

Ononis spinosa, *spring restharrow.*

Onopordum acanthium, *cotton thistle.*

its deep roots are most at home in sandy soil that is very alkaline. Cattle are kept off the herb by the sharp thorns and farmers therefore try to get rid of the plant on their land, although the deep tap root makes this difficult. Those who like flowers will be rewarded by this 50cm (20in) tall bush with abundant pink (sometimes red or white) butterfly blooms on the branches between June and August. The flowers are superb in both form and markings. The plant, which contains saponin and other substance, has been used to make herbal tea since early times. These days, some dried root is added to infusions to act as a diuretic. This ability to drive out liquid from the body can be used to treat oedema, kidney complaints, rheumatism, and gout. Some patients are helped greatly by the herb while others see no change. The cause is likely to be the great variation in the constituency of the volatile oils in the herb. Others believe the method of preparation plays a role. If the medicine is heated too long, they argue, the volatile oils lose their effectiveness. Do not leave an infusion of restharrow brewing for too long.

Onopordum acanthium syn. *Onopordum nervosum*

COTTON THISTLE, SCOTTISH THISTLE

The leaves of this thistle of about 200cm (79in) are so densely covered with felt-like hairs that they were once harvested for cushion and pillow stuffing. There is no time these days for such labour and time intensive chores. For the same reason, the cooking of the flowerheads as alternatives to artichoke has also fallen off. The flowerheads are fairly large at 3–4cm (1¹/₂in) across but not in the same league as those of artichokes. Thistle oil can be pressed from the seeds, which can be used as a lamp oil.

Tannin and other bitter substances in the leaves help to heal wounds and infusions of the leaves are useful for coughs. A decoction of the roots helps to clear catarrh. Young shoots can be blanched or fully cooked and eaten.

The cotton or Scottish thistle originates in western Europe but long since became naturalised from escape from cultivation and with the plant popular once more for natural gardens this is likely to increase. The robust shape of the greyish-white leaves and purple flowerheads are well suited to rugged gardens where they will attract many bees. Some authorities claim *Onopordium acanthium* is not a separate species from *Onopordium nervosum* but there are clear differences between them. The range of *O. acanthium* is far wider than that of *O. nervosum*, which is mainly restricted to the Iberian Peninsula.

Onopordum acanthium, *cotton thistle.*

Origanum laevigatum 'Herrenhausen', marjoram.

Origanum laevigatum 'Herrenhausen'

MARJORAM, OREGANO

This marjoram or oregano is rarely used as a culinary herb unlike its related species. The leaves also exude the wonderful fragrance of marjoram and also have antiseptic properties. This species originates in southern Turkey and Cyprus. A number of attractive cultivars have been selected, such as 'Herrenhausen' which has purple stems in spring and winter. The main flowering is in summer when pale lilac blooms are borne. The plant is easily grown in either the ornamental or herb garden and whereas the species can only withstand frosts of minus 5–10°C (14–23°F), while 'Herrenhausen' is more hardy.

Origanum majorana

SWEET MARJORAM, KNOTTED MARJORAM

The Greek *oregano* means "joy of the mountain" and it is entirely apt for anyone who walks through the Greek mountains in summer will regularly encounter the delightful fragrance of the various

Origanum majorana, *sweet marjoram.*

types of oregano or marjoram. The herb has been used by man so long that no-one is entirely certain where the plants originated. Botanists consider the most likely home was south-western parts of Asia. The ancient Egyptians knew of the herb and used it to preserve food and to disinfect wounds.

Sweet marjoram can be used medicinally. For uses, see *Origanum vulgare* (wild marjoram).

Sweet marjoram has a more refined taste for culinary use than the wild marjoram. The taste is sweeter (hence the name) and milder and the herb is ideal for adding to meat dishes. The fragrance of marjoram is unsurpassed and is not entirely lost when dried. Chopped leaves in pot-pourris and entire stems in fragrant bouquets spread the summer mountain fragrance throughout the house.

Sweet marjoram is less hardy than wild marjoram and does not survive hard winters. The plant is a perennial but is usually grown as an annual. Sow seed indoors in March to April or outside but not before late May. This plant prefers a lime-rich soil in a sunny but sheltered position.

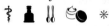

Origanum 'Rosenkuppel', marjoram.

Origanum vulgare, *wild marjoram.*

Origanum vulgare, *wild marjoram.*

Origanum 'Rosenkuppel'

MARJORAM

Origanum 'Rosenkuppel' is just one of many culti-vars which have been selected for different charac-teristics, sometimes for use or otherwise for orna-mental value. This cultivar falls into the latter category. It grows to about 50cm (20in) high, has red tinged stems and leaves, with small pink–lilac flowers which bloom in late summer. Although the emphasis is ornamental, the leaves can be used for both medicinal and aromatic purposes.

Origanum vulgare

WILD MARJORAM, OREGANO

The wild marjoram, also known as oregano, is one of the most important culinary herbs of southern Europe. The leaves have a pungent taste that is especially regarded in tomato salads, on pizzas, and in pasta sauces. The herb is cooked with the meat and used to flavour mushroom or *funghi* dishes, herb vinegar, beer, and spirits.

Origanum vulgare also smells of sunny holidays in the mountains of southern Europe. The dried leaves are added to pot-pourris, and entire stems continue to be fragrant for a long time in dried flower arrangements. Marjoram oil is incorporated in perfumes and cosmetics. If added to bath water it will relax you superbly and a few drops on your pillow help the restless to sleep.

Wild marjoram is used as a stimulating tonic with antiseptic properties. Infusions are drunk to aid digestion, stimulate gall bladder function, and to combat internal infections. For this reason, decoctions are also useful for coughs and sore throats. The herbal tea or decoction also relieves spasms and is prescribed for diarrhoea, period pains, and tense headache. Ointments based on wild marjoram help babies with colic to sleep and relieve rheumatic aches for adults. Pregnant women are advised not to take the herb internally. A purple dye for wool can be won from the herb. Dry marjoram in a shady place rather than the full sun, to prevent the volatile oils being lost.

Wild marjoram originally only grew in southern Europe but because of its uses was brought over the Alps in the sixteenth century, since when it has spread to the whole of Europe. The plant grows to about 70cm (27^1/$_2$in) and is mainly found on dry grassland scrub and hedge banks on chalky soil. Several hardy cultivars are listed below.

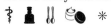

Origanum vulgare 'Album'

WHITE WILD MARJORAM

The best known white-flowering variety of wild marjoram is much lower than the species, reaching a maximum of 30cm (12in) in height. The plant grows in a woody clump with striking pale green foliage. It flowers in late summer. For uses, see *Origanum vulgare*.

Origanum vulgare 'Aureum'

GOLDEN WILD MARJORAM

The foliage of golden wild marjoram is particularly golden in spring. If planted in the full sun, the leaves can wither so that they turn white, then brown. Protect this 30cm (12in) high cultivar from the scorching midday sun. When the plant flowers in July, the leaves have turned green. The lavender to pale pink flowers are not especially striking. For uses, see *Origanum vulgare*.

Origanum vulgare 'Album', white wild marjoram.

Origanum vulgare 'Aureum', golden wild marjoram.

Courtesy The Kruidenhof, Buitenpost.

Origanum vulgare *'Charlie Gold', golden wild marjoram.*

Origanum vulgare creticum, *wild marjoram.*

Origanum vulgare 'Charlie Gold'

GOLDEN WILD MARJORAM

This golden marjoram grows more or less as a ground cover plant, with smaller leaves than *Origanum vulgare* 'Aureum'. The leaves have the same disadvantages as the earlier golden cultivar so that in a sunny position they turn white, then brown as a result of burning.
For uses, see *Origanum vulgare*.

Origanum vulgare 'Compactum'

WILD MARJORAM

The compact growth and abundant flowering of this cultivar make it one of the most popular forms of marjoram. What is more it has dense foliage which is ideal as culinary herb. This ground cover plant has a height of not more than 20cm (8in) and it had violet to pink flowers in late summer. This cultivar makes an ideal plant to spread out to provide cover, for a border plant, or a pot plant.
For uses, see *Origanum vulgare*.

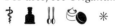
Origanum vulgare *'Compactum', wild marjoram.*

Origanum vulgare var. creticum

WILD MARJORAM

The name is derived from a specialised collection of marjoram plants in Kent where they call it *Origanum creticum*. The plants are 30cm (12in) high and they catch the eye with their dense panicles of many tiny florets. These are white suffused with pale pink and they attract many insects, especially hover flies.
For uses, see *Origanum vulgare*.

Origanum vulgare 'Hortense'

WILD MARJORAM

A large range of widely varying cultivars are sold under this inappropriate name. Different marjoram varieties cross readily with each other when they are in close proximity. A range of cultivars from these hybrids have been selected. The form illustrated is almost 100cm (39in) tall with fairly large, fresh-green leaves and bright red flowers.
For uses, see *Origanum vulgare*.

Origanum vulgare 'Hortense', *wild marjoram.*

Origanum vulgare *var.* samotrake, *wild marjoram.*

Origanum vulgare var. *samotrake*

WILD MARJORAM

The flower stems of this variety grow to 40cm (16in) long. In late summer they are covered in a mass of white florets which are popular with insects. The leaves are grey-green. For uses, see *Origanum vulgare.*

Origanum vulgare 'Thumble's Variety'

WILD MARJORAM

The leaves of this variety are pale yellow in spring but once the sun becomes stronger they change to green-yellow and by the time they flower, the foliage is pale green. Unlike other golden cultivars, 'Thumble's Variety' does not suffer from burning by the sun. The plants grow to 30–40cm (12–16in) high and have insignificant white flowers in late summer.

For uses, see *Origanum vulgare.*

Origanum vulgare *'Thumble's Variety', wild marjoram.*

Ornithogalum longibracteatum, *false sea onion.*

Oryza sativa, *drying rice.*

Ornithogalum longibracteatum syn. *O. caudatum*

FALSE SEA ONION

A plant with unusual characteristics grows in Cape Province, South Africa. False sea onion, with wide ribbon-like leaves, contains substances which help to heal burns and prevent the blisters which often accompany burns from forming. A decoction of the herb is held against the burnt skin.

Ornithogalum longibracteatum is perhaps better known under its old name of *Ornithogalum caudatum,* which indicates the large bulb which protrudes slightly from the ground. This is surrounded by lax semi-succulent green basal leaves. In summer, flowering shoots develop between these leaves which can reach 150cm (59in), bearing up to three hundred flowers. These are similar in appearance to European species of star of Bethlehem, with light-green stripes. The plant has to be grown as a container plant in northern Europe and kept free from winter frosts.

Oryza sativa

RICE

The world's number one food is rice. It is the seeds or grain (husked or not) which are eaten. Rice is

Ornithogalum longibracteatum, *false sea onion.*

cultivated throughout the tropics where there is sufficient water, usually on paddy fields or terraces which can be flooded with the water level being artificially controlled. Dry cultivation of rice is carried out where the paddy method is not practicable. Rice is even grown on a large scale in Europe, particularly in the Po delta in Italy. The Italians grow a sub species *Oryza sativa* ssp. *japonica,* which is hardier than the topical sub species *Oryza sativa* ssp. *indica.* There are more than 1,000 different known cultivars of rice.

In addition to its primary role as staple foodstuff, rice has a long history of importance in medicine. Rice water is used for treating stomach problems with enema and rice shoots have been used for generations for indigestion, feeling bloated, lack of appetite, and coughs. Rice seeds are diuretic and the roots have been traditionally used in Chinese medicine to treat pneumonia and tuberculosis.

Rice is also fermented to make alcoholic drinks such as Japanese rice wine or saki.

Osmunda regalis

ROYAL FERN, FLOWERING FERN

Our large native fern eventually acquires fronds of 150–200cm (5ft–59in) long but this takes tens of

Oryza sativa, *rice.*

Osmunda regalis, *Royal fern.*

Rice terraces.

Osmunda regalis, *Royal fern.*

years to achieve because the plant grows extremely slowly. Each autumn, the growth above ground dies back to be replaced in late spring by slightly larger leaves. Royal ferns can easily be one hundred years old. In the wild, they are found on acid soil or moorland, occasionally growing out of walls but more often in boggy places or in shallow water. Because of its slow growth and its harvesting for potting compost for growing orchids, this fern has become rare in many parts of Europe but has made a comeback in Britain's West Country.

Cultivated plants can be purchased which grow slowly but steadily in bog gardens or at the edge of a pond. Ensure they are planted with some shade in soil that is free of lime. The flesh of the main roots was once cooked to make a nutritious porridge like substance. A decoction of the roots was prescribed for the runs, jaundice, colic, ailments of the spleen, coughs, and lung complaints. Ointments with *Osmunda* help to heal wounds and bruises.

According to tradition you could prevent toothache by biting the first leaf to appear of the fern. It was said to protect you for the whole year. Royal fern can be used to dye wool yellow to brown.

$\mathcal{P}, \mathcal{Q}$

Paeonia lactiflora, *Chinese peony.*

Paeonia officinalis, *common peony.*

Paeonia lactiflora, *Chinese peony.*

Paeonia officinalis

COMMON PEONY

The two to three pistil carpels which together form the fruit of the common peony radiate a secretive light by night. This phenomenon was described by the ancient Greeks. There were of course conclusions drawn from this so that for centuries the plant was only collected for medicinal purposes at night. Its use was to combat nightmares, hallucinations, St Vitus dance, and mental illness. This use has disappeared but the roots in particular of the plant contain substances with real healing properties. The dried root is used to help to induce labour, to encourage the afterbirth to come away, but also to cause a foetus to abort.

Paeonia officinalis is a southern European perennial with large red flowers which are about 10cm (4in) across. By selection and hybridising double-flowered and other garden varieties have been created but these are currently less popular than those from *Paeonia lactiflora*. The common peony needs a very fertile well worked and deep dug soil. The upper side of the root ball should be planted not more than 2cm ($^3/_4$in) beneath the surface of the soil. Leave the plant undisturbed and feed it every spring with plenty of humus and other nutrients (such as horse manure).

☤

Paeonia lactiflora syn. *P. albiflora, P. japonica*

CHINESE PEONY

The flowers sold as peonies are almost invariably cultivars of the Chinese peony. Although they originate from China, Tibet, and Siberia, they can be grown in the same way as the common peony (see *Paeonia officinalis*). The colours of the cultivars vary widely but are usually in the range between white and pale pink. The flowers are 7–10cm (3–4in) across, usually solitary single, cup, or bowl-shaped.

The Chinese have used the plant medicinally for many centuries. The white flowering plants are used to form a tonic which also relieves pain, calms the liver, and helps with menstruation problems.

☤

Paeonia suffruticosa syn. *P. moutan*

TREE PEONY, MOUTAN PEONY

The tree peony is becoming one of the most highly regarded ornamental plants while in China it is so commonplace that there are entire fields filled with the plant. The Chinese also value the beauty of the flowers and have cultivated the plant since well before the birth of Christ, resulting in constant new varieties and colours. The fields of tree peonies though are grown for the chemical substances in

Paeonia suffruticosa, *tree peony.*

Papaver rhoeas, *corn poppy.*

their roots. The dried roots are used to make decoctions to treat feverish infections and eczema.

The common tree peony grows wild in the mountains of China, Tibet, and Bhutan, where the leaves appear after the snow thaws. In northern Europe, the plant gets a warmth stimulus earlier and starts to grow in early spring, followed quickly by flowering. This means that late frosts can damage the leaves and large flowers. The 200cm (79in) shrub itself is hardy except in the first winters after planting. New plants need protecting from hard frosts with pine branches or fern fronds. Tree peonies prefer very fertile and well-drained soil.

New cultivars arrive continuously from the orient. The flowers are single, cup, or bowl-shaped in every conceivable colour and shape. Yet these cultivars disappear just as fast as they appear so that it is difficult to find a particular variety again to buy.

Papaver rhoeas

CORN POPPY, FIELD POPPY

A new road embankment will suddenly blossom in May with poppies, often making the earth red with thousands of the flowers. These demonstrate the amazingly long period which poppy seeds can endure, keeping its ability to germinate for a decade or more until the soil in which it is sees the light of day. When this happens, the annual plant germinates on a massive scale. Once the poppy was a widespread weed of arable land, now it appears and then disappears for a time, waiting until a piece of ground is disturbed. This is what happened in France during World War I when the trenches were dug and shell craters pockmarked the landscape. The battlefields at Verdun and elsewhere were first red with blood and then later red with poppies. This is why the poppy has become an annual symbol or remembrance on "Poppy Day".

Papaver rhoeas, *corn poppy.*

The dried petals of corn poppy were once dried to make infusions for deadening pain and helping people to sleep. A syrup of poppy is still one of the constituents of certain cough mixtures, especially those to help children sleep. The sap from the petals is also used as a colouring in drinks and syrups.

Papaver somniferum

OPIUM POPPY

If the seed heads of the opium poppy are cut before they are ripe, a sticky white milky substance exudes which when exposed to oxygen dries to a brown resin. This is opium. The substance has been smoked in opium dens in China for centuries as a sleep inducing drug. There was even a state monopoly in its supply, which led to the so-called opium wars between China and Britain in the second half of the nineteenth century. The British prevented foreign merchants from trading in opium in China. Today, trade in opium is illegal in almost every country in the world because of the addictive nature of morphine, the most important constituent of opium. Despite this, there is an active trade in opiates (drugs derived from opium) because of the many drug users. In certain parts of the world (such as Afghanistan and the so-called "golden triangle" of the borders of Thailand, Burma, and Laos), the opium poppy is grown on a vast scale.

The farmers are able to extract the maximum percentage of morphine from the seed heads by cutting them in late morning. The concentration is highest at about 10 o' clock after which it drops quickly until the following morning.

Morphine has acquired a bad name because of drugs misuse but before this re-emergence as narcotic, it was one of the most useful painkillers available to medicine. Terminally ill patients are still give pain relieving morphine in the form of pills, pessaries, patches, or by injection).

Once, children who cried or would not sleep were given a drink from an infusion of the seed heads. This sometimes led to overdoses and serious accidents.

The ripe seeds do not contain morphine and opium poppies are widely cultivated in Europe for these seeds and the oil from them. The seeds are baked with bread, while the oil is added to paint, soap, and ointments.

Papaver somniferum, *opium poppy.*

Papaver somniferum, *opium poppy.*

Papaver somniferum, *opium poppy.*

Parietaria judaica, *pellitory-of-the-wall.*

The opium poppy is easily grown as an annual and will self-seed itself year after years on loose clay or sandy soil. The species type has mauve flowers but there are also red and white varieties available to buy for the garden.

Parietaria judaica syn. *P. diffusa*

PELLITORY-OF-THE-WALL

Pellitory-of-the-wall was ritually burned on certain nights of the year in Medieval times because the smoke was said to drive off the devil. When burned, the plant exuded the smell of "hellfire." The plant contains sulphur, potassium, and nitric acid. This combination was found very useful by many housewives of the past, who cleaned their lamp glasses with the leaves.

The importance of the herb medicinally is indicated by it former name of *P. officinalis.* Pellitory was used to treat urinary and gall stones. It is diuretic, heals the urethra, and was useful for treating oedema. The herb was taken as an infusion or decoction. Although its use has fallen off considerably, the herb is still a respected treatment for chronic urinary complaints.

Parietaria judaica, *pellitory-of-the-wall.*

Parietaria judaica, *pellitory-of-the-wall.*

Parietaria judaica is a native plant of southern Europe which also grows further north. It is likely that the plant's spread is related to its use as a herb. It is found growing on old walls and in ruins of old castles, manor houses and former settlements. The flowers are insignificant and the plant dies back above ground in autumn.

Paris quadrifolia

HERB-PARIS, DEVIL-IN-THE-BUSH

Paris quadrifolia has an extremely secretive appearance: not just because it is always found in the shade of a wood. A single stem emerges from the creeping root in spring, usually with four leaves in the form of a Maltese cross at its top. In May to June, this produces one flower from which one black berry is formed. The entire plant is very poisonous but the berry and roots are most toxic. There have been fatal accidents after children have discovered what they imagine to be a bilberry. When the first symptoms appear (which include vomiting) medical treatment is still possible because the poison works very slowly.

In the Middle Ages, the plant was considered to be

Pastinaca sativa, *wild parsnip.*

Paris quadrifolia, *herb-paris.*

one that could break witches spells. A berry was sewn into clothing. The same was done to ward of epidemics of the great plague.

Today, *Paris quadrifolia* is solely used in homeopathic medicine for nervous headaches and chronic respiratory and bronchial infections. *Paris quadrifolia* is found in damp woodland on chalk hills throughout Europe and Britain.

Pastinaca sativa syn. Peucadeneum officinale, Peucadeneum sativum

WILD PARSNIP

Before the potato conquered Europe, the parsnip was the most important vegetable. The pale tap roots could be stored and were of great importance in winter. Parsnips have regained popularity and are particularly in vogue within the organic food movement.

The plant grows to about 100cm (39in) high and is a biennial or occasional perennial that flowers from July with umbels of yellow blooms. The dried seeds are ideal for use as a culinary herb, using them in salads, vegetable soup, or adding before serving to sauerkraut. Combined with sauerkraut, parsnip seeds can prevent possible wind. Infusions of the dried seeds have been used in herbal medi-

cine for stomach and intestinal problems, oedema, and kidney and bladder complaints. Some people are allergic to the plant and come out in a rash.
Wild parsnip grows throughout Europe on clay and chalk soils, preferring sunny positions, often appearing profusely on roadside verges.

꽃 ♊ ✳

Passiflora foetida *var.* galapagensis, *fetid passionflower.*

Passiflora foetida

FETID PASSIONFLOWER

The stems of this passionflower are covered with fine hairs. When these are disturbed by touching, a foul smell is emitted. The plant originates from South and Central America and provides delicious fruit. The species is extremely variable with more than fifty different varieties described. Illustrated is *Passiflora foetida* var. *galapagensis* from the Galapagos Islands. Both the bud and yellow-orange fruit are surrounded by leafy, branched calyxes. The flowers are white with a purple centre. The fetid passionflower has to be grown under glass in northern Europe with a minimum winter temperature of 5°C (41°F).
The roots of this passionflower are prescribed in America as a treatment for relieving spasms and appear to calm hysteria, free catarrh, and are used for women's illnesses. A puree of the leaves placed on the skin reduces inflammations.

꽃 ♊

Passiflora 'Incense'

PASSIONFLOWER

The ornamental plant *Passiflora* 'Incense' resulted from an attempt to create a passion flower with tasty fruit and good resistance to the cold. This latter objective failed but the fruit are moderately successful. *P.* 'Incense' is a cultivar from the most important medicinal passionflower: *Passiflora incarnata*. The parts of the plant above ground are used either dried or fresh in remedies for sleeplessness, anxiety, and Parkinson's disease. Tinctures are used in homeopathic medicine to relieve pain

Passiflora 'Incense', passionflower.

and spasms. *Passiflora incarnata* grows wild in North America and in a sheltered, dry position, will withstand frosts down to minus 16°C (3.2°F). The plant dies back fully above ground following frost and then slowly re-emerges the following spring so that it does not flower until autumn. For this reason it is better grown as a container plant. Place it where it can get plenty of light during the winter with a minimum temperature of 12°C (53°F). Under these circumstances, this climbing perennial will remain green.

꽃 ♊

Pelargonium capitatum

WILD ROSE PELARGONIUM

The clusters of pink to mauve flowers of the wild rose pelargonium are borne above the velvety, curly leaves. The flowers are about 2cm (³/₄in) across, which is large for a scented pelargonium, because they are not grown for their blooms. The fragrance is exuded by the leaves, especially when they are brushed against. This is why these plants are grown alongside paths where passers-by disturb the leaves in warm climates.
For use and cultivation, see *Pelargonium graveolens.*

꽃 ♟ ♊ 🍶 ✳

Pelargonium capitatum, *wild rose pelargonium.*

Pelargonium graveolens, *rose pelargonium.*

Pelargonium graveolens

ROSE PELARGONIUM

The discovery of *Pelargonium graveolens* in South Africa was a sensation. The volatile oils from the leaves exuded a powerful fragrance of roses which was stronger than roses themselves. Perfume makers were excited and have since used rose pelargoniums to make geranium oil, which is also widely used in cosmetics, soap, and pharmaceutical products. The name geranium oil has stuck despite the mistaken confusion with the true *Geranium* genus, species of which are widespread in Europe, which is quite separate from *Pelargonium* which is of African origin.

The *Pelargonium* species can withstand very little frost and need to be brought in during winter. Place them somewhere cool and give them hardly any water. This way they have a period of rest and will make fine new growth in spring. Any shoots which do form during the winter should be removed in their entirety in spring.

The foliage of the rose pelargonium can be infused to make a disinfecting herbal tea which is also a tonic, stimulating the circulation. A compress with the infusion can be placed on the skin to treat eczema or acne.

The fragrance of the leaves helps to keep midges and other insects away.

The young leaves in particular can be added to ice cream, desserts, liqueurs, and soft drinks. The leaves are ideal for adding to pot-pourris. Geranium oil placed in an oil burner will spread an uplifting vapour through the house which is also calming and especially beneficial for pre-menstrual tension. The oil can also be added to the water for a relaxing and uplifting bath.

Pelargonium odoratissimum, *apple pelargonium.*

Pelargonium *'Rober's Lemon Rose'.*

Pelargonium odoratissimum

APPLE PELARGONIUM

The small white flowers (with a tinge of red) of apple geranium contrast strongly with the bright green leaves. The leaves are large, curly, and almost round in shape and they exude the fragrance of apple. For use and cultivation, see *Pelargonium graveolens*.

Pelargonium 'Rober's Lemon Rose'

The downy-haired leaves of this cultivar contain essential oils with the fresh aroma of lemon and rose, which is reminiscent of the rose pelargonium. This is not so surprising, since the cultivar originates from that species. The two plants look similar, although 'Rober's Lemon Rose' is more vigorous but has smaller flowers than the species. For use and cultivation, see *Pelargonium graveolens*.

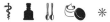

Pelargonium tomentosum

PEPPERMINT PELARGONIUM

The leaves of peppermint pelargonium are each about 6cm (2½in) wide and they are entirely covered with bristly hairs. The flowers, which are white with purple markings, have little decorative value. The plant is mainly grown for its foliage, which gives off a peppermint aroma when touched. For use and cultivation, see *Pelargonium graveolens*.

Pelargonium tomentosum, *peppermint pelargonium.*

Pelargonium tomentosum *'Chocolate'.*

Pelargonium tomentosum 'Chocolate'

There is a large chocolate brown patch at the centre of each leaf of this cultivar of the peppermint pelargonium from which the plant gets its name. The fragrance of the leaves is similar to the species.
For use and cultivation, see *Pelargonium graveolens*.

Perilla frutescens

BEEFSTEAK PLANT, SHISHO

The beefsteak plant is related to basil and also has an aromatic leaf yet it is rarely used in western cooking. The red-leafed varieties are mainly grown as ornamental plants. *Perilla frutescens* 'Atropurpurea' has reddish-purple shiny leaves. *Perilla frutescens* var. *nankinensis* is the same colour but has curly and sharply indented leaves.
Perilla is an important herb in Japanese cooking. The red leaves flavour cooked food, and are served fresh with raw fish together with the seeds from the herb. The herb has a laxative and also expecto-

Perilla frutescens *'Atropurpurea', beefsteak plant.*

rant effect and is also anti-bacterial. It is particularly used to treat colds and stubborn catarrh. The oil from the plant is used as an aromatic with food, tobacco, and cosmetics.

🜍 ⚗ ⚔ ☕ ✳

Polygonum bistorta syn. *Persicaria bistorta*

COMMON BISTORT, SNAKEWEED, ENGLISH SERPENTARY

The contorted rhizomes of common bistort sit on the surface of the soil. This resembled snakes so it was thought the herb should help to treat snake bites. The doctrine of signatures was once much in vogue in herbal medicine but disproved by modern science and only followed now by the most died-in-the-wool new age devotees.

The rhizome of bistort does have healing properties though, with tannin being the most important of the substances contained in the herb. This is astringent and can also be used to treat diarrhoea. Because its action is mild, infusion of bistort is suitable to be given to children and weak persons but is less suitable for those with stomach troubles.

Polygonum bistorta, *common bistort.*

Petasites hybridus, *butterbur.*

A gargle for dealing with inflamed gums or throat can also be prepared from the herb.

Common bistort grows wild throughout Europe in damp meadows. Where this perennial finds a suitable site it can cover large areas. It is most eye-catching from May to September when its pink flower spikes tower above the grass.

🜍

Petasites hybridus

BUTTERBUR

Butterbur was associated with the plague for a long period of time. By placing the leaves on plague boils, the sufferer was supposed to prevent the "black death". It was accepted later that the leaves may at least have reduced the boils because it was discovered that the plant does contain disinfecting and healing substances. This may have been known as long ago as the Iron Age, judging from a discovery of butterbur in a pre-historic miner's encampment in Austria.

In the last few centuries, butterbur was chiefly used to treat coughs, and bronchial and other respiratory system infections, although colt's foot (*Tussilago farfara*) is a better choice. Medical science discovered new uses for butterbur: the herb relieves spasms, in particular in the stomach and gall bladder and also reduces pain.

The herb is prescribed in homeopathic medicine as an expectorant, painkiller, and to relieve spasms.

Butterbur is a native plant throughout Europe, growing by preference in alkaline soil, always in moist places, especially beside water. The flower spikes, looking for all the world like brushes, appear in early spring, followed by the leaves, which can cover an entire bank.

🜍

Petroselinum crispum, *parsley.*

Petroselinum crispum, *parsley.*

Courtesy The Kruidenhof, Buitenpost.

Petroselinum crispum

PARSLEY

Finely chopped parsley sprinkled on a cream soup just before its served must be known to everyone. Parsley is perhaps the most widely used culinary herb. It is often used as an edible garnish with fish and egg dishes. The dried root is used during cooking as a constituent of *bouquet garni*. Drying does not improve parsley but it can be frozen satisfactorily for later use. The herb can be harvested out of doors for a great deal of the year: if sown in March, it can be picked from May until the end of summer. By sowing again later, the picking season can be extended into the start of winter. By growing under a cloche or in a cold frame, it can even be picked when there is a frost. Parsley is extremely healthy, having high concentrations of vitamins A and C. Eating the leaves helps to freshen the breath. The herb aids digestion and is also diuretic. For this reason it is useful for people with oedema, bladder, kidney, or rheumatic disorders. Pregnant women must not use any concentrated herbal preparations of parsley or the oil. The oil from parsley is used to flavour foodstuffs and as fragrance in perfumes.

Parsley is a biennial umbelliferous plant from southern Europe which is grown as an annual in northern Europe. The seed, which is slow to germinate, is sown in March on the surface but must not dry out. The plants themselves also cannot tolerate dry soil. It makes them flower immediately and flowering plants are of no culinary use. Plant them therefore in moisture-retaining, fertile soil by preference in partial shade.

The are scores of cultivars of the species. The flat-leaved forms have the strongest taste but the curly-leaf varieties are perhaps better known. There is also *Petroselinum crispum* var. *tuberosum*, which is grown for its edible root.

Phaseolus vulgaris, *French bean.*

Physalis alkekengi, *Chinese lantern.*

Phaseolus vulgaris

FRENCH BEAN

The French bean is the ancestor of quite a few different types of vegetables or pulses. The plant originated in tropical America and is grown in Europe as an annual. In its normal form, it is a climber which can grow to 4m (13ft) around its supports. It has white, pink, or crimson flowers in summer.

Apart from being cooked as beans, the seeds and especially the pods can also be dried and used as medicine. They are strongly diuretic and are therefore beneficial for oedema, kidney, and bladder ailments, plus rheumatism and gout. What is more, the beans contain glucocinin which can replace insulin for treating diabetes.

Physalis alkekengi, *Chinese lantern.*

Physalis alkekengi syn. P. franchetti

CHINESE LANTERN, WINTER CHERRY, BLADDER CHERRY

Branches of Chinese lantern are popular decorations for the home in autumn and winter. They are picked as soon as the bladder-like calyxes surrounding the berries begin to take their colour. The "lanterns" are also widely used in floral decorations or to decorate fruit.

Inside each "lantern" is an orange berry, which was once widely used as medicine. The berries were dried and eaten as a diuretic in order to ease rheumatic complaints, arthritis, and gout. A tincture of the berries is used in homeopathy to treat jaundice, bladder, and kidney problems.

Physalis alkekengi grows wild in southern Europe and western Asia but is hardy in northern parts of Europe. This perennial of about 50cm (20in) high spreads by creeping roots and can develop to plague proportions in a garden. After the summer flowers, the fruits ripen in autumn.

227

Physalis alkekengi, *Chinese lantern.*

plant grows to 4m (13ft). Usually it is between 150–200cm (59–79in) tall. Elongated plumes of white florets appear in summer that turn into purple-black fruits with dark burgundy colour juice. These are eaten by birds which ensures the seed is distributed. It usually germinates in places that are rich in nitrogen, such as the foot of a wall.

☦ ✎

Phytolacca americana, *Virginian pokeweed.*

Phytolacca americana, *Virginian pokeweed.*

Phytolacca americana syn. *P. decandra*

VIRGINIAN POKEWEED, POKEROOT, RED-INK PLANT

Virginian pokeweed is one of the many herbs used by the native North Americans which were later found to have beneficial effect in treating various illnesses. The indigenous people chewed the fruit and seeds of the plant to treat arthritis and as a drastic laxative. They knew the correct dose precisely, since too much can cause poisoning. For this reason all parts of this plant should only be used under medical supervision.

Today the dried roots are used to treat rheumatism, rheumatoid arthritis, and also to cleanse the lymph system as a treatment for glandular fever. Preparations of the herb are used externally for scabies, eczema, psoriasis, and fungal infections. Pregnant women are advised to avoid pokeweed.

The berries are suitable for use as a natural dye for colouring wool and textiles red to purple. *Phytolacca americana* grows wild in North and Central America but has been cultivated in Europe for several centuries. In fertile and humus-rich soil, the

Picea abies *'Diedorfiana', spruce.*

Pimpinella anisum, *anise.*

Picea abies

COMMON SPRUCE, NORWAY SPRUCE

The spruce is one of the most useful trees in Europe. Most people know the tree as a Christmas tree but it is also an important source of softwood timber. Additionally, turpentine is also produced from the resin for use as a paint thinner and brush cleaner.

The needles contain a volatile oil which acts as an expectorant and this is added to boiling water for inhalations to help breathing during colds, asthma, and whooping cough, and generally for respiratory infections. Added to bath water, it provides for a wonderfully fragrant and relaxing soak.

Extracts of *Picea abies* are used in homeopathic medicine to protect the mucous membranes, and as an expectorant.

Pimpinella anisum

ANISE, ANISEED

The seeds of anise contain 2 per cent oil with a characteristic aniseed flavour. The seeds and oil have been used since the times of the ancient Egyptians as culinary herb. Now the seeds are baked with bread, added to cabbage to improve its digestion, and used in pickling gherkins to prevent them causing wind.

The oil is used as an aromatic in liqueurs (anisette, aquavit), with sugar lumps added to milk as a nightcap, and also in cough syrups. Aniseed does have medicinal properties. The oil relieves spasms and prevents infections (especially of the stomach and intestine), enhances the appetite, is an expectorant, soothes coughs, and has a mild painkilling effect. Nursing mothers find that drinking an infusion of the herb aids milk production.

Aniseed is an annual umbelliferous flowering plant from southern Europe and neighbouring regions. It is cultivated mainly in drier regions on lime-rich soil. The plant does not thrive in the moist climate of northern Europe. Sow in position in April–May in a warm, sheltered position, in well-worked, well-drained, and lime-rich soil.

Pimpinella major

GREATER BURNET SAXIFRAGE, GREATER PIMPERNEL

Greater burnet saxifrage once had, just like the lesser burnet saxifrage or synthetic anethole

Pimpinella major, *greater burnet saxifrage.*

(Pimpinella saxifraga), a reputation as a treatment for kidney stones, cholera, and the plague. Research has subsequently found these claims to be unfounded.

Currently only the use of the herb for treating bronchial and respiratory problems are still recognised. An infusion of the dried roots helps with a cold, hoarseness, bronchitis, asthma, throat infections, and as an expectorant. Although the greater burnet saxifrage has a strong aroma, the fresh leaves are used to flavour soups, sauces, with fish and cheese, and with salads (especially with tomato). The plant grows to about 100cm (39in) high and has a preference for moisture-retaining clay soil. This perennial grows in Europe where this type of soil is to be found, especially in western and central Europe. It is often found in roadside verges.

Pinus mugo

MOUNTAIN PINE

The volatile oil from the needles of the mountain pine can be inhaled to help bronchitis sufferers. The oil is also an important constituent in creams for treating rheumatism.

Pinus mugo *'Zundert', mountain pine.*

Pinus sylvestris, *Scot's pine.*

The mountain pine grows as a low bushy tree in the mountains of southern and central Europe. Because of its compact size, it is a favourite for smaller gardens. Growers have developed hundreds of cultivars over the years with widely varying characteristics. *Pinus mugo* 'Zundert' is one of the most popular, growing no taller than 100cm (39in). The needles are strikingly yellow in winter but turn green again in summer. Do no plant the mountain pine in acidic soil. Ensure the soil is pH6 or higher.

Pinus sylvestris

SCOT'S PINE

The trunk of the Scot's pine contains resin from which turpentine is formed. This is used as paint thinners by professional decorators. The volatile oil also helps the breathing of bronchitis sufferers and it is incorporated in salves for treating rheumatism.

Scot's pine grows naturally in the colder parts of Europe and neighbouring Asia. The tree was planted widely in the nineteenth century to prevent soil erosion. The large scale plantations that resulted have little natural value but do provide pine timber. Scot's pine is extremely susceptible to acid rain so that the plantations of the trees in milder parts of Europe are now being replaced with woods of trees that are more natural.

Pistacia lentiscus

MASTIC TREE, LENTISE

The bark of the mastic tree contains a very pure resin, known since ancient times as the "mastic of Chios" from the Greek island where the resin is harvested. *Pistacia lentiscus* also grows elsewhere in the Mediterranean region. The bushy tree, which can reach about 4m (13ft) keeps its leaves in winter and is not hardy in northern Europe where it is grown as a container plant which needs to be kept under glass in the winter.

A varnish made from the resin or mastic is ideally suited for protecting paintings. The mastic is also placed in compresses because of its antiseptic and blood clotting properties. The mastic is both diuretic and expectorant. The resin, which smells of pine, is also used for treating bronchitis. The resin is a well-known flavouring in liqueurs, tobacco, and is used in the perfume industry to bind the fragrant substances.

Pittosporum viridiflorum

CAPE CHEESEWOOD

The bark of the Cape cheesewood contains substances that appear to be beneficial for treating diarrhoea and dysentery. This shrub grows wild in South Africa and bears large evergreen leaves. The yellow-green flowers have a wonderful jasmine-like fragrance. *Pittosporum viridiflorum* has to be

Pistacia lentiscus, *mastic tree.*

Pittosporum viridiflorum, *Cape cheesewood.*

grown as a container plant in northern Europe and kept under glass in winter.

Plantago afra

GLANDULAR PLANTAIN

The seeds of glandular plantain have a remarkable outer case in which there are mucous cells that absorb water. This is useful to the plant in its natural habitat in southern Europe to give the seed longer to germinate after a shower of rain. This mucous substance has soothing properties and is incorporated in cosmetics. The most important use though is as a bulky laxative with which constipation is relieved naturally and in a gentle manner. The oil from the seeds was also once used for cough mixtures.

Plantago afra is an annual plant of 20cm (8in) that originates from southern Europe. It thrives best in a sunny position on dry soil.

Plantago lanceolata

RIBWORT PLANTAIN

Plantains were traditionally used for cough mixture. The mucilaginous substances in plantains are

Plantago afra, *glandular plantain.*

soothing while the bitter substances act as a tonic. The substances are also bactericidal. Infusions can be made of the fresh or dried leaves.

Pharmaceutical use is concentrated mainly on the ribwort plantain, which has a high concentration of the active substances for the creation of extracts. Tinctures of *Plantago* are used in homeopathy for ear infections. The bruised leaves are held over shallow wounds and grazes to hasten healing and rubbed on insect bites to stop them itching.

Ribwort plantain is a widely distributed wild plant throughout grassland and roadside verges. The leaves reach about 20cm (8in) with the flower spikes protruding slightly above them. Ribwort plantain often flowers from spring through summer to autumn.

Plantago major ssp. *major*

GREATER PLANTAIN, RAT-TAIL PLANTAIN

The greater plantain contains the same active substances as the ribwort plantain (see *Plantago lanceolata*) but in lower concentrations so that the pharmaceutical industry prefers to use the rib-

Plantago lanceolata, *ribwort plantain.*

Plantago lanceolata, *ribwort plantain.*

wort species. The fresh or dried leaves are used generally in herbal medicine with fresh leaves being rubbed on insect bites to soothe the itch and pain.

The tannin in the leaves hardens skin and people once placed the leaves in their boots before long treks to prevent sore feet.

Greater plantain is found widely throughout Europe on fertile soil and particularly alongside paths. The wide leaves often lay recumbent on the ground except when between other vegetation when the plant grows more erect. It is one of the

Plantago major *ssp.* major, *greater plantain.*

few plants that can withstand being trodden on. Since other plants are more susceptible to this, the greater plantain experiences less competition and consequently grows well on paths. Greater plantain blooms from spring to late autumn with unremarkable flower spikes.

℞

Plantago media

HOARY PLANTAIN

The hoary plantain contains the same active substances as the other types of plantain but in lower concentrations than ribwort plantain. See *Plantago lanceolata* for properties.

The hoary plantain is somewhere between greater and ribwort plantains in terms of its leaves but when this type flowers (May–August) it appears quite different from these other species. The flower spikes are long, have a wonderful fragrance, and are pale lilac in colour. Hoards of bees are attracted to the flowers. Hoary plantain is also grown as an ornamental plant. It grows in the wild in dry, chalky grassland and lime-rich meadows.

℞

Plantago media, *hoary plantain.*

Platycodon grandiflora, *balloon flower.*

Platycodon grandiflora

BALLOON FLOWER, CHINESE BELLFLOWER

The balloon flower or Chinese bellflower is perhaps best known as an attractive ornamental plant with late summer purple flowers (occasionally white or pink). The foliage of this plant emerges late in spring and produces shoots of about 50cm (20in) which hang down slightly under the weight of the balloon-like buds. This hardy perennial prefers well-drained fertile soil and a sunny position.

Podophyllum hexandrum, *Himalayan mayapple.*

233

The plant originates from eastern China, Manchuria, and Japan. It is an important medicinal herb in eastern Asia and is available from some specialist Oriental shops. The substances contained act as an expectorant and are widely used in cough mixtures.

Podophyllum hexandrum

HIMALAYAN MAY APPLE

The Himalayan may apple is found in the wild in the woods on the lower slopes of the Himalayas. Grown in Europe, it prefers moisture-retaining acid soil and partial shade. This rather special plant is highly regarded by those creating woodland gardens. Solitary open cup-shaped pink flowers appear before the leaves unfurl in late spring and bloom until midsummer. In late summer the flowers are transformed into elongated red-orange fruits that resemble elongated tomatoes. The entire plant contains podophyllotoxin and a resin known as podophyllin that can destroy tumours so that they are of importance in treating cancer.

Podophyllum peltatum

AMERICAN MANDRAKE, MAY APPLE, WILD LEMON

In spring the new growth of American mandrake looks like newly germinated horse chestnuts. The plant expands by underground creeping roots and can cover a large expanse. This is precisely the growth habit of the plant in its natural habitat in the woods of eastern parts of North America. The fragrant flowers are white. The only parts of the plant that are not dangerous are the ripe yellow fruits. They are in fact edible. The remaining parts of this plant contain a toxic resin which is a strong purgative. Powdered root, known as podophyllin, is used medicinally as a purgative. This was copied from the native North Americans, who also used it

Podophyllum peltatum, *American mandrake.*

to worm themselves, to induce vomiting, and utilised the toxins as insecticide. If you decide to harvest the roots make sure you wear gloves and protect your eyes because the sap can cause severe skin rashes.

Polemonium caeruleum

JACOB'S LADDER, GREEK VALERIAN, CHARITY

Jacob's ladder is a European plant of chalk downland, scree, and rocky ledges, found mainly in Derbyshire and the Yorkshire Dales in Britain but sometimes discovered elsewhere having naturalised from garden cultivation. This perennial self-seeds itself readily in fertile, moisture-retaining soil. It grows to about 100cm (39in) high in cultivation and blooms in June–July with cerulean blue and sometimes white flowers. The flowers of *Polemonium caeruleum* 'Album' are pure white.

Jacob's ladder is a popular ornamental plant because of its superb flowers. Also known as Greek valerian, the herb was used for a wide range of ailments such as epilepsy, syphilis, hydrophobia, and dysentery.

Polemonium caeruleum, *Jacob's ladder.*

Polygonatum multiflorum, *Solomon's seal.*

Polemonium caeruleum *'Album', Jacob's ladder.*

Polygonatum multiflorum, *Solomon's seal.*

Polygonatum multiflorum

SOLOMON'S SEAL

The various forms of Solomon's seal contain chemical substances such as asparagin and convallaria-glycoside. This latter compound is named after the lily-of-the-valley which is a close relative of the Solomon's seals. These chemicals have a beneficial external effect for blood blisters, bruises, haemorrhoid, and sprained limbs. Internal use is as a diuretic, for gout, rheumatism, coughs, and diabetes.

The plant grows throughout Europe in copses, often in drier places at the edge of a wood. The roots expand a stage further each year and push up new shoots in spring of about 45cm (18in). White-green flowers dangle between the leaves in May–June, followed by poisonous blue-black berries.

Polygonum aviculare

KNOTGRASS

Herbal tea made with knotgrass has been popular for a long time as a remedy for colds and coughs. The herb is also added to body purifying infusions because it is diuretic, cleanses the blood, and therefore is beneficial for rheumatism and gout. Internal bleeding and diarrhoea can be stopped with the herb too. However modern medicine makes no use of the herb.

Knotgrass is a general agricultural weed which grows as an annual on ploughed or bare soil wherever the seeds fall, which can be between paving. One stem springs from the roots which then branches out to form a mass of green shoots. This low habit plant bears miniscule green-white flowers in May.

Polygonum hydropiper

WATER-PEPPER

The value of water-pepper is its ability to ward off plagues of insects. The substances contained in the plant are effective on wheat galls *(Anguina tritici)* among other insects. Polygodal is also derived from the plant, which is a biodegradable insecticide for treating aphids.

Infusions of the herb are used medicinally for painful periods with heavy bleeding and also as a diuretic and antiseptic. The herb contains astringent substances which can cause irritation of the skin and mucous membranes.

Polygonum aviculare, *knotgrass.*

Polygonum hydropiper, *water-pepper.*

Water-pepper grows in much of Europe in moist to wet areas. This annual only germinates where other plants are low growing. Water-pepper itself reaches about 80cm (31¹/₂in) and has insignificant flowers from July.

Polygonum persicaria

SPOTTED LADY'S THUMB

In common with many herbs that contain tannin, spotted lady's thumb is used as an astringent in herbal medicine: externally for treating wounds, varicose veins, and haemorrhoid, and internally for diarrhoea. The herb is also diuretic and therefore used for kidney and bladder stones and rheumatism.

Dyers of textiles and wool use the flowering herb eagerly to create vivid yellows and greens.

Spotted lady's thumb grows in much of Europe as a wild plant, specially in damp soil that has been disturbed, such as arable land, and beside water. This annual grows to about 80cm (31¹/₂in) high and blooms from June to autumn with soft pink flower spikes.

Polygonum persicaria, *spotted lady's thumb.*

Polypodium vulgare

POLYPODY

This fern has little problem with drought. The 20cm (8in) high plant grows in moderate regions of Europe on hills and at the edges of woods. During dry periods and frosts, the fronds roll themselves up, although the plant is hardy. In addition to reproducing by spores, the plant also sends out creeping roots.

Those roots taste sweet and have been used in herbal tea for a long time to treat coughs, bronchitis, asthma, hoarse throats, and other lung and

Polypodium vulgare, *polypody.*

breathing difficulties. Consumption of the herb also has side effects: the herb acts as a purgative and stimulates the gall bladder so that the herb is rarely used medicinally.

Potentilla anserina

SILVERWEED, TRAVELLER'S EASE, TRAVELLER'S JOY

Silverweed is particularly useful for helping women with period pains and the herb is also good for relieving painful spasms, including those of the stomach and intestine, which can be treated with an infusion of the leaves.

Potentilla anserina grows close to the ground. Runners spread out from the rosette of feathery leaves, which have a silvery appearance because of their hairs. Where the runners touch the ground, a new rosette of leaves is formed.

Because it hugs the ground, silverweed cannot withstand competition from taller plants but given an open and sunny position, it can cover an entire area. This happens on waysides, in waste places, and where soil is trodden, where it can become rampant Silverweed always flowers with one flower at a time but spread over a long period from May to September. It is found growing throughout Europe.

Potentilla erecta

TORMENTIL

Both the red dye and medicinal properties of tormentil make it a valued herb. The dye is used by dyers of cloth to create a yellow-brown colour and the red dye has also found to be antiseptic so that decoctions of the roots from which the red dye is derived can be used as a gargle for infections of the mouth and throat. The roots also contain almost 20 per cent of a mild tannin which has an astringent healing effect on wounds but can also be taken

Potentilla anserina, *silverweed.*

Potentilla erecta, *tormentil.*

Potentilla reptans, *creeping cinquefoil.*

internally. Decoctions of the root are used for diarrhoea and stomach or intestinal infections.

Tormentil grows throughout Europe on moist soil in damp meadows, wet heaths, moorland, and at the edges of woods. This perennial grows to about 30cm (12in) high and blooms between May and October with small yellow flowers which can be recognised by their four petals. Related species have five petals.

Potentilla reptans

CREEPING CINQUEFOIL, CREEPING TORMENTIL

Creeping cinquefoil contains the same substances as tormentil but in lower concentrations. These work both antiseptically and as an astringent and can be used in the same ways as tormentil (see *Potentilla erecta*).

In addition to the medical properties of creeping cinquefoil, it is deemed to have magical properties too which will protect the user from evil.

Potentilla reptans has larger flowers than tormentil which consist of five petals which overlap each other to form an almost closed calyx. The flowers bloom between May and September. The leaf forms of creeping cinquefoil are slightly broader than tormentil, New shoots emerge from the leaf rosettes which form new plants where they touch the ground. Creeping cinquefoil is common on waysides and waste ground throughout Europe, but is restricted in Britain to England and Wales.

Primula elatior

OXLIP

The roots of oxlip contain different substances to the flowers. The roots and flowers are therefore used for quite different medical purposes. The roots particularly contain high concentrations of saponins which are expectorant.

Extracts or infusions of the roots are still added to cough syrup and medicines for bronchitis. Decoctions of the roots are used in wet compresses for painful joints (especially with arthritis) to ease the pain and reduce swelling.

The flowers contain no saponins but have bitter substances instead. Herbal tea made with the flowers has been prescribed for centuries for anxiety state and nervousness, migraines, and sleeplessness. A bath with *Primula* oil is very relaxing and helps to get a good night's rest.

Oxlip flowers early in spring in broad-leaved woodland and damp meadows. There are no leaves on the plant in March so the flower can fully benefit from the early spring sunlight. The plant prefers moisture-retaining loam, or chalky soil, and prefers partial shade. Oxlips have a wide distribution in Europe (particularly found in southern and central parts) and are virtually restricted in Britain to eastern parts. All *Primula* species are popular garden plants.

Primula elatior, *oxlip.*

Primula vulgaris

PRIMROSE

Primroses are a much loved wild and garden plant. A tremendous variety of widely differing forms and colours have been derived from the wild primrose: dark yellow, orange, pink, red, purple, and white, almost always with a yellow centre. The primrose grows abundantly in southern Europe and in much of England, although its distribution is irregular. Generally the plant prefers moist conditions with partial shade. The wild flowers bloom in March but cultivated varieties and hybrids flower at all times of the year. The medical properties are the same as *Primula elatior*.

Prunella vulgaris

SELFHEAL, HEAL-ALL

Selfheal has a long history of use in herbal medicine. This perennial is often found skulking amidst the grasses where it grows somewhat recumbently, putting down fresh roots from the leaf buds. *Prunella vulgaris* is widely found in areas with a moderate climate, where it prefers moist soil and a sunny position or partial shade.
The plant blooms between June and October with violet (but sometimes pink) flowers and is often

Prunella vulgaris, *selfheal*.

Courtesy The Kruidenhof, Buitenpost.

Primula vulgaris, *primrose*.

239

Prunella vulgaris, *selfheal.*

grown as an ornamental plant or in association with beekeeping. Where not competing, the plant grows to about 20cm (8in) high.

Selfheal has proven itself as a herb for wounds over many centuries. A weak infusion can also be gargled for bleeding or inflamed gums. The crushed fresh leaves are placed on clean, bleeding cuts to close the wound, stem the bleeding, and to disinfect the wound (or alternatively heated and used in a dry compress).

Prunus dulcis syn. *P. amygdalus*

ALMOND

There are a number of cultivated forms of almond. The bitter almond usually has white flowers and small seeds, which contain prussic acid among other substances. The oil from the seeds is used as a bitter flavouring in foodstuffs and drinks and is also added to some medicines.

The sweet almond contains virtually no prussic acid and is considered as a great delicacy. Flaked almonds garnish salads, hot dishes, and decorate and flavour cakes, providing a slightly bitter taste.

The oil is used in cough mixtures, especially for children, and almond oil is particularly used for nervous coughs and relieving tension and spasms. The oil is also a popular constituent in salves, skin creams, and other cosmetics.

Almond trees only provide good harvests in certain climates. A cold winter is necessary but spring must come quickly so that the almond blossoms do not get frost burned. The tree is therefore grown in countries surrounding the Mediterranean, southern Australia, and California. In northern Europe, the blossoms are usually lost to frosts and the tree is susceptible to all manner of diseases.

Prunus dulcis, *almond.*

Prunus dulcis, *almond.*

Prunus spinosa, *blackthorn.*

Pulicaria dysenterica, *common fleabane.*

Prunus spinosa

BLACKTHORN, SLOE

Herbal tea from the leaves but especially the flowers of the blackthorn or sloe has been a known traditional medicine for centuries. The tea is reputed to help all manner and variety of ailments but the generally recognized properties of the herb are much more restricted. The tea is laxative and slightly diuretic. The fruits or sloes can make tasty jam which aids digestion and stimulates the appetite. The raw fruit contains a great deal of tannin and is poisonous for humans.

The bark provides a dyestuff which can be used to colour wool and other textiles brown.

Countless white blossoms suddenly appear on the dark branches of the blackthorn in March–April before the leaves have emerged, so that they are even more striking. Some of the blossoms mature in autumn into blue-black sloes which are eaten by birds. The plant grows as a bushy tree of about 5m (16ft) high but can be pruned to required size and shape. It is a native European species that is also found in neighbouring parts of Asia and Africa.

Pulicaria dysenterica

COMMON FLEABANE

The botanist Linnaeus named common fleabane after dysentery because a Russian general had told him the herb cured his soldiers of the disease during their war with the Persians. Indeed there are substances in the plant which may well have stopped diarrhoea but not too much must be expected of this herb. Today common fleabane is rarely used as a medicinal herb.

The plant grows wild throughout Europe, particularly in the west, and with its preference for moist soil, the plant is often seen close to water. The plant has delightful yellow flowers from July and

grows about 50cm (20in) tall. Common fleabane is an ideal ornamental plant for the garden, especially next to a pond.

Pulmonaria officinalis

LUNGWORT, JERUSALEM COWSLIP, SOLDIERS AND SAILORS

The speckled leaves of lungwort were associated in the doctrine of signatures with the lungs (for more

Pulmonaria officinalis, *lungwort.*

Pulmonaria officinalis, lungwort.

Pulsillata vulgaris *var. 'Alba', white pasque flower.*

about this doctrine see *Polygonum bistorta).* This meant the plant must be beneficial for lung diseases. In fact the herb does contain saponins and tannins which acts respectively as an expectorant and soothe infected mucous membranes but there are far more effective herbs for these purposes, so that lungwort is rarely used.

New leaves can be added to salads and soups, imparting a flavour of vermouth.

Pulmonaria officinalis is common in marshes, meadows, and ditches in southern Britain and Ireland and is found in woodland in central and eastern Europe. Elsewhere the plant sometimes escapes from cultivation. The plant is often planted in gardens for its fine silver-flecked foliage and early flowering. Pinkish-red flowers emerge from March but they change colour to violet as they mature. This plant is best grown in partial shade because in a dry sunny position it will often become infected with a white mildew. With this exception, it is a trouble-free plant.

Pulsillata vulgaris, *pasque flower.*

Pulsillata vulgaris syn. *Anemone pulsillata*

PASQUE FLOWER

The blue-violet silver-haired blooms of the pasque flower make it a much appreciated garden plant. The white-flowered *Pulsillata vulgaris* 'Alba' is also a popular garden plant. Unfortunately these April-flowering plants are not easily cultivated. *Pulsillata* needs a dry sunny position, preferably on lime-rich soil, which approximates to the dry chalky grass-covered slopes on which it grows wild. The plant is mainly found in central Europe but small groups can be found in Britain scattered on old grassland in chalk and limestone areas.

The fresh plant is poisonous and will cause inflammation if the sap comes in contact with the skin or mucous membranes. Eating the fresh plant is life-threatening. The dried herb was once used by

242

herbal healers to treat infections of the stomach, intestines, and sex organs. It was also used as a tonic for the nervous system and was dispensed to those who were too easily angered and to people who were sad, particularly for post-natal depression. In view of the toxicity of the herb, it is now virtually restricted to homeopathic use, for depression, pre-menstrual tension, migraine, stomach and intestinal problems, short or irregular menstruation, white secretions in young women, varicose veins, aching joints, rheumatism, gout, and chronic inner ear infections.

Punica granatum

POMEGRANATE

In classical times, the pomegranate was a symbol of fertility, so that women who wanted children but were unable to, ate the fruit. Perhaps today they would drink grenadine, which is the drink added to cocktails made from the seeds.

The root bark, trunk, and branches contain alkaloids which paralyse tapeworms. An extract of the herb is followed by a drastic purgative which flushes the paralysed worms from the system. The bark

Punica granatum, *pomegranate.*

can also cure diarrhoea and is used for treating dysentery.

Today, the pomegranate is principally an edible garnish with desserts and ice cream. When sliced through, a cluster of juicy cells are revealed, each containing a seed. The contents of the cell are eaten with some difficulty. Pomegranate has a sharp, fresh taste.

The pomegranate originated in Asia but is now grown throughout the sub-tropics. Cultivars which remain compact are popular in Europe to be grown as container plants. They need to be kept cool under glass in winter (5–10° C/41–50°F).

Quercus robur

COMMON OAK, ENGLISH OAK, PEDUNCULATE OAK

The bark of the oak tree is renowned for the tannin it contains. This is important to the leather tanning industry but also important for herbal medicine. Tannins work astringently, reducing infection, and strengthening the mucous membranes. The fresh or dried bark from thin branches is used to make a decoction or infusion for a gargle to treat mouth and throat infections, or infusions for combating diarrhoea.

The oak is extremely useful for dyeing wool and other textiles. Large galls the size of marbles are often found on oak trees and these are used as grey or bronze-coloured dyestuff. The bark provides a warm brown colour, rotted wood gives bronze, and the leaves enable grey to beige colours to be produced.

The oak is part of the natural flora of central and western Europe. In other words, if man allowed nature its full reign, wherever the soil was suitable, an oak wood would result. Oaks grow to about 45m (150ft) high and can live to be 1,500 years old.

Quercus robur, *oak.*

Raphanus sativus, *radish.*

Raphanus sativus

RADISH

Radish give a spicy flavour to summer salads. The spherical or elongated tubers are usually sliced for addition to salads but the whole bulb can be eaten although these are very pungent and not appreciated by everyone. The fieriness varies from type to type and also depends on the soil in which the radish is grown. Clay soil imparts a stronger taste. Depending on the sort, radishes can be red, white, or black, which provides many possibilities for decorative garnish. Radishes are often sliced or sculpted into flowers and other forms for decorating oriental dishes such as fish. The origin of the radish is uncertain as it has been cultivated for thousands of years as a hardy annual. For medicinal use see *Raphanus sativus* ssp. *niger.*

� ⚭

Raphanus sativus ssp. niger

BLACK RADISH

The leaves and flowers of the black radish are virtually identical to those of the species but the difference lies under the soil. The black radish forms a long grey to black tuber which can be eaten as a vegetable. Slices of the black radish can also be eaten on bread, sprinkled with salt. The black radish also has a fresh pungent taste.

Both types of radish are rich in vitamin C and eating them is healthy for the gall bladder and liver. Juice pressed from the radish, if preferred

Left: Ricinus communis, castor-oil plant.

Raphanus sativus *ssp.* niger, *black radish.*

Courtesy The Kruidenhof, Buitenpost.

sweetened with honey, is drunk fresh for indigestion and also helps to reduce wind, a bloated feeling, and can be beneficial for infections of the gall bladder.

Black radishes are also grown as annuals from seed. They are hardy and can therefore also be added to the winter table without need for heating of a greenhouse. Black radish makes a welcome alternative to vegetables flown in or grown artificially under glass. These demand a great deal of energy and are responsible for contributing to greenhouse gases in the atmosphere.

☠ ⚭

Reseda lutea

WILD MIGNONETTE

The botanical name *Reseda* is derived from the Latin *resedare,* meaning "to return to rest". A long time ago, it was considered that the herb brought the entire body into a beneficial balance and also recognised a calming effect of the herb. Today the herb has no use in herbal medicine.

Wild mignonette principally grows in southern Europe but was brought north by man. In northern

Europe, it is only found on sunny dry chalky sites, particularly where rubbish is deposited, alongside railways, and chalk embankments. The plant grows in northern Europe as a biennial or occasional perennial that reaches 70cm (27½in) high. The green-yellow flowers are borne in spikes between June and August. Their sweet fragrance attracts many bees so that the plant is often grown as an adjunct to beekeeping.

Reseda luteola

WELD

Weld is very similar to wild mignonette but grows much taller. On average, the flower spikes shoot up to 150cm (5ft) high but can be as tall as 200cm (79in). This biennial plant likes a similar position to the wild mignonette but can be grown in garden soil provided it is alkaline or has lime added. Weld is not just an attractive ornamental plant that is fragrant and important for beekeeping, it also provides important dyestuffs. The entire herb, if picked at the start of flowering, is a well-known dye for colouring wool and other textiles. It provides a warm yellow colouring which with the

Reseda luteola, *weld.*

Rhamnus frangula, *alder buckthorn.*

addition of other herbs can be used to dye cloth orange, salmon pink, or even green.

Extracts from the plant are incorporated in skin creams and other cosmetics.

Rhamnus frangula syn. Frangula alnus

ALDER BUCKTHORN

Before the bark of alder buckthorn is suitable for use as a laxative, the dried rolls of bark must be heated for hours at boiling point to change the vomit inducing substances into merely purgative. The same can be achieved by keeping the bark for at least one year before using it. The dried bark is often contained in herbal teas prescribed as a spring and autumn tonics to cleanse the system but is also sold on its own for making infusions. These have a mild yet powerful laxative effect which is especially suitable for cleaning the large intestine.

The bark can also be used as a brown dye for cloth and was once used to treat head lice.

Alder buckthorn grows mainly as a bush on acid soil and is found throughout Europe on moist soil. The insignificant flowers change during the summer from green to red, and then black berries.

Rheum palmatum

CHINESE RHUBARB, CHINGHAI RHUBARB

When Chinese rhubarb arrived in western Europe in the eighteenth century, it already had a long history behind it as medicine. The Chinese were using the roots before the birth of Christ. After its arrival from the east, the herb became an important medicinal herb in Europe. The root was cut into pieces and dried before use in infusions which are laxative in effect. Currently extracts of the root are

Rheum palmatum, *Chinese rhubarb.*

Courtesy The Kruidenhof, Buitenpost.

Rhododendron ferrugineum, *alpenrose.*

more commonly used for a more precise dose for the treatment of inflammation of the stomach and intestinal linings and menstruation problems. Pregnant women and nursing mothers must not use the herb. Homeopaths prescribed the very dilute extracts for diarrhoea.

Rheum palmatum is a very large perennial which reaches 200–300cm (79in–10ft) during flowering. It grows wild in mountainous north-west China and when grown in a garden prefers a moist fertile soil with plenty of humus that does not become sodden in winter. Under the right circumstances, the plant will withstands frosts of minus 15°C (5°F).

⚕

Rhododendron ferrugineum

ALPENROSE

The alpenrose is found growing on lime-free slopes of the Alps and Pyrenees. This shrub can grow to 150cm (5ft) high but usually is no taller than 100cm (39in). Dark pink flowers can be anticipated from May to August but the spectacular flowering of the mountains rarely occurs in garden settings.

There are more attractive rhododendrons as ornamental plants but with *R. ferrugineum* the interest is the dark green leaves which have brown scales

on their undersides. This contains *arbutin*, which is beneficial for treating kidney and bladder ailments and also purifies and acts as a diuretic to relieve rheumatism and gout. All rhododendrons are poisonous and so should only be used as a herb under medical supervision.

Rhus radicans

POISON IVY

The native North Americans coated the tips of their arrows with this plant, which is one of the most poisonous of all American plants. The sap causes severe rashes when in contact with skin so that this low shrub must be handled with great care. The shrub grows wild in North America, China, and Japan and is fully hardy when grown in northern Europe. It is occasionally planted in gardens for the superb autumn colouring of its leaves. The leaves are dried and used in homeopathic medicine for treating skin complaints such as eczema, but also fever, infected mucous membranes, rheumatism, and nerve pains.

Ricinus communis

CASTOR-OIL PLANT

The oil from *Ricinus communis* has been used for thousands of years to deal with serious constipation, with the castor-oil plant being known at the time of the earliest of the Egyptian Pharoahs. The considerable toxicity of the seeds from which the oil is derived was of equally great concern to them then as today. The seeds contain a highly toxic protein, ricin, one of the most deadly natural poisons there is. Eating five to ten seeds can proved fatal while touching the leaves or seeds can cause skin irritations.

Use of castor oil as prescribed has no dangers for health but the dose should never be exceeded. Castor-oil is added to a wide range of products such as soap, candles, cosmetics, and lubricating oil.

The origins of the castor-oil tree are probably in Africa where it grows as a bushy shrub. In northern Europe it can be grown as an annual by sowing the seed indoors and planting out only well after the last frost in fertile soil that is rich in humus, moisture-retaining, and in the full sun.

Rhus radicans, *poison ivy.*

Ricinus communis, *castor-oil plant.*

Rosa canina, *dog rose.*

Rosa canina

DOG ROSE

Herbal tea from rose hips looks much like water and yet it is an ideal tonic and pick-me-up, guarding against colds and influenza. The hips are rich in vitamin C and also contain abundant vitamins A, B, and K. It is no surprise then that the hips are made into rose hip syrup and fruit drinks, especially for children. Adults also enjoy rose hip jam.

The Romans prescribed the herb to treat hydrophobia or rabies (hence the name *R. canina* or dog rose). Science has found no therapeutic link with fatal disease.

In all other respects, the dog rose has the same uses as the other roses which follow. The shrub grows to about 3m (10ft) high and flowers for just a few weeks in July with white to pink blooms. These are succeeded by the hips of which the calyx falls away once they are ripe. The dog rose is a native plant throughout Europe except the coldest northern parts.

Rosa x *damascena*

DAMASK ROSE

The damask rose is so old that it is difficult to be certain of its botanical origins. It is generally re-

Rosa damascena, *damask rose.*

garded to be a hybrid. The semi-double to double flowers are striking with their abundant petals for most wild roses merely have five. Whatever its background, the damask rose had already been cultivated for centuries when the crusaders brought it back with them to western Europe in the fourteenth century. The damask rose has the same beneficial properties as the apothecary's rose (see *Rosa gallica*) but is the premier rose used for its fragrance by the perfume industry. Vast areas of damask rose can be seen growing in Bulgaria from which countless rose petals are collected in the three weeks of flowering for distillation into rose water for the perfume industry. Rose water is also used as a flavouring in food and added to other cosmetic products for its fragrance.

The damask rose flowers for just three weeks in July and grows to about 200cm (79in) high.

Rosa gallica var. *officinalis*

APOTHECARY'S ROSE, RED ROSE OF LANCASTER

Although countless other roses contain the same medicinally active substances as the apothecary's

Rosa gallica, *red rose of Lancaster.*

Rosa gallica, *red rose of Lancaster.*

rose, it is this rose which is most widely grown for herbal use. *Rosa gallica* var. *officinalis* is a cultivar which remains low and has semi-double flowers.

The petals contain tannin and other astringent substances which are antiseptic. The flowers are incorporated into medicines that ease diarrhoea and sore throats in a mild manner but these are not suitable for pregnant women. The addition of rose oil to a bath engenders relaxation and can lift temporary depression caused by PMT and menopause. The fragrance can also evoke sexual feelings and push aside feelings of shame about one's own body. For other uses of the oil see *Rosa damascena*.

Rosa gallica generally forms a dense erect shrub of 100cm (39in) high and flowers fairly long for a species rose, between the end of May and early August with pink to crimson blooms which are succeeded by brick red hips. The red rose of Lancaster is a native of central and southern Europe.

Rosa eglanteria syn. *R. rubiginosa*

SWEET BRIAR, EGLANTINE

When the leaves of sweet briar are touched the fresh aroma of apple is released and can sometimes

Rosa eglanteria, *sweet briar.*

Rosa eglanteria, *sweet briar.*

be detected even when in proximity of the shrub. By contrast, the flowers give off little fragrance. These flower for a few weeks in July, followed by red-orange hips which are edible and can be made into jam, syrup, or fruit juice. The shrub mainly grows on lime-rich soil where it can reach 200cm (79in). This rose can be used for all the other uses listed previously but the shrub is mainly grown in gardens for its apple scent. Sweet briar grows wild in much of Europe and is found scattered throughout the British Isles, mainly in hedgerows and scrub on chalk soil.

Rosmarinus officinalis, *rosemary.*

Rosmarinus officinalis

ROSEMARY

Rosemary conjures up thoughts of summer and the Mediterranean. The herb is widely used with roasted meat (especially lamb) in the countries of the Mediterranean. It contains a strongly aromatic and flavoured volatile oil in the folded grey-green leaves. Meat roasted above a fire of old rosemary bushes acquires a very special flavour.

Rosemary gave even the decorous ladies of Victorian England a flush as they prayed it would work on the man into whose pocket they secretively slipped the herb. If the liaison succeeded and they became pregnant (after marriage!) then the lady would have to cease using rosemary in any quantity for it is astringent and can bring on labour. Always use rosemary in moderation. A little provides a wonderful aroma for meat, game, soups, sauces, and cheese dishes. Too much brings a camphor-like smell to the foreground. The herb can be kept mild by adding a sprig to vinegar or oil. When the plant remains have been strained off, the rosemary vinegar or oil can be used as flavouring. The herb is often added to white wine for medicinal uses.

Large doses of rosemary taken internally can be harmful, especially for pregnant women. Moderate doses aid digestion, strengthen the nervous system, improve circulation, and help to reduce blood pressure. The herb is antiseptic and diuretic. Spirit of rosemary can be rubbed on the skin to improve circulation and thereby reduce muscular aches, rheumatism, arthritis, and nerve pains. The volatile oil is suitable for use in oil burners that spread the fragrance through the vapour or for adding to the morning bath. Rosemary oil is added to countless cosmetic products and perfumes. *Rosmarinus* literally means "dew of the sea". The low bushes often grow against rocks at sea level along the Mediterranean coat. The herb can withstand frost but not in combination with moisture which makes the roots rot away in severe winters. The shrub will survive in an unheated greenhouse, cold frame, or conservatory, where the plant will survive low temperatures and flower in May to June with blue blooms. Rosemary remains compact by regular cutting for culinary use. Any shoots that have gone to seed should be cut back hard in spring.

Rubia tinctorum

MADDER

Alizarin or Turkey red are other names for the red madder pigment derived from the roots of madder. The red is unusually clear and bright for vegetable pigments and was extremely popular with dyers of cloth for many centuries in large parts of Europe and Asia. The plant was grown commercially on a major scale. The plant was dug up after two to five years and the roots were carefully dried. This took at least a year before they were dry enough to pulverise. The resulting powder was then used for dyeing in a hot bath. The dried root is still available from specialists for use as a dye. The extensive madder cultivation in Turkey, the Balkans, France, and elsewhere ended suddenly after the discovery in 1868 of ways to synthesise alizarin.

Madder is a laxative, diuretic, and antiseptic, and was therefore previously used to heal wounds. It was also taken internally for bladder and kidney stones. The urine of those taking the herb turned bright red and if used for a period of time, even the bones turned red. This characteristics was used to identify bone diseases.

Madder is a perennial of about 100cm (39in) from Asia Minor and the neighbouring Mediterranean. It is fully hardy and can still be found naturalised where it was once cultivated, growing on dry arable land, on clay or sand. The plant has little ornamental value for the garden.

Rubus fruticosa

BLACKBERRY, BRAMBLE

In late summer and autumn, blackberries can be picked and eaten from their thorny stems growing in hedges, or taken home and made into tarts or preserves. The healthy properties of the blackberry leaves are rather less well known. After drying, they can be used to make an infusion that is both tasty and good for you. It stops diarrhoea, cures inflamed mucous membranes, and eases cold symptoms. Gargling with a strong infusion of blackberry leaves helps with tonsillitis, sore throat, and gingivitis.

Rubia tinctorum, *madder.*

Rubus fruticosa, *blackberry.*

The bramble is a native plant throughout Europe, growing with long woody stems which root wherever they touch the ground. White to pink flowers appear on the thorny stems from May to late autumn and they are followed by the well-known fruit.

♀ ⚎

Rumex pseudoalpinus syn. *R. alpinus*

MONK'S-RHUBARB

Butter was once wrapped in the large leaves of monk's-rhubarb (a type of dock or sorrel) to preserve it. The leaves contain a bitter substance which has preservative properties. The roots contain substance which are mildly laxative and are used for this purpose in central Europe.

Monk's-rhubarb grows in the mountains of Europe, often close to farms and cottages where the soil is fertile and moist. The leaves grow about 50cm (20in) long and 20cm (8in) wide. Flower plumes appear on stems of about 100cm (39in) high in early summer. The plant is a hardy perennial.

♀

Rumex obtusifolius

BROAD-LEAVED DOCK, LAPATHUM

With its modest flowers and green leaves that blend into the background, broad-leaved dock

Rumex pseudoalpinus, *monk's-rhubarb.*

Courtesy The Kruidenhof, Buitenpost.

Rubus fruticosa, *blackberry or bramble.*

253

does not readily catch the eye. Yet it is one of the most commonly occurring plants. This dock grows throughout Europe, especially where the soil is rich in nitrogen and by preference in partial shade. While flowering, the broad-leaved dock can reach a height of 100cm (39in).

The young leaves are sometimes appreciated as a vegetable although their use as a yellow or green dye for cloth is more important.

Rumex acetosa ssp. *ambiguus* syn. *R. rugosus*

GARDEN SORREL

Garden sorrel *(R. acetosa* ssp. *ambiguus)* is a cultivated form of common sorrel but with broader leaves. It is grown as a vegetable and may be offered as *Rumex rugosus.* The leaves are tender and edible before the flowers appear and are added to salads and raw cabbage for its fresh but sharp taste. Previously sorrel was cooked and eaten as a vegetable but this is less healthy because of high concentrations of oxalic acid which is especially unhealthy for people who suffer with rheumatic complaints.

Rumex obtusifolius, *broad-leaved dock.*

Rumex acetosa *ssp.* ambiguus, *garden sorrel.*

Courtesy The Kruidenhof, Buitenpost.

Rumex is virtually restricted to homeopathic medicinal use for sinusitis and catarrh, diarrhoea, and other stomach and intestinal complaints.

This member of the *Rumex* family also provides green to yellow dye for cloth.

Ruta graveolens

RUE, HERB OF GRACE, HERBYGRASS

Dogs, cats, and evil spirits all hate rue. If this is not reason enough to plant this herb you can enjoy the attractive deeply-divided leaves and late summer green-yellow flowers. Bees and other insects throng to the flowers for the nectar, while the dried and powdered leaves are an effective insect repellent.

In the countries of southern Europe, rue was once an important herb, used by artists to improve their vision, while chopped leaves were added to salads, soups, and sauces (particularly with fish). Northern Europe rarely used the fresh leaves because of the bitter taste and stomach and intestinal disorders that followed excessive consumption. Pregnant women should not use the herb in any circumstances.

Sprigs of rue are still placed in wine or vinegar for

Ruta graveolens, *rue.*

Courtesy The Kruidenhof, Buitenpost.

Ruta graveolens, *rue.*

Ruta graveolens, *a hedge of rue.*

a pungent flavouring. The volatile oils from the plant are also added to liqueurs such as the Italian grappa and as a constituent in certain perfumes.

Only use rue as a medicinal herb under medical supervision. Its effect is calming, sleep inducing, and cramp relieving, and is also used to stimulate appetite, and as a diuretic. Rue is used in homeopathic medicine for treating rheumatism, bruising, and eye infections. Contact with rue can cause an allergic skin rash.

Ruta graveolens grows wild in dry, sunny places in southern Europe, especially the Balkans. Rue will happily accept similar or even less favourable places in a garden, growing to about 50cm (20in) tall. The plant is hardy but can be frost damaged in severe winters, requiring hard pruning the following spring. Rue can be readily pruned so that it is often grown as a low hedge in herb gardens.

S

Salix alba, *white willow.*

Salix alba

WHITE WILLOW

Willow bark led pharmaceutical companies to the development of aspirin which is synthesised from salicylic acid which occurs naturally in willow. The painkilling effect of willow bark had been known in herbal medicine for generations which led to research into its properties. The most important active substance in the bark is salicin which is converted in the human body into salicylic acid. Aspirin is a chemically synthesised form.

In addition to salicylic acid, willow bark also contains tannin and other compounds of medical importance. An infusion of dried willow bark induces perspiration, reduces fever temperature, prevents infection, and has an astringent action so that it is beneficial for stomach 'flu and diarrhoea.

Solidago canadensis, *Canada goldenrod.*

Salix species, *stripped willow on Madeira.*

In addition to the painkilling effect, willow bark is also of importance for rheumatic disorders. The bark is peeled in spring from young branches from which the leaves have emerged. Both the bark and leaves of willow can be used to dye cloth green or yellow.

Young willow shoots are harvested in places as diverse as Madeira and the Somerset levels for weaving into baskets.

Salix alba can be distinguished by the striking grey-green leaves but other willows can be used in the same ways. Because willows cross with each other readily it is very difficult to keep the species separated. There are countless hybrids and cultivars. Willows are often pollarded every few years with the small timber being used around the farm or for hurdle making. Willows are extremely easy to propagate: if a branch is sawn off and pushed into the soil before the leaves have emerged, a newly rooted tree will almost invariably result.

Willow baskets being woven.

257

Salvia officinalis, *common sage.*

Sage is widely used as a culinary herb. Apart from the renowned poultry stuffing, try a little finely chopped leaf in soups or fish sauces. The herb is often added to sausage and vol-au-vent fillings.
Salvia officinalis originated from the hotter climate of the Mediterranean but has grown in northern Europe since the Middle Ages. It was an important herb in the monastery gardens that were established in the Renaissance and spread from these to private gardens where it was once grown as a culinary and medicinal herb. Today this perennial is mainly grown for its ornamental value because of its grey-green foliage. This plant is

Salvia officinalis

COMMON SAGE

It is said that planting sage in a garden will grant the gardener a long life. In ancient times, sage was associated with old age. The herb was taken as a tonic to ward off loss of memory associated with ageing.

In the Middle Ages common sage was seen as a cure-all for every ill. It was used to aid digestion and to get rid of the associated wind. Further uses were relief of spasms, perspiration, catarrh, increasing lactation for nursing mothers, and diarrhoea, together with curing infection and providing relaxation. Today, common sage is rarely used medicinally, although infusions are ideal for gargling to treat mouth, gum, and throat infections, or to use in a compress to help slow-to-heal wounds to heal.

Salvia is used homoeopathically to counter excessive perspiration, as an antiseptic for mouth and gum infections, and to reduce lactation in nursing mothers. There are no side-effects from sage when used homoeopathically but taking large amounts of the herb can induce labour in pregnant women and is therefore best avoided. No-one should take *Salvia* in large amounts because it contains thujone which is toxic in large doses and can cause epileptic fits.

Salvia officinalis *'Icterina'.*

Courtesy The Kruidenhof, Buitenpost.

Salvia officinalis *'Purpurascens'.*

Salvia officinalis, *common sage.*

Salvia officinalis *'Purpurascens'*.

Salvia officinalis *'Purpurascens'*

Salvia officinalis *'Tricolour'*.

Courtesy The Kruidenhof, Buitenpost.

hardy although some damage can occur in severe winters. There are numerous cultivars on sale, usually with different leaves of great ornamental interest. These include: *Salvia officinalis* 'Icterina' with yellow-green leaves with golden margins, *Salvia officinalis* 'Purpurascens' is the most widely used cultivar for medicinal purposes because it contains higher concentrations of the active substances. The leaves are dark red to purple. The new leaves of *Salvia officinalis* 'Tricolor' are pink suffused with purple but during growth they gradually change to grey-green with creamy margins.

☧ ⚕

Salvia pratensis, *meadow clary.*

Salvia pratensis, *meadow clary.*

Salvia pratensis

MEADOW CLARY

Superficially, meadow clary resembles sage but it has much less attractive leaves although the upper lip of the flowers of this species are much larger than those of sage. Meadow clary's purple to blue flowers appear between May and July.

The herb originates from southern parts of Europe and it grows mainly in rocky places on sunny grasslands such as roadside verges, and on slopes. The main distribution is to central Germany with a few isolated pockets as far north as Scandinavia and naturalised in pockets in southern, eastern, and western Britain.

Meadow clary is not used as a culinary herb. It contains the same substances as sage but not in the same concentrations. The herb has the same medicinal uses as sage.

Salvia sclarea

CLARY SAGE, CLEAR EYE, MUSCATEL SAGE

Clary sage is currently a much appreciated garden plant because of its large grey-green leaves and lengthy three-coloured flower spikes (white, pink, violet). The flowers are also extremely aromatic but opinions are divided about the fragrance. Men in general find the plant stinks while most women find the fragrance pleasant. It is possible that the herb exudes a "masculine" scent. The "muscatel oil" from the plant is a constituent in male fragrances. Perfumes are really sexual signals and many male fragrances, lotions, and after-shaves contain the aroma of musk, which is never used in fragrances for women.

Muscatel oil from the herb is used to add flavour to certain Rhine wines but other than this, the herb has virtually no culinary uses. Medicinal uses are also a thing of the past, although the plant does contain the same substances as sage and is certainly useful for treating throat infections or gum disorders.

Salvia sclarea grows wild in south-east Europe and in neighbouring parts of Asia, in dry and rocky places. In northern Europe the plant is normally grown trouble-free in ordinary garden soil as a biennial. The flowering starts in July and continues into August.

Salvia sclarea, *clary sage.*

Salvia sclarea, *clary sage.*

Sambucus ebulus

DWARF ELDER

Dwarf elder looks like a shrub of 100–200cm (39–79in) high but is really an herbaceous perennial. The stems die back to the ground in winter. This plant grows in very fertile soil in moist places in western, central, and southern Europe and adjoining parts of Asia and Africa. It is possibly native in Britain where it is found scattered throughout the country. After the flowering in June to August, black berries are formed. These berries are poisonous, as are the other parts of this plant. Once they were used as a drastic laxative but due to accidents which occurred this practice has ceased. The roots are dug up to be dried for use in infusions to use as laxative or diuretic, with beneficial effects on oedema and rheumatism.

Dyers of cloth use the leaves and stems to form a yellow dyestuff and the unripe berries are used to produce a blue colour.

The dwarf elder is easily to cultivate in fertile soil and can even become rampant through underground runners. Virtually no other plant will grow under dwarf elder.

Salvia sclarea, *clary sage.*

Sambucus ebulus, *dwarf elder.*

261

Sambucus ebulus, *dwarf elder.*

Sambucus nigra *'Laciniata', common elder.*

Sambucus nigra

COMMON ELDER

There is a feast for the starlings in late summer when the elder is a mass of ripe black berries. When they gorge themselves on the berries which often ferment in their stomachs, the alcohol formed makes them rush about noisily, flying here and there.

Humans cannot eat the raw berries except when we are constipated, because they have a laxative effect. Once cooked this effect is removed and elderberries can be used to make conserves. Ripe berries that are allowed to ferment with apples make a delicious fruit wine.

The large flower umbels can also be harvested in June to make elderflower wine which is lighter, with a subtle taste. Alcohol-free elderflower syrup can be added with mineral water to make a refreshing summer drink. The syrup is made by cooking the flowers briefly in sugar water with lemon and then steeping in the liquid for forty-eight hours. Elderflower fritters are cooked by dipping the flowers in batter and then frying. Elderflower is used medicinally to help a patient "sweat off" a fever. Because the active substances contained also help to improve resistance to illness, dried flowers are often added to herbal tea mixtures for colds and 'flu.

The berries and leaves of elder are widely used for dyeing of cloth. The juice from the berries produces lilac-purple to grey-black and the leaves produce yellow to yellow-green.

Sanguisorba minor

SALAD BURNET

The pollen of salad burnet is spread by the wind so that the extremely small flowers do not need colourful petals to attract insects. But if you take the trouble to look at the flowers closely you will see their beauty. The flowers are arranged together in dense terminal spikes with the male flowers below and female above. The plant grows to about 40cm (16in) in May–June when the flowers are borne. This perennial of chalky meadows is found in most of Europe except the colder north. Its has pinnate leaves which are picked while new to be added to salads, fruit salads, herb butter, and soft cheeses.

The taste is similar to cucumber but more pungent. Chopped leaves are added just before serving to soups and sauces, especially with fish.

Sambucus nigra, *elder.*

Sambucus nigra, *elder.*

Sanguisorba minor, *salad burnet.*

Sanguisorba officinalis, *great burnet.*

Salad burnet is slightly astringent and able to stem bleeding, stop diarrhoea, and is beneficial for treating haemorrhoid and for the digestion. This mild herb has few other medicinal uses.

Sanguisorba officinalis syn. *Poterium officinalis*

GREAT BURNET

Great burnet was once the most highly regarded herb for stemming bleeding. The dried root, which has the highest concentrations of tannin, was especially used for this purpose. The above ground parts of the plant have a weaker effect but were also dried to make infusions for treating diarrhoea.

Sanguisorba officinalis, *great burnet.*

Sanicula europaea, *sanicle.*

fused with pink. The perennial reaches 50cm (20in) during flowering and it can be readily cultivated in shade or semi-shade in moist, humus-rich soil.

Santolina chamaecyparissus

LAVENDER-COTTON, COTTON LAVENDER

Cotton lavender grows in arid, sunny places in the western and central parts of the land surrounding the Mediterranean. In northern Europe the low shrubs (growing to about 50cm (20in) high are able to withstand frosts but not in combination with wet soil so that they are best grown as a container plant. Provide they are not pruned, the shrubs produce yellow flowerheads in summer. In mild parts of Europe where they are hardy in dry soil, the shrubs are often trimmed to form hedges but then do not flower.

The trimmings from the shrub have a wonderfully sweet fragrance and used to be strewn on floors. The herb has a delightful fragrance in a pot-pourri and is reputed to drive insects away. For this reason, twigs were placed between clothes to keep moths away.

The flowers were once used to get rid of worms but these days the herb has virtually no medicinal use.

 ✳

The infusion can also be used to gargle for treating infections of the mouth, throat, or gums and are used particularly in homeopathic medicine for varicose veins.

Great burnet grows virtually throughout Europe in moist grassy places but is mainly restricted in Britain to the Midlands, South Wales, and the north. This perennial grows about 100cm (39in) tall and has flower spikes filled with reddish-brown florets from June.

Sanicula europaea

SANICLE

The tannin, other bitter substances, and saponins in sanicle are astringent and antiseptic. An infusion of the dried herb (or dried root) stops diarrhoea and wind, and is beneficial for stomach and intestinal disorders, and excessive bleeding during menstruation. As a gargle, the herbal tea is useful for infections of the mouth, throat, or gingivitis of the gums, and in a wet compress can be used to treat bruises and skin rashes.

Sanicula europaea is native throughout almost all of Europe and found scattered in Britain in ash and beech woods on alkaline soils. During its flowering in May–June, the plant bears very compact umbels of white pink florets, sometimes suf-

Santolina chamaecyparissus, *lavender-cotton.*

Saponaria officinalis, *soapwort.*

Saponaria officinalis, *soapwort.*

Saponaria officinalis

SOAPWORT, BOUNCING BET

Saponaria contains high concentrations of saponin, which creates foam in water and has mild cleansing properties. Before the soap-making process was known, the crushed roots of soapwort were soaked in water in order to do the laundry. Today soapwort is only used by restorers to clean very old wall hangings and historical clothing.

The use of soapwort as medicine has also become less important. The herb is laxative, blood purifying, and expectorant but saponin is toxic so incorrect use can lead to inflammation of the stomach and intestines. Internal use of the plant is therefore not advisable.

A decoction of the roots can be added to bath water to treat psoriasis and other flaky skin disorders. It is also a popular treatment for dandruff.

The flowers, which appear between June and August, spread a superb fragrance and are therefore wonderful cut flowers. The flowers are large and a delightful soft pink to white.

Although soapwort probably originated in the woods of southern Europe, it has become widely naturalised. The perennial grows about 100cm (39in) high and is most at home in fertile, moisture-retaining soil at the edges of woods or in hedges. Soapwort makes an indestructible, delightful garden plant.

   ✳

Satureja hortensis

SUMMER SAVORY

Summer savory could be found in every single herb garden in the Middle Ages because it was regarded as a cure-all for all illnesses. Ideas have retreated somewhat from this position since but the different forms of savory are still important as medicinal and culinary herbs.

Dishes made with pulses such as beans can often be difficult to digest and cause wind. By adding a little savory to the dish, this problem is removed. The herb stimulates digestion, increases the appetite, and stops diarrhoea. Herbal tea from the dried herb is expectorant and helps with coughs. A teaspoon of honey added makes the tea taste delicious. Honey can acquire the fragrance of savory when bees derive their nectar from the plant. Bees are extremely fond of the herb. When savory is ready to flower in late summer, it is time to harvest for drying. Use the herb sparingly because of its pungent taste. *Satureja hortensis* is milder in

Satureja hortensis, *summer savory.*

flavour than *Satureja montana*. Pregnant women should avoid using these herbs.

Summer savory comes from south-eastern parts of Europe and neighbouring Asia Minor. This annual can be sown indoors in spring or out of doors in a sunny and sheltered position from mid April. This herb prefers fertile and well-worked soil.

Satureja montana, *winter savory*.

Satureja montana

WINTER SAVORY

Winter savory can be used in the same way as *Satureja hortensis* (see there). Winter savory has a more pungent taste than summer savory and has therefore to be used very sparingly.

Winter savory grows as a small shrub of about 50cm (20in) high. It originates from southern Europe but is sufficiently hardy to survive northern European winters provided the soil is not too wet. The herb lends itself to being grown as a low hedge next to paving laid on sand, where water will drain away quickly. The hedges can be clipped back into shape when the herb is harvested. This is done at the expense of the pale pink flowers, which appear in late summer.

Schisandra chinensis

SCHISANDRA

Schisandra spreads a delightful sweet fragrance from its white to pink flowers at the end of May. This deciduous climbing shrub originates from north-eastern parts of China where it has long been used medicinally. The herb increases energy (including sexual energy) and is beneficial for a wide range of ailments: diarrhoea, incontinence, coughs, heart tremors, and memory loss. The fruit are harvested for these purposes and only grow on female plants. In northern Europe, schisandra forms a fine

Satureja montana, *winter savory*.

Schisandra chinensis, *schisandra*.

shrub which when grown against a south-facing wall will reach 5m (16ft) and entirely screen the wall with its attractive foliage. Ensure sufficient watering and humus to retain moisture, especially when grown against a wall. The soil needs to be very fertile.

Scopolia carniolica syn. *S. atropoides*

SCOPOLIA, JAPANESE BELLADONNA

Scopolia does not readily catch the eye because it is predominantly green with bell flowers which are purple-brown on the outside and yellowish-green inside. This herbaceous perennial dies back above ground in the winter but the roots survive. These used to be dug up for the alkaloids hyoscine and hyoscyamine. These substances are hallucinogens that are also found in henbane *(Hyocyamus niger)* and deadly nightshade *(Atropa belladonna)*.

In the Middle Ages both witches and witch hunters uses the substances (see *Hyocyamus niger)*. Patients were put into a stupor by using the herb before operations. Today hyoscyamine is used

Scopolia carniolica, *scopolia.*

medicinally to relieve spasms and the shakes associated with Parkinson's disease. Used externally, the herb can be beneficial for rheumatic aches and other pains but because of its highly toxic nature the entire plant should only be used under medical supervision.

This perennial grows well in partial shade in normal moisture-retaining soil.

Scopolia carniolica, *scopolia.*

Scopolia carniolica, *scopolia.*

Scorzonera hispanica, *scorzonera.*

Scrophularia nodosa

COMMON FIGWORT

The flowers of common figwort are normally busy with bees and wasps in summer, which find an abundance of nectar. The insignificant perennial grows to between 100–200cm (39in–79in) tall and is found in the wild in clearings in woods but also manages to survive on sunny to slightly shady places if the soil is fertile. The plant dies back above ground in the winter. Its short pale rhizomes can be found just beneath the surface.

The rhizome and the tops of the plant have been used since the Middle Ages as a purifying medicine. Infusions of the chopped and dried foliage is said to heal eczema, acne, psoriasis, and swollen lymph glands.

Scutellaria galericulata

SKULLCAP

The blue-flowered skullcap grows beside water and in marshes throughout virtually the whole of Europe. The violet flowers appear on this perennial in pairs above the leaves from mid summer.

Scrophularia nodosa, *common figwort.*

Scorzonera hispanica

SCORZONERA, BLACK SALSIFY, SPANISH SALSIFY

The thin and extremely long tap roots of scorzonera are white on the inside with black skin. The name is derived from Italian, with "scorza" meaning bark and "nera" black. The roots of this plant were once widely grown as a vegetable but are enjoying a revival. The vegetable can be eaten by diabetes patients because the sweet substances in the root have little influence on blood sugar levels. Another explanation of the name is that it is derived from the old French "scorzon" which means snake. The plant was used for a long time to treat poisonous snake bites. Today the main use is to deal with excessive perspiration.

Scorzonera hispanica is a perennial from southern Europe and neighbouring parts of Asia. It grows naturally in dry soil but is content with normal garden soil. Depending on the fertility of the soil, it can grow to between 50cm (20in) and 120cm (47in) and bears yellow flowers in summer.

Stems of about 50cm (20in) long are formed from the creeping roots.

Skullcap is virtually unused these days even though it contains the same substances as such recognised medicinal herbs as it close Asian relative *Scutellaria baicalensis* and *Scutellaria laterifolia* from America.

The herb was once used for epilepsy, nerve pains, delirious fever, St. Vitus dance (chorea), and hysteria. The foliage from the plant is still used as a general tonic for the nervous system and in homeopathy the herb has a similar use.

Sedum acre

BITING STONECROP, COMMON STONECROP, WALLPEPPER

Stonecrop, also known as wallpepper, grows on the most improbable places: on walls, roofs, and at the edges and central reservations of motorways (especially where water washes the winter salt off the highway). This succulent forms a mass of vegetation in these places and flowers between May and July, turning its sites into a swathe of yellow. Sedum acre is an evergreen perennial which grows throughout Europe in dry, sunny places, especially on thin, sandy soil.

Stonecrop is used in very small amounts as a purgative, especially for headache and also reduces blood pressure. In any quantity, the herb induces

Scutellaria galericulata, *skullcap.*

Scutellaria galericulata, *skullcap.*

Sedum acre, *stonecrop.*

Sedum rupestre, *stone orpine.*

vomiting because of the toxic alkaloids it contains. This means there is danger associated with using the herb with the exception of homeopathic use to treat haemorrhoids.

Sedum rupestre syn. *S. reflexum*

STONE ORPINE, REFLEXED STONECROP

The stone orpine grows in very dry and rocky places or sandy places where there is only occasional moisture. In these short periods, the plant stores the liquid in its rounded succulent leaves which are deliciously juicy with a cool freshness that makes them ideal for adding to salads. The young upper shoots are harvested in spring for this purpose.

Previously, the leaves were also applied externally to soothe painful haemorrhoids and inflamed skin but these medicinal uses have been largely forgotten.

Sedum rupestre grows throughout Europe, including Britain where it has become naturalised, but only in an open, sunny position, on rocks or sand. It flowers from June to August. The plant can easily be grown in gardens provided it has poor but open soil. This plant is ideal for a rock garden but can become very rampant.

Sedum rupestre, *stone orpine.*

Courtesy The Kruidenhof, Buitenpost.

Sedum rupestre, *stone orpine.*

Sedum telephium

ORPINE

The orpine is a succulent which stores moisture in its leaves. This liquid contains alkaloids among other substances which cause vomiting when ingested in large quantities. Because of the toxicity of this plant, its use in salads or as herbal medicine is most certainly ill advised. It used to be cooked in milk to stop diarrhoea and improve kidney function.

Orpine has been used externally for centuries as a wound herb. it promotes circulation of the blood and the tannins in the sap are slightly astringent, ensuring a wound closes quickly. The herb also has antiseptic properties, so that the leaf can be held against inflamed skin, haemorrhoid, or burns.

Succulents almost always grow in very sunny and dry places. Orpine is the exception, being found in woods and hedgebanks but also rocky places. This perennial dies back in winter. The plant grows to about 60cm (24in) and has purple to violet flowers in July–August. This herb is easily grown in the garden and can become rampant.

Sedum telephium, *orpine.*

Sedum telephium *ssp.* maximum, *orpine.*

it can often be seen. For uses see *Sedum telephium.*

☥

Sempervivum tectorum

COMMON HOUSELEEK

The common houseleek has been planted on the roofs of houses for almost as long as human history. The Latin *tectum* means "roofs" and *sempervivum* means "always living" because the plant remains green summer and winter. Planting houseleek on the roof was said to prevent lightning from striking and some people still believe in this property for the succulent. Even if you have more confidence in a lightning conductor, houseleek does look good growing on the roof. The species originates in the Alps and is grown elsewhere as a garden plant but also on roofs and in walls where it can survive for a long time. Common houseleek grows best in a sunny, dry position. It is just one species of the genus *Sempervivum*, which are all known as houseleek.

The sap from the leaves of common houseleek contain substances which are cooling and astringent so that it is a perfect wound herb. The crushed leaves are placed on bleeding wounds and burns, inflamed skin, or insect bites. Internal consump-

Sedum telephium ssp. *maximum*

ORPINE

The orpine is an extremely variable plant with significant differences in the leaves and colour of the flowers. This pale sub species has purple-tipped flower buds but when the flowers open they are cream to pale yellow inside. Because the orpine does not readily produce seed in northern Europe and reproduces mainly via its creeping roots, it does not easily cross with other varieties or cultivars. This pale orpine is popular in gardens so that

Sedum telephium *ssp.* maximum, *orpine.*

Sempervivum tectorum, *common houseleek.*

Courtesy The Kruidenhof, Buitenpost.

271

Sempervivum tectorum, *common houseleek.*

tion of the herb is ill advised because of the toxic alkaloids it contains. The herb is prescribed in homeopathic medicine for menstruation problems.

Senecio jacobaea

RAGWORT, TANSY RAGWORT

Ragwort was an important medicine for a long time for provoking menstruation and for relieving severe period pains. The powdered root acted as a laxative, while the plant itself was prescribed for diarrhoea and coughs. The herb should not be taken internally under any circumstances because taking large doses over a period of time can cause liver damage (both to humans and grazing cattle). Furthermore, it has been proven that the alkaloids in the plant are carcinogenic. The herb is still used as a yellow dyestuff for cloth.
Senecio jacobaea grows virtually throughout Europe in meadows and other grassland. The biennial or occasionally perennial plant comes into flower in June, when it is about 100–150cm (39–5ft) high.

Senecio jacobaea, *ragwort.*

Serratula tinctoria, *saw wort.*

Courtesy The Kruidenhof, Buitenpost.

Serratula tinctoria

SAW WORT

Saw wort is one of the better known plants from which dyestuffs are derived. The above ground vegetation is used to produce a yellow dye for wool and other textiles. Harvesting of this thistle presents no problems because it does not have prickles. Saw wort flowers from July with small purple-pink flowerheads on stems of up to 100cm (39in). Saw wort is a native plant in much of Europe including the British Isles. The plant survives in the wild on very poor soil but is happy growing in good garden soil where it can then reach 150cm (5ft) high.

Silphium perfoliatum

CUP PLANT

If the disc-floret of the cup plant is cut or broken, an aromatic resin oozes out. The native North Americans chewed this resin to freshen bad breath. A side-effect of this is strongly-smelling urine. Substances in the resin are diuretic and also act as an expectorant for patients with a cough. The herb is used to treat both malaria and pneumonia but the

dose needs to be determined by a specialist because excessive use causes vomiting.

The plant originates in the damp woodland of North America and is only grown in Europe as an ornamental plant, requiring fertile, moisture-retaining soil. Cup plant flowers in late summer with blooms of 5cm (2in) diameter on stems of more than 200cm (79in).

Silybum marianum

MILK THISTLE

The milk thistle's veins were formed, according to legend, by the Virgin Mary's milk running down the leaves (hence also the Latin *marianum).* The plant is found most readily on the Atlantic cliffs of France and the British Isles, although this imposing thistle can also be found inland where it is invariably in a sunny position. The plant grows both as an annual and biennial, in the latter case, the leaves emerge in spring with clearly defined white veins. The reddish-purple flowers emerge on 100cm (39in) high stems from June on.

The flowerheads form black seed case with hairy tufts towards the end of the summer when the downy tuft is harvested for drying and use in infusions. The infusion is very beneficial for the liver, preventing fat forming, which can cause health problems. Many people regard the milk thistle as a wonder cure. The herb is used homoeopathically for

Silybum marianum, *milk thistle.*

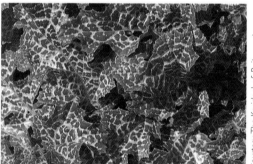

Courtesy The Kruidenhof, Buitenpost.

Silybum marianum, *milk thistle.*

Silybum marianum, *milk thistle.*

Sisymbrium officinale, *hedge mustard.*

Courtesy The Kruidenhof, Buitenpost.

Sium sisarum, *skirret.*

Courtesy The Kruidenhof, Buitenpost.

the same purpose and also for stimulating the gall bladder, treating gall stones, and depression.

Sisymbrium officinale

HEDGE MUSTARD

Hedge mustard is a common plant of waysides and rough terrain. This annual or perennial plants bears very small yellow flowers on its 100cm (39in) high stems between May and October. The young leaves and shoots of the plant before flowering can be used in salads to impart a mustard flavour and are also suitable for adding a pungent flavour to sauces and soups. The herb acts as a general tonic for the entire body and also stimulates digestion, is mildly laxative, diuretic, and expectorant. It is also beneficial in use with bladder disorders, cough, and bronchitis.

Sium sisarum

SKIRRET

Skirret acquires its sweet taste after the first frosts of autumn. The name derives from the Dutch name "suikerwortel" or "sugarroot". Skirret was once an important winter vegetable which was harvested in early winter for storage in moist sand through the winter months when few other vegetables were available. The roots were eaten raw, steamed, or briefly boiled, sliced like carrots or sometimes cooked with minced pork or beef. They were also pickled in vinegar for serving with cold dishes. The young tender leaves are ideal for stir-frying.

Skirret is a purifying and diuretic herb that is especially beneficial for persons suffering from liver complaints including jaundice.

The origins of this plant are unknown but its has been cultivated for a long time. It was highly regarded in ancient Rome and has been in use as a culinary and medicinal herb in China since very early times. This perennial is fully hardy in northern Europe, grows to about 100cm (39in) tall, and flowers in summer. Cultivate it in fertile garden soil which must not be allowed to dry out.

Solanum dulcamara

BITTERSWEET, WOODY NIGHTSHADE

Bittersweet can be found in hedges and the edges of damp woodland. The purple flowers with yellow stamens are borne in summer on long stems which climb up to 200cm (79in) long into bushes. The flowers are followed by green berries which turn scarlet in late summer. Only the ripe berries or relatively non toxic. All the other parts of the plant are extremely poisonous and can even prove lethal for both humans and animals if sufficient is ingested. In the appropriate doses, the plant has beneficial medicinal value. Infusions of the stems are used in herbal medicine to treat rheumatism, gout, jaundice, oedema, skin inflammation, eczema, stubborn catarrh, blocked airways, coughs, and asthma. Although the herb is useful for all these ailments, it should only be used under supervision of a skilled specialist.

Solanum dulcamara, *bittersweet.*

Solanum dulcamara, *bittersweet.*

Solanum melongena

AUBERGINE, EGGPLANT

Solanum melongena is one of the many forms of aubergine, a vegetable brought to Europe from south-east Asia in the thirteenth century. The fruits of the aubergine that is commonly cultivated are a brownish shade of purple, which is a colour also known as "aubergine". *Solanum melongena* more closely resembles the original eggplants brought from the Far East with fruits the size of a hen's egg that are white at first, changing to yellowish-

Solanum melongena, *aubergine.*

orange as they ripen. The fruits are prepared in precisely the same way as commercially grown aubergines. Small amounts, diced and fried in olive oil, impart their flavour to salads.

Solanum melongena is a perennial but is grown in northern Europe as an annual. Sow the seed under cover in spring but do not plant out until June and then in a sheltered, sunny position. Because of the plant's need of warmth, cultivation in a greenhouse is more successful.

Solanum tuberosum

POTATO

Everyone knows the potato, which is the staple diet of Europeans and North Americans. Before the potato was discovered in the Americas, Europeans had to rely on other staples. The native peoples of the Americas had developed numerous cultivars of the species and there is greatly renewed interest in these early forms, which are less susceptible to disease.

Apart from use of the tuber as a rich source of nutrition, the potato is also a medicinal herb. The starch in potatoes relieves spasms, and reduces burning stomach acid. The potato is used in homeopathic medicine for the same purposes: reducing stomach acid, inflammation of the stomach lining, loss of appetite, and stomach ache.

Seed potatoes are planted in spring, producing a

plant with foliage of about 50cm (20in) high which bear purple or white flowers in summer. The foliage is allowed to die back (or chemically killed off) and the tubers that have formed on the roots are then harvested from the soil. These are the potatoes.

Solidago canadensis

CANADIAN GOLDEN ROD

The Canadian goldenrod (and better-known goldenrod or *Solidago virgaurea*) are well-known garden plants which can become rampant in open soil to fill large areas with their yellow flowers in late summer on tall stems of 150cm (5ft) high. The plant

Solidago canadensis, *Canadian goldenrod.*

Solanum tuberosum, *potato.*

Solidago canadensis, *Canadian goldenrod.*

Solidago virgaurea, *goldenrod.*

readily becomes naturalised in dry, sunny positions, such as railway embankments. Unlike the native species, *S. canadensis* originates from North America where the indigenous people used it as a wound herb and to treat sore throats.

The North America species of goldenrod is virtually never used medicinally in Europe but is an important source of yellow dyestuff for colouring wool and other textiles.

Solidago virgaurea

GOLDENROD

The native goldenrod is even more widely used as a yellow dyestuff for colouring wool and textiles. In addition, this species has long been an important medicinal herb that provides a blood purifying herbal tea. The top shoots of the plant provide substances which are diuretic, so that rheumatic complaints and skin conditions can be treated with the herb. What is more, the herb stimulates kidney function and can be beneficial in treatment of kidney and bladder infections. The herb has similar uses in homeopathic medicine.

Goldenrod is a native of dry grassland, wayside verges, rocky places, and sandy soil throughout Europe and most of the British Isles. The plant flowers in late summer and grows taller than 100cm (39in).

Sorbus aucuparia

ROWAN, MOUNTAIN ASH

The orange berries of the rowan or mountain ash contain tannin and prussic acid among other substances so that they are inedible raw. With cooking, the prussic acid disappears and the structure of the other substances is changed. Puree or conserve of the berries is very healthy. Birds have no difficulties digesting the raw berries and thrushes and blackbirds in particular gorge themselves on the fruit.

The tasty preserve stimulates secretion of gastric juices in the stomach, which aids digestion. Rowan berry puree or conserve will help overcome lack of appetite and is also delicious in small quantities with game.

The rowan grows mainly in cooler parts of Europe, including the extreme north. The low tree often reproduces itself from seed eaten by birds and has a preference for acid soil.

Stachys officinalis, *betony.*

Stachys officinalis syn. S. betonica, Betonica officinale

BETONY, BISHOPSWORT

It was once thought that sneezing had a strong cleansing effect so that snuff was taken to clear the airways, and help prevent headaches. Betony is one of the plants that was ground to form snuff. In those times there were some ninety different ailments that betony was said to cure. The plant was important among those uses as a wound herb, and improved the supply of blood to the brain which is beneficial for those who are mentally exhausted. It was also prescribed for menopause difficulties in women. Pregnant women should not use the herb. Today infusions of the herb are still used, which in moderation can help with diarrhoea (excess can cause severe diarrhoea and vomiting). The herbal tea can also be used as a gargle for mouth and throat infections.

Stachys officinalis grows virtually everywhere in Europe south of southern Sweden, being widespread in England and Wales but more scattered elsewhere in the British Isles. This perennial of 50cm (20in) high has striking reddish-purple flowers between June and September and can be cultivated easily in gardens in partial shade, preferring open soils.

Stachys palustris

MARSH WOUNDWORT

Marsh woundwort is found widely beside rivers and ponds. This perennial grows to about 100cm (39in) high and flowers in June to August. The foliage has a strong and unpleasant smell.

The plant has been used in herbal medicine for a long time, being regarded as one of the best wound herbs. The herb is harvested at the start of flowering. The crushed plant, a tincture, or an infusion of the dried leaves are placed against the wound. Substances in the herb are astringent and ensure speedy healing of wounds.

Stachys sylvatica

HEDGE WOUNDWORT

Hedge woundwort grows in moist, shady places. When the flowers bloom from July in a hedgerow or at the edge of a wood, the plant can at first glance be taken for an orchid. The flowers are borne on a rectangular stem which can grow to 100cm (39in). The leaves are wider than that of the marsh woundwort and has the appearance of a

Stachys palustris, *marsh woundwort.*

Stachys sylvatica, *hedge woundwort.*

Stachys sylvatica, *hedge woundwort.*

stinging nettle. Hedge woundwort can be used as a wound herb in the same manner as the marsh woundwort (see *Stachys palustris).*

Succisa pratensis

DEVIL'S-BIT SCABIOUS

Both the vegetation and thickened roots of devil's-bit scabious contain the same substances, which include saponin, tannin, bitter substances, and glycoside. The plant is used as a culinary herb with the raw leaves being added to salads or cooked as spinach. However, given the cocktail of substances contained within the plant this does not seem to be without its dangers. Cows suffer inflamed tongues and mouths from eating large quantities of the herb. Devil's-bit scabious is especially used in herbal medicine. Infusions of the dried leaves or root are a proven treatment for coughs and stubborn catarrh. The herb also has a purifying action, is diuretic, a laxative, and gets rid of worms.

Devil's-bit scabious is a typical plant found in moist pasture left for hay, at the edges of woods, and poor grassland. Depending on the position and competition from surrounding plants, it can grow to between 15–100cm (6–40in). The flowers

Succisa pratensis, *devil's-bit scabious.*

are blue, sometimes lilac-pink, white, or yellowish and they appear between June and October.

Symphytum officinale

COMMON COMFREY, KNITBONE

The herbalist Culpeper was delighted with comfrey in 1653. He wrote in *The English Physitian Enlarged* that it is "special good for ruptures and broken bones; yea it is said to be so powerful to consolidate and knit together, that if they be boiled with dissevered pieces of flesh in a pot, it wil join

Symphytum officinale, *common comfrey.*

them together again." Herbal specialist today are a little more modest, although the properties of comfrey are still praised. The plant is unsurpassed as a wound herb. The active substances include allantoin, which is contained in the roots. These are cooked, either fresh or dried, with the decoction being used in a compress. Wounds heal extremely rapid after this treatment, even when suppurating. The herb is frequently incorporated in ointments and creams for bruising, varicose veins, haemorrhoid, rheumatism, and gout. The herb is used in homeopathic medicine for muscle and joint pains.

The young leaves of comfrey are tasty whether eaten raw or cooked. Infusions of the leaves are also used to treat a variety of illnesses. Internal use of the herb is best avoided however now it has been proven that liver damage can occur and risk of tumours is increased by ingesting the herb. Comfrey is also added to shampoos, soaps, and skin creams. *Symphytum officinale* grows wild throughout Europe except Scandinavia and northern Scotland, being found generally in moist grassland and on the banks of streams, rivers, and ponds. This perennial grows to about 100cm (39in) and has purple or occasionally white, yellow, or pink flowers between June and August.

Symphytum x *uplandicum* syn. *S. peregrinum*

RUSSIAN COMFREY

Russian comfrey is a cross between common comfrey and rough comfrey *(Symphytum asperum)*, which originates from the Caucasus mountains. The flowers of Russian comfrey are initially pink but they turn to a delightful blue. The plant can be encountered as an escapee from cultivation but is not native to northern Europe. This perennial contains the same active substances as common comfrey (see *Symphytum officinale).*

Symphytum officinale, *common comfrey.*

Symphytum *x* uplandicum, *Russian comfrey.*

Syzygium aromaticum, *clove.*

Syzygium aromaticum, syn. *Eugenia caryphyllata*

CLOVE

Chewing on a clove helps to ease toothache. The dried flower bud (for that is what a clove is) not only releases its characteristic aroma and taste but also volatile oils and tannin, which lessen the pain. The spicy aroma of clove was highly valued by the Chinese before the birth of Christ. Nobles were only permitted to approach the emperor after they had perfumed their breath with clove.

The distinctive taste and aroma of clove is so strong that very little needs to be used to spice a dish. A few cloves baked with ham or added with onion to cabbage changes the flavour consider-

ably. This is why cloves are also ground for more precise use. Ground clove does not keep very long because the volatile oils quickly evaporate. The volatile oils remain much better in oil of clove. This can be added to food such as pies and tarts and other baking, and to drinks. A taste resembling vanilla is also created by using oil of clove. Oil of clove is also used to clean optical instruments and is often added to cosmetics. Clove is frequently added to pot-pourris and other aromatic decorations, such as a hedgehog made of an orange with cloves stuck in it.

The active constituents in clove have a slightly antiseptic characteristic and also soothe the stomach. Once far more medicinal value was granted the clove. Doctors used to treat plague patients with a clove gripped between their lips.

In the Far East, and in particular Indonesia, aromatic "kretek" cigarettes with clove extract are commonly smoked.

The tree on which cloves grow can develop into a large tree. The trees are cultivated in plantations as bushes of pyramid form but platforms are still needed to pick the flower buds before they open. If the flowers do open, they appear to consist of a tuft of stamens and pistils.

The clove tree only thrives in tropical coastal areas with a very consistent even temperature. Today, most cloves come from Zanzibar and Madagascar.

Syzygium aromaticum, *clove.*

Syzygium aromaticum, *clove.*

Tagetes tenuifolia, *signet marigold.*

Tagetes patula

FRENCH MARIGOLD

If the flower of a French marigold is rubbed over a sheet of paper it will leave a red, orange, or yellow mark, depending on the specific cultivar. The flowers and dead flower heads are used as a dyestuff to produce yellow to red colours.

For those who wish to garden without using chemicals, plagues of insects and weeds can be kept under control by planting French marigolds. The roots of plants that are at least three months old exude a substance that effectively kills pests in the soil. This has been scientifically established. French marigolds can be planted around sensitive plants, such as between tomato plants to ward of white fly.

French marigolds are among the easiest of all annuals to grow from seed. In spite of the name, these plants originated in Central America, and in particular from Mexico. They are not hardy and should be sown out of doors in May or indoors in March. Young plants grown indoors can be planted out in mid May.

 *

Tagetes tenuifolia

SIGNET MARIGOLD

Tagetes tenuifolia is naturally slightly taller than the French marigold, although there are dwarf forms of this species, which is normally up to 80cm (31^1/$_2$in) high. This species does not contain substances shown to ward off pests such as *Tagetes*

Left: Tagetes patula, *French marigold.*

---

minuta, Tagetes erecta, and *Tagetes patula* (see by this last species). The flowers, dead flower-heads, and stems do contain natural dyestuff which can be used for colouring wool and other textiles.

Tanecetum balsamita syn. Balmsamita major

ALECOST, COSTMARY

Alecost is a bitter, astringent herb, that gets rid of worms, and lessens menstruation pains. Pregnant women should not use the herb because of its diuretic functioning. The herb was dedicated to the Virgin Mary.

Today, alecost is principally an ornamental plant with leaves that have a mint-like aroma. The leaves can be added with discretion to meat dishes. Dried leaves emit a balsamic fragrance and are therefore ideal for adding to pomanders and pot-pourris.

Before hops were used to make beer, alecost was added for its bitter taste.

Alecost is a hardy perennial that originates from eastern Europe and Asia. It flowers in late summer,

Tanacetum balsamita, *alecost.*

Tanacetum balsamita, *alecost.*

grows to about 80cm (31¹/₂ in) tall, and is easily grown in almost any soil that is not too wet.

Tanecetum parthenium syn. Matricaria parthenium, Chrysanthemum parthenium

FEVERFEW

Superficially, feverfew resembles alecost but the leaves of feverfew are pinnately lobed, in four segments, with clearly rounded lobes.

This perennial originates from south-eastern parts of Europe but was taken elsewhere long ago as medicinal herb and ornamental plant.

In previous eras, many women died during labour of puerperal fever and other complications. Drinking an infusion of the bitter herb could speed up labour. The herb contains substances that induce contractions and which help the afterbirth to be delivered. Because the herb contains toxic substances, it must never be given in large doses.

It was recently discovered that feverfew was very effective for getting rid of certain types of migraine. The migraine goes away but the patient sometimes gets mouth ulcers in exchange. If the herb is first heated briefly (like stir-frying), this problem is resolved. Pregnant women must not use the herb.

There are numerous cultivars available of feverfew, often with double flowers. This perennial grows trouble-free in any soil, becomes 50cm (20in) tall, and flowers throughout the summer.

Tanacetum parthenium, *feverfew.*

Tanecetum vulgare

TANSY

The unpleasant smell of tansy gave people the idea that insects would find it unpleasant too so that the top shoots were placed where animals with fleas usually lay down, such as dog baskets, and also to ward off midges and moths.

Better known use of tansy was to expel worms and to cause a foetus to abort. Those who used the herb in these ways were risking danger, because the substances contained can be deadly in sufficient quantity.

The tops of flowering plants contain pigments which can be used as dyestuff for colouring wool and other textiles green or brown.

Tanacetum vulgare, *tansy.*

Tanacetum vulgare, *tansy.*

Tansy is a wild flower throughout Europe, growing on waysides, waste places, and hedgebanks where this perennial grows to about 150cm (59in). It blooms in later summer with clusters of button-like yellow flowers.

Taraxacum officinale

DANDELION

The appendage *officinale* in the botanical name of a plant indicates that it is or was regarded as a medicinal herb. This is certainly true of the humble dandelion which can be found widespread colouring meadows yellow in April–May.

The plant is strongly diuretic and has blood purifying properties, which made it popular for spring and autumn "cures". Rheumatism patients are especially helped by the herb which activated the liver and kidneys and expels considerable amounts of urine. Herbal tea made of the dried roots and leaves is also a laxative, stimulates the appetite and is a general tonic. The fresh leaves are rich in vitamin C and can be eaten raw in salads. The bitter taste can be lightened by blanching the leaves first with a pot over the plant before picking them.

The white sap in the flower stem can cause skin irritations, especially in children. Theoretically, the dandelion contains substances which can be toxic in large doses, causing fluctuations in heartbeat.

Taxus baccata

COMMON YEW

Yew grows as a native shrub or tree throughout Europe, except the extreme north. Insignificant summer flowers are succeeded in late summer by "berries" which turn red. In reality, these are seeds surrounded by a fleshy aril which is the only part of the plant which is not poisonous. There are countless cases of cattle and horses that have died from eating yew.

Yet for all this, the yew tree can save life too. The bark of the tree contains taxol, which is particular-

Taraxacum officinale, *dandelion.*

Taxus baccata, *common yew.*

Teucrium chamaedrys, *wall germander.*

ly promising in the treatment of ovarian cancer. Until recently the substance was derived from the Pacific yew *(Taxus brevifolia)* that grows on the west coast of America. So many trees had to be felled to produce the drug that the US government demanded a search for an alternative. The foliage of our common yew was found to be a source and suddenly there was a tremendous demand for the prunings and clippings from yew trees and hedges to supply to pharmaceutical companies. *Taxus baccata* is one of a few fully hardy evergreen trees and shrubs which can withstand severe frosts, although it is best planted where it is sheltered against the cold easterly wind. The shrubs can be readily clipped to form a dense evergreen hedge. Topiary with yew is a true art form, which has a steadily growing band of enthusiasts.

Teucrium chamaedrys, *wall germander.*

Taxus baccata, *common yew.*

Teucrium chamaedrys

WALL GERMANDER

Wall germander has a distinctive fragrance all of its own, which is sometimes used to flavour liqueurs. This use is forbidden in some countries since it was discovered that large quantities of this herb can lead to liver damage.

The herb contains bitter substances including tannin, making it an ideal stomach remedy. It stimulates the appetite, gall bladder, and kidneys, and also aids digestion. An infusion of the dried herb is used as a diuretic and cleansing "cure", with beneficial effects for rheumatism, gout, skin rashes, and bronchitis.

Wall germander grows on limestone rocks and chalk grassland southern and central Europe and is native in the British Isles, where it predominates in the south. This perennial grows to about 40cm (16in), flowering between June to September. It is easily grown in gardens.

☤

Teucrium scorodonia

WOOD SAGE

Wood sage is one of the few plants that rabbits do not eat. It contains an involved cocktail of ingredients, including tannin and other bitter substances, but it is not known why rabbits leave it undisturbed.

Wood sage has a similar beneficial effect on digestion as *Teucrium chamaedrys* (q.v.), but is also considered a wound herb. Rubbing the fresh leaves on a wound causes it to close more quickly and prevents infection. An infusion of the leaves soothes a cough and frees catarrh.

Wood sage is widely found in parts of Europe with a maritime climate but is less common further east. This approximately 50cm (20in) high perennial is found in the British Isles too in woods, hedgerows, hilly areas, stable shingle and sand dunes, preferring acidic soil. The pale greenish-yellow flowers with purple stamens emerge in July and bloom until September.

☤

Teucrium scorodonia, *wood sage.*

Teucrium scorodonia, *wood sage.*

Teucrium x *lucidrys*

GERMANDER

This hybrid results from crossing the wall germander *(Teucrium chamaedrys)* with *Teucrium lucidum* which originates in the Alps and is fully hardy. This hybrid can be readily clipped to form low hedges which are evergreen. Although the plant has the same substances in theory as the parents, little is known of any medicinal use.

✳

Teucrium x lucidrys, *germander.*

Thalictrum aquilegifolium, *French meadow-rue.*

Thalictrum flavum *ssp.* glaucum, *yellow meadow-rue.*

herb contains at least two poisonous alkaloids: berberine and magnoflorine, so that it can only be administered under strict medical supervision. Since there are less dangerous medicines available, the herb has fallen into disuse. The highest concentration of the toxic alkaloids is in the roots.

Wild yellow meadow-rue is taller at 120cm (47in) than the subspecies *Thalictrum flavum* ssp. *glaucum* grown in gardens, which is a 60cm (24in) perennial. This plant originates from the Iberian Peninsula and North Africa, where it also prefers fertile soil.

Thalictrum flavum *ssp.* glaucum, *yellow meadow-rue.*

Thalictrum aquilegifolium

FRENCH MEADOW-RUE

The flowers of French meadow-rue resemble those of the columbine *(Aquilegia)* and indeed the two plants are related: both belonging to the family of Ranunculaceae. The resemblance of the foliage of French meadow-rue to *Aquilegia* is so close that the plant has been dubbed *aquilegifolium*, meaning "leaves of *Aquilegia*".

French meadow-rue can reach heights of 150cm (59in) on fertile, moisture-retaining soil. This perennial grows wild at the edge of bushes and against rocks in hilly and mountainous areas, especially in central and eastern Europe but is found naturalised in a scattering of other places. The plant bears flowers between May and June that consist almost entirely of lilac (occasionally white) stamens, which soon fall.

French meadow-rue has been used as a natural dye for wool and other textiles for a very long time.

Thalictrum flavum ssp. *glaucum* syn. *T. speciosissimum*

YELLOW MEADOW-RUE

In principle, yellow meadow-rue should be able to treat jaundice and epilepsy but unfortunately the

Theobroma cacao, *cocoa.*

Thuja occidentalis *'Danica'*, American arbor-vitae.

Theobroma cacao

CACAO, COCOA, CHOCOLATE TREE

A bar of chocolate can only be called chocolate if it contains at least twenty-five per cent cacao, since this is what chocolate is made from. Efforts are under way from food manufacturers to lower this percentage and the European Community is set to reduce the proportion to the disgust of the cacao producing countries in South America and Africa. Countries such as Ghana and the Ivory Coast are strongly dependent on the export of cacao.

Theobroma cacao originated in South America but the low evergreen tree now grows in other tropical countries. The fragrant white blossoms develop on the trunks and thicker branches where they are eventually replaced by torpedo-shaped fruits of up to 30cm (12in) long. These fruit contain the cacao cocoa beans from which cocoa and chocolate are made.

The fruit and seeds also produce a fatty substance known as cocoa butter which is incorporated in creams and the casing of suppositories. The shells of cocoa beans are now being widely sold as a garden mulch.

Thuja occidentalis

AMERICAN ARBOR-VITAE, EASTERN WHITE CEDAR

This conifer, which forms the boundary between many gardens, contains toxic substances yet can also be used as a medicinal herb. Using an infusion of the young scale-like leaves as a diuretic is best avoided because of the poisonous nature of this tree. Medical science has gained drugs for treating cancer from this cedar and homeopaths prepare tinctures and salves of the herb for external use in treating warts, reactions to injections, after-effects from infections, excessive perspiration, and greasy skin.

The American arbor-vitae or eastern white cedar is an evergreen tree, which grows to a giant of 20m (65ft) in North America but remains much smaller in western Europe. There are also numerous dwarf cultivars available. *Thuja occidentalis* can more easily withstand wet soil than other conifers.

Thymus x citriodorus

LEMON-SCENTED THYME

Lemon scented thyme is a cross between *Thymus pulegioides* (large thyme) and *Thymus vulgaris* (garden thyme), with a noticeable lemon taste and fragrance. Because of its refreshing taste, the leaves of lemon-scented thyme are a popular addition to salads and more especially fruit salads. Many people use too much of the herb, which contains the same substances as garden thyme and can therefore be used for the same purposes as *Thymus vulgaris*. A range of cultivars have been selected from the hybrid with decorative foliage. *Thymus x citriodorus* 'Aureus' has golden yellow leaves, which are at their finest in winter and early spring. During the course of the summer the leaves gradually become greener, eventually losing the yellow colouring. *Thymus x citriodorus* 'Silver Queen' has a more lasting colour with leaf margins that are silver white.

Thymus *x* citriodorus 'Aureus'.

Thymus *x* citriodorus 'Silver Queen'.

Thymus praecox

CREEPING THYME, WILD THYME

Creeping thyme is closely related to common thyme. Both are creeping in habit. *Thymus praecox* is found from the extreme north to the mountains of central Europe. Sub species can be found in different parts of Europe. *Thymus praecox* ssp. *arcticus* is found on Greenland, and Iceland, and in Scandinavia; *Thymus praecox* ssp *praecox* is the central and eastern Europe sub species; and *Thymus praecox* ssp *britannicus* is found

Thymus praecox *ssp.* arcticus, *creeping thyme.*

throughout the British Isles. The plant has suffered from fertiliser and organic manuring in areas of intensive agriculture. The plants flower from late May into July. They contain the same active substances as garden thyme although the aroma is less pronounced so that more needs to be used. For other information, see *Thymus vulgaris*.

🜍 🝆 ⚗ ⚭ ✳

Thymus pulegioides, *large thyme*.

Thymus pulegioides, *large thyme*.

Thymus pulegioides

LARGE THYME, BROAD-LEAVED THYME

Large thyme remains more compact than creeping and garden thyme, grows more vigorously, and bears slightly larger flowers. Otherwise the plant has broadly the same characteristics as the others. Because of this compact growth, large thyme is popular for ornamental gardens, where it is often grown as ground cover or as border plant. Many insects are attracted to large thyme, especially bees, and the honey which they make from the herb has a distinctive aroma of thyme. The heart of great thyme's distribution is in central Europe but with a range that extends to southern Scandinavia, the British Isles, Portugal, and the Balkans, where it is generally found growing on chalk hillsides, but elsewhere on sand. For uses, see *Thymus vulgaris*.

🜍 🝆 ⚗ ⚭ ✳

Thymus serpyllum, *wild thyme*.

Thymus serpyllum

WILD THYME, CREEPING TIME, MOTHER OF THYME

Thymus serpyllum and *Thymus praecox* are difficult to tell apart. This wild thyme is typically northern European, and in contrast with the Mediterranean species of thyme, it prefers lime-free, acidic and sandy soils, and a warm, dry, sunny position, against a slope in dunes, on heaths, or sparse grassland. This wild thyme is lost between higher vegetation and has been threatened by intensive agriculture with its high nitrogen feeds. *Thymus serpyllum* flowers between May and September and is eagerly visited by bees.

This thyme has a noticeable lemon fragrance in spring in particular, so that the leaves are very suitable for adding to fruit salads and certain desserts. The spasm relieving properties of this species are more pronounced than garden thyme and it can be used to ease period pains. Pregnant women are advised to avoid using the herb. For other uses see *Thymus vulgaris*.

🜍 🝆 ⚗ ⚭ ✳

Thymus vulgaris, *garden thyme*.

Thymus vulgaris, *garden thyme.*

Thymus vulgaris

GARDEN THYME, COMMON THYME

Mildews and bacteria do not get a look in with garden thyme. It is little wonder then that the ancient Egyptians used the herb when they mummified their Pharoahs, because thyme helps to preserve them. The leaves of thyme contain between one and three per cent volatile oils which create the aromatic scent of the plant. The taste is so sharp, that only small quantities are needed. The herb has a broad range of culinary uses in soups, sauces, meat, poultry, game, and also egg dishes, vegetables, and pulses. Thyme is especially useful with less easily digested foods because it aids digestion and prevents wind. Thyme is sometimes used diluted in oil or vinegar to prevent using too much.

Herbal tea of thyme aid digestion, prevents and stops diarrhoea, calms the stomach, is antiseptic, treats mouth and throat infections, eases coughs, asthma, and bronchitis. A bath with thyme oil added can also be used for these complaints and for rheumatism, or general debility.

Thyme oil is also used in some cosmetics and is often a constituent of massage oils for stomach and respiratory disorders, or nervous headache. Preg-

nantwomen should only used thyme in moderation.

Thymus vulgaris originates from the Mediterranean region. This perennial is often cultivated as an annual because it quickly becomes woody, although this can be prevented by regularly cutting the 20–30cm (8–12in) high shrub back hard after flowering. Plant garden thyme in a sunny position. The plant will not survive hard winters in wet soil but can withstand frosts of minus 15°C (5°F) or lower in dry soil.

Tilia x *europaea*

COMMON LIME

At the height of mid-summer you can prepare yourself for winter ailments. The blossoms of lime trees spread their delightful fragrance in June–July. This is the time to pick the blossom, complete with the elongated calyx. Store them dry, in an airtight container, then in winter they can be used to make herbal tea which can both prevent and cure colds. Lime blossom also increases perspiration, reduces fevers, and is also diuretic.

Common lime is a cross between *Tilia cordata* (small-leaved lime) and *Tilia platyphyllos* (broad-leaved lime). All three trees have blossom which spreads a delightful fragrance, and which can be used to make a delicious and healthy herbal tea.

Tiarella cordifolia 'Oakleaf'

FOAM FLOWER

The foam flower is a popular garden plant which can be found in most garden centres. Clusters of white to pink flowers are borne on stems above the

Tilea x europaea, *common lime.*

292

Tiarella cordifolia *'Oakleaf', foam flower.*

attractive foliage in May. This perennial grows wild in fertile moist woodland soil in eastern parts of North America and spreads by means of underground runners.

An infusion of the leaves acts as a tonic, is diuretic, stimulates liver function, and aids digestion. The herb is especially used to treat bladder stones.

Tragopogon porrifolius

SALSIFY

The long tap root of salsify can be used in the same way as scorzonera or black salsify (see *Scorzonera hispanica*). The young flower stems can be picked before flowering, sliced in half lengthways, and cooked. They taste similar to asparagus.

Salsify is a biennial to perennial from southern Europe which has become naturalised in northern Europe. The plant can be found at scattered locations throughout the British Isles, especially southern England. The first purple flowers appear on stems of 100cm (39in) in June.

Salsify is sown in March in order to harvest the long, yellowish roots that autumn. These can be lifted and stored for winter or remain in the soil, for the plant is fully hardy.

Tragopogon porrifolius, *salsify.*

Tragopogon pratensis, *goat's beard.*

Tragopogon pratensis

GOAT'S BEARD

The interest in goat's beard, just as with scorzonera and salsify, is in the long edible tap root of the plant. For preparation see *Tragopogon porrifolius*. The medicinal interest is in the young foliage which is pressed for the juice to use as a medicine for excessive gall bladder functioning.

Goat's beard grows virtually everywhere in Europe on very varied sites from grassy to rocky, in meadows, embankments, and beside railway lines. This perennial to perennial has flowers of 5cm (2in) diameter in May to July which form impressive seed plumes. For cultivation, see *Tragopogon porrifolius*.

Trifolium pratense

RED CLOVER, PURPLE CLOVER

If you suck the flower of red clover you can enjoy the nectar which also attracts bees to the flower. Red clover was once an important fodder crop but intensive modern agriculture has pushed clover aside with the other wild flowers. Red clover is still widely found though in moist waysides and also in

Trifolium pratense, *red clover.*

meadows left for hay. This perennial has a long tap root and flowers throughout the summer.

An infusion of the dried flowers is antiseptic and used externally for treating wounds and burns, or internally for coughs, sore throat, and diarrhoea. Clover tea is considered a good purifier of the blood.

The flowers can be used as a yellow to brown dyestuff for colouring wool and other textiles.

Trifolium repens syn. *Amoria repens*

WHITE CLOVER

Grass growing close to clover is far greener than elsewhere because the plant absorbs nitrogen from the air and releases it for the grass roots. It is therefore no surprise that white clover has been grown as green manure for a long time. The plant is widely found in mown and grazed grasslands, and often appears in lawns. The summer-flowering plant disappears in longer grass.

White clover contains the same substances as red clover and can be used medicinally in the same way as *Trifolium pratense* (q.v.). What is more, the Herb is used to treat rheumatism.

Trifolium repens, *white clover.*

Trigonella foenicum-graecum, *fenugreek*.

Tropaeolum majus, *garden nasturtium*.

Trigonella foenicum-graecum

FENUGREEK

A literal translation of *foenicum-graecum* would be "Greek hay". The plant is indeed an important form of fodder in southern parts of Europe. The dried seeds are ground and used as a culinary herb in southern and eastern Europe. It has a powerful taste so has to be used sparingly. The germinated seed and cooked leaves are milder in taste and can be used in larger quantity.

Fenugreek is an ancient medicinal herb, the use of which spread from Asia Minor into China, southwards to North Africa, and westwards throughout Europe, although its use is less common in northern Europe. This has recently changed as a result of the discovery that the herb reduces the blood sugar level and claims by some that it can be used to treat cancer. The herb is especially used in the orient and North Africa for impotence and problem periods. Fenugreek helps lactation for nursing mothers but they must not take it until after the birth. A compress with a puree of ground fenugreek seeds can be placed on boils to heal them.

Fenugreek is an annual plant that grows to about 50cm (20in) high. The precise origin is unknown but it grows wild throughout southern Europe. The unimposing flowers appear from April to June and are followed by 10cm (4in) long seed pods.

Tropaeolum majus

GARDEN NASTURTIUM, INDIAN CRESS

Nasturtium leaves have a bitter taste and they are sometimes added to salads, and soft-cheese to provide a spicy flavour. The young tender leaves are best to pick and should be used in moderation to avoid irritating the stomach and gut. The flowers have a mild taste and are an ideal edible garnish.

They can also be preserved in vinegar to retain their colour, and the seeds can be prepared and eaten in the same way as capers.

Tropaeolum majus originates from the Andes mountains in Colombia, Ecuador, Peru, and Bolivia, where it has long been used as a wound herb. The herb closes the wound and prevents it becoming infected.

Because of the bactericidal properties of this herb, it is also taken for internal infections, especially those of the urinary tract and bladder. The plant also raises the general resistance of the body to disease.

The plant is well-known in Europe as an attractive annual for gardens. There are numerous different forms from climbing to ground cover. Garden nasturtiums flower from June until the first frost, when the plant instantly turns into pulp. The seeds that have been dropped will readily germinate after a dry winter.

Tropaeolum majus, *garden nasturtium*.

U-Z

Urtica dioica, *stinging nettle*.

Urtica dioica

COMMON NETTLE, STINGING NETTLE

Stinging nettles have tough, thin hollow tubes in their leaves and stems containing formic acid. When the plant is touched, the tubes are broken, releasing the formic acid onto the skin, causing at first a strong burning feeling, followed by swelling, a rash, and itching. The concentration of formic acid is especially strong in early spring.

This is just the time when the tender young leaves are harvested as vegetables, for cooking or making nettle soup and nettle tea. Stinging nettles also contain high concentrations of chlorophyll, vitamins A, B, and C, and minerals (particularly calcium and iron). The herb is a general tonic for the entire body and especially beneficial for combating anaemia. Nettle tea is often drunk as part of a spring cleansing "cure" for the body, especially by those who suffer from rheumatism and gout. In serious

Left: Verbascum phlomoides, *orange mullein.*

cases, fresh leaves are placed on the painful places. A decoction of nettle is useful for both dandruff and hair loss. Nettles are also commercially exploited for their chlorophyll, that is used as a colouring in foods and medicines. It is recognised for this purpose by the European Community and indicated on packing by the E number E140. Wherever the common nettle grows, the soil is rich in minerals. This perennial can claim large areas at the edges of woods and other places that are in partial shade, spreading itself by underground runners. The plant is 50–150cm (20–59in) high. The plant is particularly abundant on lime-rich soil, or where stable litter has rotted down. The common nettle is regarded as a troublesome weed yet it is also one of the most important food plants for the most beautiful of butterflies such as the red admiral, tortoiseshell, and peacock.

  ✳

Urtica urens

SMALL NETTLE

The small nettle grows to about 50cm (20in) high. It probably originates from southern Europe but is now a general weed throughout parts of Europe with a moderate climate. The plant is an annual

Urtica urens, *small nettle.*

Vaccinium vitis-idaea, *cowberry.*

Vaccinium vitis-idaea, *cowberry.*

Valeriana officinalis, *common valerian.*

but remains green in summer and winter. Several generations of the plant are formed each year. The small nettle is especially prevalent in arable land and vegetable gardens, where manure is added to the soil. This nettle is very venomous, containing the same substances as the common nettle. For uses, see *Urtica dioica.*

Vaccinium vitis-idaea

COWBERRY

Cowberry grows as a low shrub, often creeping, throughout northern Europe and in the mountains of central Europe. The plant prefers acid soil and is found on heaths, moorlands, and in woods. The blossoms are followed by small, bright-red berries which can be used to make conserves but are not as tasty or as widespread in the British Isles as the bilberry *Vaccinium myrtillus.* The cowberry does, however, contain arbutin, a urinary antiseptic, which also lowers blood-sugar levels, which is not found in the bilberry. Infusions of the dried leaves of cowberry are a proven remedy for urinary disorders. It is beneficial with bladder infections and kidney stones although high doses of the leaves can cause poisoning.

Valeriana officinalis

COMMON VALERIAN, GARDEN HELIOTROPE

Valerian is renowned for its calming effect although it is not known which substance is responsible. It is considered that a combination of volatile oils or iridoids known as "valepotriates" is responsible. Sceptics think the alcohol in which valerian root is dissolved has a role to play. Valerian is not only used as a tincture though. Herbal valerian tea is also successful in overcoming sleeplessness. Such infusions also help to loosen catarrh and are prescribed for coughs.

Valerian must not be taken continuously over a period of time in high doses because it can become addictive and also causes headaches and palpitations for some people. Those who are sensitive to it are better advised to take homeopathic preparations.

Oil of valerian is added to some perfumes and is also used as flavouring in many sweet dishes and drinks. *Valeriana officinalis* is a widespread plant of damp meadows throughout Europe and is often on banks beside freshwater ponds and streams. The many branched roots act as natural bank protection. The tight, compact roots make it difficult to harvest so the plant is cultivated for medicinal use, This perennial grows 50–150cm (20–59in) high and has pale pink or white flowerheads between June and August.

Vanilla planifolia

VANILLA

Vanilla pods are in reality the elongated fruits of the orchid *Vanilla planifolia*. These orchids root in the soil but climb with long stems, densely covered with foliage, into trees in Central America. The pale yellow-green flowers are of little decorative value but their fragrance is overwhelming. After pollination, long pods of 15–20cm (6–8in) develop. These turn black during drying and fermentation. Inside the pods there is an aromatic jelly with seeds. By cooking the vanilla pods during preparation of desserts, the characteristic vanilla flavour is released. This is also synthetically made these days but vanilla is still commercially cultivated in many tropical countries.

Veratrum album

FALSE HELLEBORE, WHITE HELLEBORE

The dried root of false hellebore was once ground into powder to make one of the most important cleansing herbs, used as snuff. Small amounts of the powder were sniffed up the nostrils; too much could cause heavy nose bleeds. It became apparent to people that the plant was poisonous and the entire plant, but especially the roots, contain very toxic alkaloids, which are still dangerous in the

Valeriana officinalis, *common valerian.*

Vanilla planifolia, *vanilla pods.*

dried herb. If the herb is found in hay, it can kill cattle. The dried roots were once important medicinally for reducing high blood pressure. The herb has a cleansing action and was used for oedema, rheumatism, asthma, psoriasis, and depression. Salves from the roots of the close American relative *(Veratrum viride)* were incorporated in ointments and tinctures for nerve pains. In homeopathy, false hellebore is used for blood pressure that is too low rather than too high, and also for depression, bronchitis, sciatica, diarrhoea, and nerve pains.

Veratrum album grows in the mountains of northern Scandinavia, central, and southern Europe, and adjoining parts of Asia as far as Siberia, and also the mountains of North Africa. In these areas, the powdered root is used as an insecticide. The perennials often grow in mountainous terrain, near becks and mountain lakes. The plant can also be cultivated in gardens if planted in moisture-retaining soil but it takes eight to ten years before a seed matures into a flowering plant. Quicker results can be achieved by taking root cuttings. Flowering plants reach 50–150cm (20–59in) high and bear spikes of white flowers with green markings.

⚕ ✳

Veratrum album, *false hellebore.*

Veratrum album, *false hellebore.*

Veratrum nigrum.

Veratrum nigrum.

Veratrum nigrum

When not flowering, *Veratrum nigrum* closely resembles false hellebore *(Veratrum album)*. Once the plant starts to flower after eight to ten years, the flowers of *Veratrum nigrum* prove to be dark purple. The flowers exude a strong smell of rotting fruit. Beetles and flies come from far and wide to the plant, ensuring its pollination.

Veratrum nigrum generally grows somewhat higher up the mountains than *Veratrum album* and is less dependent on water. This plant does not attract attention in the partial shade at the edge of a wood or a clearings in the middle of summer but continues growing into a stately plant of 150cm (59in). It grows wild in a ring of territory of the central massif of France eastwards to eastern Asia. The plant can be grown as a fully hardy perennial in northern Europe. Ensure it has fertile, moisture-retaining soil.

The herb contains the same toxic alkaloids as false hellebore and can be used for the same purposes (see *Veratrum album).*

♄ *

Verbascum nigrum

DARK MULLEIN

The various type of mullein are difficult to differentiate from each other, especially since the plants readily cross with each other in gardens to form many hybrids. Dark mullein is by contrast easily recognised by the striking purple hairs on the stamens.

This plant flowers in late summer, from June to September. The plant is slender in appearance and grows to between 50–150cm (20–59in) tall. It is always found in the wild in open landscape on sandy or lime-rich soil. Dark mullein grows throughout Europe to southern Scandinavia, and is locally common in the Channel Islands, central and southern Britain.

The leaves of dark mullein have virtually no hairs so that no fibres can be harvested from them but other uses are the same as orange mullein (see *Verbascum phlomoides).*

♄

Verbascum phlomoides

ORANGE MULLEIN

Orange mullein is often included in herbal tea cough and bronchitis remedies.

301

Verbascum nigrum, *dark mullein.*

Verbascum phlomoides, *orange mullein.*

Verbascum phlomoides, *orange mullein.*

The plants contain saponin, which acts as an expectorant and other substances that are bactericidal. Consequently, the herb is used to treat throat infections, other bronchial ailments, tonsillitis, and infections of the linings of the stomach and intestines. The flowers can be used to cleanse the kidneys of excessive uric acid and are diuretic. Only the yellow petals are picked and dried. They can easily be removed from the green calyx.

Oil from the petals can be used to cleanse wounds, stem infections, and soothe nerve pains. The calming action of the oil is beneficial for treatment of both sinus and earache.

Verbascum is prescribed in homeopathy for the previously mentioned ailments and also for children who continue to wet their beds when they grow older.

The entire plant can be used to form a dyestuff for colouring wool and other textiles yellow, orange, or brown. The leaves have also been smoked in the past as a surrogate for tobacco, while the woolly hairs were combed to make wicks for oil lamps. The leaves contain substances which prevent fish breathing through their gills, thus driving them to the surface. This property was once used throughout southern Europe in particular as a way of catching fish in lakes and ponds.

Verbascum phlomoides is a native wild flower of central, eastern, and southern Europe, but has become naturalised in pockets in the British Isles after introduction. The biennial flowers from late June to August and reaches 200cm (79in) in height.

Verbascum speciosum

HUNGARIAN MULLEIN

The botanical name of this introduced garden species of mullein is sometimes used as a catch-all name for all the differing cultivars and hybrids which have been developed and arisen spontaneously. These plants all have precisely the same characteristics as herbs as the other mulleins and contain the same chemical substances. For uses, see *Verbascum phlomoides*.

Verbascum thapsus

GREAT MULLEIN, AARON'S ROD

Great mullein, orange mullein, and dense-flowered mullein readily cross with each other. This pre-

Verbascum speciosum, *Hungarian mullein.*

Verbascum speciosum, *Hungarian mullein.*

sents no problems in their use because they all have the same properties. For uses see *Verbascum phlomoides)*. Dense-flowered mullein *(Verbascum densiflorum)* has flowers of 4cm (1¹/₂in) diameter, which are twice the size of those of great mullein and orange mullein. Great mullein originates in southern parts of Europe but has spread throughout most of the moderate climate zone of Europe. It is often found alongside railway lines but is not an adventitious plant spread by train to new areas, such as a seed transported with agricul-

Verbascum thapsus, *great mullein.*

Verbascum thapsus, *great mullein.*

Verbena hastata, *blue vervain.*

tural products. The plant finds its needs fulfilled by railway embankments: plenty of sun, warmth, and well-drained soil. It grows in similar situations elsewhere, such as dunes, and chalky soil near the coast.

This biennial reaches about 200cm (79in) high but only 100cm (39in) on dry dunes (as illustrated). On more fertile soil, the plant makes many more shoots. It flowers from late May to early September.

Verbena hastata, *blue vervain.*

Verbena hastata syn. *Glandularia hastata*

BLUE VERVAIN

This North American plant grows in swampy woods and the moist banks of rivers and lakes. It can be cultivated easily in Europe in fertile moisture-retaining soil. Because of its decorative value, blue vervain is more popular for gardens than our native vervain *(Verbena officinalis).* This perennial grows to about 150cm (59in) high and flowers in late summer.

The blue vervain was once used as a cold remedy and is still utilised for liver problems and period pains, although rarely. Pregnant women should avoid use of the herb.

Verbena officinalis syn. *Glandularia officinalis*

VERVAIN

A number of cultures regard vervain as a magical plant. The herb is used to purify altars for rituals and in the not so far distant past men and women secretively placed the herb in the drink of those

Verbena officinalis, *vervain.*

Verbena officinalis, *vervain.*

Veronica officinalis, *common speedwell.*

Courtesy The Kruidenhof, Buitenpost.

Veronica officinalis

COMMON SPEEDWELL, HEATH SPEEDWELL, FLUELLEN

Infections of the mouth or throat, coughs, colds, stomach and liver complaints, rheumatism, gout, inflamed kidneys, and diarrhoea should according to folk legend all be eased by drinking an infusion of dried common speedwell. Today this is seriously questioned but even if the herb does not have healing properties, it makes a tasty herbal tea. Once speedwell was used instead of real tea.

Common speedwell is part of our native flora and grows happily in moist places but is very much appreciated too in the ornamental garden. Successions of new blue flowers bloom on the plant in June, July, and August.

Veronicastrum virginicum syn. Veronica virginica, Leptandra virginica

CULVER'S ROOT, BLACKROOT

With its regularly-spaced leaves along its stem and white to blue flower racemes which reach to 200cm (79in) high, culver's root is a highly regarded and popular garden plant. It originates from eastern parts of North America, where is grows wild in moist meadows, edges of woods, and forests. This hardy plant does well in Europe in any soil that is not too dry.

The fresh roots of the plant can be used as medicine for stimulating liver function, dissipating excessive gall fluid, and settling upset stomachs. The bulbs are best avoid though because they are a powerful laxative and in quantity induce vomiting.

they loved. The herb was deemed to arouse the ardour. In this day and age, no-one can understand what all the fuss was about. Now, the herb is almost exclusively used to aid digestion, for treating stomach upsets and diarrhoea. An infusion of the herb is used for these purposes. This perennial of about 60cm (24in) high grows throughout Europe, especially in dry grassland in the east, centre and south. It is locally common in southern Britain but rarer elsewhere in the British Isles. Small pale lilac, pink, or white flower spikes appear from June.

Veronicastrum virginicum, *culver's root.*

Viburnum opulus, *guelder rose.*

Viburnum opulus

GUELDER ROSE, CRAMBARK

Many regard the guelder rose as one of our most attractive native shrubs. Clusters of creamy white florets appear in late spring and are succeeded by reddish-orange berries. The leaves have superb autumn colouring. The shrub grows to about 4m (13ft) high with a similar spread.

The berries remain on the shrub in winter because the birds are not fond of them, so that they do not eat them until late winter when other sources of food are scarce. The berries are poisonous for humans when raw, causing inflammation of the stomach and intestines but are edible once cooked or made into jam. The bark is also toxic but can be used in small doses to induce labour. Muscular pains cause by tension and constipation can both be relieved by the bark, together with period pains. Such medicines are usually not suitable for pregnant women because they can induce premature labour. In the case of guelder rose, it is used to prevent miscarriages but because of its high toxicity, the herb should only be taken strictly under medical supervision.

Vinca major

GREATER PERIWINKLE

Greater periwinkle is the larger sister of the lesser periwinkle *(Vinca minor)*. This native plant grows as a creeper and is evergreen. It is one of the most useful ground cover plants for shade. The blue flowers sometimes emerge in February and the flowering reduces over the course of the summer. The two periwinkles closely resemble each other except in their respective sizes. Greater periwinkle is a popular garden plant.

Both plants were deemed to be poisonous to humans but tests have shown this fear to be misplaced. The substances in the plant are incorporated in drugs for dilating arteries and medicines for treating leukaemia. In homeopathic medicine, greater periwinkle is prescribed to improve the supply of blood to the brain to treat headaches, dizziness, and loss of memory.

Vinca major, *greater periwinkle.*

Dog-strangling vine is a native plant of southern Europe where the perennial grows no taller than 100cm (39in). The white flowers in summer are followed by very elongated fruit pods containing the seeds.

℞

Viola tricolor

HEARTSEASE, WILD PANSY, LOVE-IN-IDLENESS

Those who sow wild pansy seeds or plant them in their garden will probably see the annual or occasional perennial plant every year from then on. The seeds of heartsease or wild pansy germinate in gravel, between paving slabs, and in sandy places. This wild plant grows in a variety of habitat throughout Europe, depending on the sub species. Garden varieties are invariably hybrids resulting from crossing with related species and bear a variety of type names. These generally contain the same active substances as the wild pansy. Heartsease flower mainly in summer but start early (in March) and continue deep into autumn.

Heartsease has developed a reputation as a treatment for nappy rash, infantile eczema, and other skin complaints. It is incorporated in creams and salves and decoctions of the herb have a purifying

Viola tricolour, *heartsease or wild pansy.*

Vincetoxicum nigrum

DOG-STRANGLING VINE

Vince means "conquering" and *toxicum* is "poison" or "toxin". *Vincetoxicum nigrum* was once used as an antidote for snake bite although the use of this herb was itself not without danger. Every part of the plant is poisonous and may therefore only be used under professional supervision. The herb is diuretic and its root induces vomiting. The same is true of *Vincetoxicum hirundaria*, the related species.

Vincetoxicum nigrum, *dog-strangling vine.*

Hybrid of Viola tricolour, *garden pansy.*

Viscum album, *mistletoe.*

action. Such herbal tea is healthy for small children. Homeopathic uses of the herb are very similar.

Viscum album

MISTLETOE

Mistletoe roots itself in the branches of trees where it taps into the sap of its host. The plant is therefore a parasite, deriving its nutrition from another plant. Mistletoe has a marked preference for trees of the family of Rosaceae, such as fruit trees, or may, but can also be found on limes, willows, and poplars. Mistletoe can be found throughout Europe except the extreme north and is common in England and Wales south of Yorkshire. Birds eagerly eat the

Viscum album, *mistletoe.*

Vitis vinifera, *grape vine.*

Zingiber officinale, *ginger.*

white berries with their sticky contents. These are poisonous for humans, as is the foliage.

Mistletoe has special powers. The leaves provide medicine for lowering blood pressure, preventing thrombosis of the arteries, and strengthening the heart. The plant also offers new promise in the form of cancer therapy, particularly lung and ovarian cancer.

Vitis vinifera

GRAPE VINE

Drinking a glass of wine per day reduces the risk of heart disease and thrombosis. Many a happy imbiber eagerly awaited the results of this research and now pops the cork with even greater pleasure. In Denmark this announcement was even followed by the introduction of a wine pill for those who wanted the health benefits without alcohol.

The leaves of the vine and the grapes were once used as medicinal herbs for treating high blood-pressure and obesity but these uses have gradually become less common. The culinary use of the vine is not restricted to the ripe grape but also includes currants, raisins, and sultanas, with the young leaves being stuffed with rice or minced meat to make *dolmades*, a tasty snack found mainly in southern European countries. Residues from wine making include wine vinegar, and *marc*, and the sediment from barrels forms cream of tartar or potassium bitartrate, used in baking powder and other economic uses. It is an important adjunct to dying of fabrics.

Grape vines have been cultivated for thousands of years, having been grown by the ancient Egyptians. The plant is a climber but is pruned and trained in commercial vineyards to keep it low. The old stems become woody. Many different cultivated forms of the grape vine have been developed by selection over the thousands of years in cultivation, each with its own characteristics, such as flavour, vigour, and resistance to disease.

Zingiber officinale

GINGER

Root ginger is candied root of the ginger plant which grows to about 150cm (59in). The plant grows wild in South-East Asia but is now cultivated in other parts of the world with a hot climate. The roots or rhizomes continually make new side-shoots from which new stems emerge with their reed-like foliage. When the foliage dies back, the roots are harvested, with the newer rhizomes providing the best ginger. The quality is dependent on both the cultivar and method of cultivation.

Ginger imparts its hot, pungent, and sweet taste to oriental cooking and can be eaten on its own with a chunk of cheese. Ground ginger is added to fish dishes, meat, sauces, soups, and also to baked foods, and drinks, including liqueurs. The fragrant volatile oils are also added to perfumes.

Ginger, known as *jiang* is very important in Chinese herbal medicine. Europeans find it an excellent stimulant for the appetite, an aid to digestion, and beneficial for stomach disorders. Even stomach ulcers respond to treatment with ginger but only under medical supervision because of possible harmful side-effects. In homeopathic medicine ginger is prescribed for bronchial asthma. The

Zinnia angustifolia, *Mexican zinnia.*

dried root also provides a basis for capsules for travel sickness and queasiness.

Zinnia angustifolia syn. *Z. haageana, Z. mexicana*

MEXICAN ZINNIA

The Mexican zinnia forms large clumps of green to a maximum of 50cm (20in) high from which countless yellow-orange flowers emerge from July onwards. The centre of each flower protrudes and is darker in colour. The flowers can be used as a yellow, orange, or red dyestuff for colouring wool and other textiles. The flowers are picked immediately after flowering for immediate use because when dried, they lose their colour. Removing spent flowers stimulates the plant to produce new ones. *Zinnia angustifolia* is a native annual plant of Mexico and the southern states of USA. It can withstand very little frost. Sow under cover in

March or in position in May. *Zinnia angustifolia* as a garden plant is known as *Zinnia haagena*.

Zinnia elegans

ZINNIA

The best-known garden zinnias are the cultivated varieties of *Zinnia elegans*. This annual plant grows to 20–70cm (8–27$^1/_2$in) high, depending on the cultivar. The taller varieties with their dahlia-like flowers are especially suitable for use as dyestuff. The flowering colour varies widely from cream, through yellow, orange, and red, to purple. This makes no difference to the outcome of the dye which always produces warm yellow shades through to red.

The flowers can be picked immediately after flowering and should be used as dye immediately because they lose the colour when dried. Removing the spent flowers stimulates the plant to produce new flowers.

Zinnia elegans also originates from Mexico and can withstand virtually no frost. Sow seed under cover in March or outside in position in May.

Zinnia elegans, *zinnia.*

Herb gardens to visit

All botanical gardens are worth visiting for herbs. The gardens listed below all have sections specialising in herbs and plants of economic value. The plant collections feature specimens from many parts of the world. *Plants may be available for sale at those gardens indicated.

Acorn Bank Garden
Penrith, Cumbria *
017683 61893
(walled herb garden)

Barnsley House
Barnsley, Gloucestershire *
01285 740281
(knot garden, potager)

Barwinnock Herbs
Barrhill, Ayrshire, Scotland *
01465 821338

Congham Hall Hotel
Grimston, Norfolk *
01485 600250
(culinary and medicinal herbs)

A herb garden.

The Cottage Herbery
The Mill House, Boraston,
Nr. Tenbury Wells, Worcestershire *
01584 781575

Geffrye Museum
Kingsland Road, London E2
0171 739 9893
(traditional domestic herbs)

Hardwick Hall
Chesterfield, Derbyshire *
01246 850430
(Herb garden in large formal garden)

Harlow Carr Botanical Garden
Harrogate, Yorkshire *
01423 565418
(herb garden, national *Rheum* collection)

Hatfield House
Hatfield, Hertfordshire
01707 262823
(knot gardens, scented gardens)

The Herb Farm
Reading, Berkshire
0118 972 4220
(medicinal and pot-pourri)

Hexham Herbs
Hexham Northumberland
01434 681483
(Roman garden, national *Thymus* and *Origanum* collections)

Hill Farm Herbs
Brigstock, Northamptonshire *
01536 373694
(herbs)

Hollington Nurseries
Newbury, Berkshire *
01635 253908
(herb gardens and plant nursery)

Iden Croft Herbs
Staplehurst, Kent *
01580 891432, (herb gardens, garden for disabled, national *Origanum* and *Mentha* collection)

Norfolk Lavender
King's Lynn, Norfolk *
01485 570384
(national *Lavendula* collection)

The Queen's Garden
Royal Botanic Garden, Kew, Surrey
(17th-century herbs)

The Royal Horticultural Society's Garden
Wisley, Surrey
(formal herb garden)

Sissinghurst Castle
Cranbrook, Kent *
(herb garden, thyme lawn)

Index

Aaron's rod	303
absinthe	53
Acanthus balcanicus	19
Acanthus hungaricus	19
Acanthus longifolius	19
Acanthus mollis	19
Acanthus mollis 'Latifolius'	19
Acanthus spinosus	20
Achillea millefolium	20
Achillea ptarmica	21
Achillea ptarmica 'Schneeball'	22
Achillea ptarmica 'Boule de Neige'	22
Achillea ptarmica 'Perry's White'	22
Achillea ptarmica 'Snowball'	22
Achillea ptarmica 'The Pearl'	22
Achillea ptarmica 'The Pearl'	22
Aconitum lycoctonum	23
Aconitum lycoctonum ssp vulparia	23
Aconitum napellus	22
Acorus calamus	23
Actaea erythrocarpa	24
Actaea nigra	25
Actaea rubra	24
Actaea spicata	25
Actaea spicata var. rubra	25
Adonis aestivalis	25
Adonis vernalis	25
Aegopodium podagraria	25
Aegopodium podagraria	26
Aegopodium podagraria 'Variegatum'	26
Aesculus hippocastanum	26
Agastache anethiodora	27
Agastache foeniculum	21
Agastache rugosa	28
Agastache urticifolia	28
Agave altissima	28
Agave americana	28-29
Agave americana 'Marginata'	29
Agave americana 'Medio Picta'	29
Agave americana 'Striata'	29
Agave americana 'Variegata'	29
Agrimonia eupatoria	29
agrimony	29
Agrostemma githago	30
Ajuga reptans	30
Alcea rosea	31
Alcea rosea 'Nigra'	31
Alchemilla conjuncta	32
Alchemilla mollis	33
Alchemilla vulgaris	33
Alchemilla xanthoclora	33
alder buckthorn	246
alecost	283
alehoof	139
alfalfa	183
Alisma plantago-aquatica	33
alkanet	43
Alliaria petiolata	34
Allium cepa	34
Allium cepa 'Proliferum'	35
Allium fistulosum	35
Allium porum	36
Allium sativum	36
Allium schoenoprasum	37
Allium schoenoprasum 'Album'	38
Allium sibiricum	37
Allium tuberosum	38
Allium ursinum	39
almond	240
aloe	40
Aloe vera	40
Aloysia citriodora	40
Aloysia triphylla	40
alpenrose	247
Althaea officinalis	40
Althaea rosea	31
alum root	135
Amaranthus caudatus	41
ambergris	86
American ipecac	137
American mandrake	234
Amoria repens	294
Anagallis arvensis ssp. arvensis	42
Ananas comosus	42
Anchusa officinalis	43
Anemone pulsillata	242
Anethum graveolens	43
angel's trumpets	68
angelica	44
Angelica archangelica	44
Angelica sylvestris	44
aniseed	229
anisette	53
Antennaria dioica	45
Anthemis nobilis	45
Anthemis tinctoria	45
Anthemis tinctoria 'Wargrave'	45
Anthriscus cerefolium	46
Anthriscus sylvestris	46
Anthyllis vulneraria	47
Apium graveolens	47
Apium graveolens var. dulce	47
Apium graveolens var. rapaceum	47
Apium graveolens var. secalinum	47

Achillea ptarmica *'Sneezewort'*

Angelica archangelica, *angelica*

Apocynum cannabinum	48
apple	181
applemint	191
Aquilegia canadensis	48
Aquilegia vulgaris	48
Arabian jasmine	161
arbor-vitae, American	290
archangel	163
archangel, yellow	163
Arctium lappa	49
Arctium minus	50
Arctium minus ssp pubens	49
aril	196
Arisaema triphyllum	50
Aristolochia clematitis	51
Armoracia rusticana	51
arnica	52
Arnica chamissonis	52
Arnica montana	52
aromatic herbs	9
aromatic oil burners	9
aromatic oils	9
Artemisia abrotanum	53
Artemisia absinthium	53
Artemisia annua	54
Artemisia dracunculus	55
Artemisia dracunculus ssp. dracunuloides	55
Artemisia dracunculus ssp. sativa	55
Artemisia ludoviciana	55
Artemisia vulgaris	55
artichoke, globe	102
arum	56
Arum italicum	56
Arum maculatum	56
asarabacca	57
Asarum europaeum	57
Asclepia curassavica	57
Asclepia incarnata	57
Asclepia syriaca	58
Asclepia tuberosa	58
ash, common	128
asparagin	59
asparagus	59
Asparagus officinalis	59
Asparagus officinalis ssp. officinalis	59
asparagus, allergic rash	59
Asperula odorata	132
Asperula tinctoria	59
Aspidium filix-mas	113
Asplenium scolopendrium	59
asthma weed	174
Atriplex hortensis	60
Atriplex hortensis var. rubra	60
Atropa belladonna	60
aubergine	275
autumn crocus	92
Avena sativa	61
avens	137
avens, water	136
avens, wood	137

Anethum graveolens, *dill*

De Kruidhof, Buitenpost

balloonflower	233
Ballota nigra ssp. foetida	62
balsamita major	283
baneberry, red	24
Baptisia australis	62
Baptisia tinctoria	63
Barbados aloe	40
Barbarea vulgaris	63
barberry, common	64
basil	205
basil, aniseed	206
basil, lemon	206
bastard balm	185
bay	164
bay laurel	164
bear's foot	146
bedstraw, great hedge	132
bedstraw, lady's	133
bedstraw, northern	131
bee balm	193
beefsteak plant	224
beggar's buttons	49
beggar's herb	89
bellbine	73
Bellis perennis	64
bellpepper	76
Berberis vulgaris	64
bergamot	193
Betonica officinale	278
betony	278
Betula	65
bilberry	298
birch	65
birch sap	65
bird's-foot-trefoil, common	176
birthwort	51
bishopswort	278
bistort, common	225
bitter almond	240
bittersweet	275
black cohosh	86
black Indian hemp	48
black root	305
black snakeroot	86
blackberry	252
black-tang	128
blackthorn	241
bladderwrack	128
blessed thistle	89
Bocconia cordata	179
bog asphodel	198
bog myrtle	195
bogbean	192

borage	66
Borago officinalis	66
Botrychium lunaria	67
bottle brush	115
bouncing bet	265
bowman's root	137
box, common	68
bramble	252
Brassica nigra	67
broom	102
Brugmansia arborea	68
Brugmansia aurea	68
Brugmansia sanguinea	68
Brugmansia suaveolens	68
Brugmansia versicolor	68
Bryonia cretica	68
bryony, white	68
buckbean	192
buckwheat	124
bugle	30
bugleweed	176
burdock greater	49
burdock, common	49
burdock, lesser	49
burnet saxifrage, greater	229
burnet saxifrage, lesser	229
burnet, great	263
burnet, salad	262
burning bush	107
butterbur	225
butterfly weed	58
Buxus sempervirens	68
cacao	289
calamint, common	70
calamint, greater	71
calamint, lesser	68
Calamintha ascendens	70
Calamintha nepeta	70
Calamintha nepeta ssp nepeta	70
Calamintha nepetoides	70
Calamintha officinalis	70
Calamintha sylvatica ssp. ascendens	71
calamus	23
Calendula arvensis	71
Calendula officinalis	72
calico bush	162
Californian poppy	118
Caltha palustris	73
Calystegia sepium	73
Camellia sinensis	74
camphor	86
Canadian fleabane	117
Canadian hemp	48
Cannabis sativa	74
cannabis, slang synonyms	74
Cape cheesewood	231
Cape jasmine	133
Capsella bursa-pastoris	75
capsicum	76
Capsicum annuum	76
caraway	78
Carbenia benedicta	89
cardoon	101
Cardus benedictus	89
Carica papaya	77
carrot, wild	105
Carthamus tinctorius	78
Carum carvi	78
Castanea sativa	79
castor oil	248
castor oil plant	248
cat's ear	45
Catha edulis	79
Catharanthus roseus	80
catmint	201
catnip	200
catnip, lemon-scented	201
catsfoot	45
cayenne jasmine	80
cayenne pepper	76
cedar, eastern white	290

Cedronella japonica	28
celandine, greater	83
celeriac	47
celery	47
celery, wild	47
Centaurium erythraea	80
centaury	80
Centranthus ruber	81
century plant	28
Chamaemelum nobile	81–82
Chamaemelum nobile 'Flore Pleno'	82
Chamaemelum nobile 'Treneague'	82
chamomile	81
chamomile lawn	82
chamomile, German	182
chamomile, ox-eye	45
chamomile, Roman	81
Chamomilla recutita	182
charity	234
checkerberry	133
Chelidonium majus	83
Chenopodium ambrosioides var. anthelminticum	84
Chenopodium bonus-henricus	84
chervil	46
chervil, Japanese wild	98
chestnut, Spanish	79
chestnut, sweet	79
chicory	85
children and poisonous plants	14
chilli	76
chilli pepper	76
Chinese bellflower	233
Chinese chives	38
Chinese hibiscus	149
Chinese lantern	227
Chinese moxa	55
Chinese rhubarb	246
Chinghai rhubarb	246
chives	35
chives, garlic	38
Christmas rose	146
Chrysanthemum leucanthemum	169
Chrysanthemum parthenium	284
Chrysanthemum segetum	85
Cichorium intybus	85
Cicuta virosa	93
Cimicifuga racemosa	86
Cinchona	27
Cinnamomum camphora	86
Cistus ladanifer	87
Cistus laurifolius	86
Citrus limon	87
clary, meadow	260
clematis	88
Clematis recta	88
Clematis vitalba	89
clove	281
clover white	294
clover, purple	294
clover, red	294
clover, yellow sweet	184
Cnicus benedictus	89
cochineal beetle	103
Cochlearia danica	89

Galium verum, *lady's bedstraw*

Sambucus nigra, *common elder*

Cochlearia officinalis	90
cocklebur	29
cocoa	289
coconut	90
Cocos nucifera	90
Coffea arabica	91
coffee	91
cohosh bugbane	86
Colchicum autumnale	92
colt's foot	225
columbine	48
comfrey, common	280
comfrey, Russian	280
common fleabane	241
common houseleek	271
compress	11
coneflower, purple	114
Conium maculatum	93
Consolida ajacis	93
Convallaria majalis	94
convolvulus	74
Conyza canadensis	117
coriander	94
coriander, Roman	204
Coriandrum sativum	94
corn cockle	29
Corydalis bulbosa	95
Corydalis cava	95
Corydalis halleri	96
Corydalis solida	96
Corydalis transsylvanica	96
cosmetic herbs	10
Cosmos sulphureus	96
costmary	283
cotton-lavender	264
cow parsley	46
Cow parsnip	147
cowbane	93
cowberry	298
cranesbill, American	135
cranesbill, spotted	135
Crataegus	97
Crataegus laevigata	97
Crataegus monostyla	97
creams	11
creeping cinquefoil	238
creeping jenny	177
cress	168
Crithmum maritimum	97
crosswort	97
Cruciata laevipes	97
Cryptotaenia canadensis	98
Cryptotaenia japonica	98
Cryptotaenia japonica	98
Cuchay	38
cuckoo pint	56
cudweed	55
culinary herbs	9
Culver's root	305
cumin, black	204
cup plant	272
Cupressus sempervirens	99
Curaçao aloe	40
Curcuma longa	100
Curcuma zedoaria	100
curcumine	100
Curcurbita pepa	98
curry plant	145
cyclamen	100
Cyclamen europaeum	100

Cyclamen hederifolium	100
Cyclamen neapolitum	100
Cyclamen purpurascens	100
Cydonia oblonga	100
Cynara cardunculus	101
Cynara scolymus	102
cypress, Italian	99
cypress, Mediterranean	99
Cytisus scoparius	102
cytostatica	80
Dactylopius coccus	103
daffodil	198
daisy, common	64
daisy, ox-eye	169
damask rose	249
dame's violet	149
dandelion	285
dandelion salad	285
Daphne mezereum	103
Daphne mezereum 'Rubra'	103
Datura metel	104
Datura stramonium	104
Datura stramonium var. tatula	105
Daucus carota	105
Daucus carota ssp. sativa	105
dead nettle	163
dead nettle, white	163
deadly nightshade	60
decoction	10
Delphinium consolida	93
devil's apple	104
devil's-bit-scabious	279
devil-in-a-bush	221
Dianthus deltoides	106
Dicentra eximia	106
Dicentra formosa	106
Dictamnus albus	107
Dictamnus dasycarpus	107
Dictamnus fraxinella	107
Digitalis ambigua	108
Digitalis grandiflora	108
Digitalis lanata	108
Digitalis lutea	108
Digitalis orientalis	108
Digitalis purpurea	109
dill	43
Diospyros kaki	110
Diospyros kaki 'Sharon'	110
Dipsacus fullonum	111
Dipsacus sativus	111
dittany	107
dock, broad-leaved	253
Dodonaea viscosa	112
Dodonaea viscosa 'Purpurea'	112
dog rose	249
dogbane	48

dog-strangling vine	307
doku-dami	152
Doronicum cordatum	112
Doronicum pardalianches	112
Drimys winteri	112
Drimys winteri var. andina	112
Drosera rotundifolia	112
dry compress	11
drying herbs	16
Dryopteris filix-mas	113
dumpling cactus	175
dungwort	146
dwale	60
dyer's greenwood	134
dyestuffs	8
E number	100
earthsmoke	128
Ecballium elaterium	114
Echinacea purpurea	114
Echinacea purpurea 'White Swan'	115
echinacea, purple	114
Echium vulgare	115
economic plants	7
eggplant	275
eglantine	250
Egyptian tree onion	35
elder, common	262
elder, dwarf	261
elder, ground	25
elecampane	156
English serpentary	225
Equisetum arvense	115
Equisetum hyemale	116
Equisetum palustre	116
Equisetum telmateia	116
Erica tetralix	116
Erigeron canadensis	117
Eriobotrya japonica	117
Eruca vesicaria	117
Eruca vesicaria ssp. sativa	118
Erythraea centaurium	80
Eschscholzia californica	118
Eucalyptus	119
Eugenia caryphyllata	281
Euonymus europaeus	119
Eupatorium cannabinum	119
Eupatorium maculatum 'Atropurpurea'	120
Eupatorium purpureum	120
euphorbia	121
Euphorbia amygdaloides	121
Euphorbia cyparissias	121
Euphorbia lathyris	122
Euphorbia palustris	122
Euphorbia stricta	123
European juniper	162
European wild angelica	44

Allium schoenoprasum, *chiver*

Butterflies on Mentha longifolia *'Buddleja'*

evening primrose, common	206
everlasting flower	145
eyebright	123
Fagopyrum esculentum	124
false hellebore	299
false indigo	62
false saffron	78
false sea onion	215
farmer's tobacco	181
felon herb	55
fennel	126
fennel	285
fennel, Florence	126
fenugreek	295
fern, male	113
fever, normal	27
feverfew	284
feverwort	80
Ficus carica	124
fig	124
figwort, common	268
Filipendula rubra	124
Filipendula ulmaria	125
flag, blue	160
flag, yellow	159
flax	173
flaxseed	173
flowering fern	215-216
fluellen	305
foam flower	292
Foeniculum vulgare	126
Foeniculum vulgare 'Giant Bronze'	126
Foeniculum vulgare var. azoricum	126
Foeniculum vulgare var. vulgare	126
food additives	100
forget-me-not, field	194
foxglove	108
foxglove, common	109
foxglove, yellow	108
foxglove, woolly	108
Fragaria vesca	127
Frangula alnus	246
Fraxinus vesiculosus	128
French bean	227
French lilac	129
fuller's teasel	111
Fumaria officinalis	128
fumewort	96
fumitory	95
fumitory	128
Galega officinalis	129
Galeobdolon luteum	163
Galeopsis segetum	129
Galeopsis speciosa	130

Galeopsis tetrahit	130
Galeopsis x tetrahit	130
Galium aparine	131
Galium boreale	131
Galium mollugo	132
Galium odoratum	132
Galium verum	133
garden myrrh	196
garden nasturtium	295
Gardenia	133
Gardenia augusta	133
Gardenia florida	133
Gardenia jasminoides	133
garlic	36
garlic cloves	37
garlic mustard	34
garlic oil	37
garlic press	37
garlic, wild	39
Gaultheria procumbens	133
Genista tinctoria	134
gentian, great yellow	134
Gentiana lutea	134
Geranium maculatum	135
geranium oil	223
Geranium robertianum	135
Geranium robertianum 'Album'	136
Geranium robertianum 'Celtic White'	136
geranium, wild	135
germander	287
germander, wall	286
Geum rivale	136
Geum urbanum	137
giant hogweed	147
Gillenia trifoliata	137
ginger	309
ginger, wild	57
gingko	138
Ginkgo biloba	138
Glaucium flavum	138

Borage officinalis, *borage*

Glechoma hederacea	139
Gloriosa superba	139
glory lily	139
Glycyrrhiza glabra	140
glycyrrhizine	140
goat's beard	294
goat's rue	129
goldenrod	277
goldenrod, Canadian	276
good King Henry	84
goosegrass	131
goutweed	25
granny's bonnet	48
grape vine	309
Gratiola officinalis	140
gravel root	120
greater pimpernel	229
Grindelia camporum	141
Grindelia robusta	141
Grindelia squarrosa	141
groats	61
gromwell	173
ground ivy	139
guelder rose	306
gum tree	119
gumplant	141
gumweed	141
gypsywort	176
Hamamelis virginiana	143
hart's tongue fern	59
hasheesh	74
hashish	74
hawthorn	97
heal-all	239
heart wort	51
heartsease	307
heath, cross-leaved	116
Hedera helix	143
hedge bindweed	73
hedge garlic	34
Helianthus anuus	144
Helichrysum angustifolium	145
Helichrysum arenarium	145
Helichrysum italicum	145
heliotrope, garden	299
hellebore, stinking	146
hellebore, white	299
Helleborus niger	146
hemlock	93
hemp	74
hemp agrimony	119
hemp rope	74
hempnettle	129
hempnettle, common	130
hempnettle, large-flowered	130
henbane	153
Heracleum mantegazzianum	147
Heracleum sphondylium	147
herb bennet	137
herb christopher	25
herb gardens	311
herb of grace	254
herb pillows	9
herb robert	135
herb vinegar	11
herbal Tea	11
herb-paris	221
herbygrass	254
Herniaria glabra	148
Hesperis matronalis	149
Hibiscus pilosella	150
Hieracium pilosella	150
Himalayan may apple	234
Hippophae rhamnoides	150
hoarhound	182
hogbean	153
hogweed	147
Hoheria populnea	151
holly	156
hollyhock	31
holy thistle	89

homeopathy	11	Iris versicolor	160	Lilium martagon var. album	172
honewort	98	iris, wild	160	lily-of-the-valley	94
honewort	98	Isatis tinctoria	160	lime, broad-leaved	292
honeysuckle, common	175	ivy	143	lime, common	292
hop	152	ivy bush	162	lime, small-leaved	292
horehound	182			Linaria vulgaris	173
horehound, black	62	jack-by-the-hedge	34	linseed	173
horehound, white	182	jack-in-the-pulpit	50	Linum usitatissimum	173
horse chestnut	26	Japanese belladonna	267	lion's foot	33
horsemint	187	jasmine tea	161	liquorice	140
horseradish	51	jasminum sambac	161	Lithospermum erthrorhizon	173
horsetail, field	115	Jerusalem cowslip	241	Lithospermum officinale	173
horseweed	117	jimson's weed	104	Lithospermum ruderale	174
Houttuynia cordata	152	joe pye weed	120	Lobelia inflata	174
Houttuynia cordata 'Chameleon'	152	Juglans regia	161	Lobelia siphilitica	174
Houttuynia cordata 'Plena'	152	juglon	161	lobelia, great	174
Humulus lupus	152	juniperus sabina 'Hicksii'	162	Lonicera periclymenum	175
Humulus lupus 'Aureus'	152	juniper, common	161	loosestrife, common	177
Hydrangea arborescens	153	Juniperus communis	161	loosestrife, purple	178
Hydrangea arborescens 'Annabelle'	153	Juniperus sabina	162	Lopanthus rugosus	28
hydrangea, wild	153	Juniperus sabina	162	Lophophora echinata	175
Hyocyamus niger	153	Juniperus sabina 'Hicksii'	162	Lophophora lutea	175
Hypericum perforatum	154			Lophophora williamsii	175
hyssop	155	kaki	110	loquat	117
hyssop, anise	27	Kalmia latifolia	162	lords and ladies	55
hyssop, blue giant	27	keck	147	Lotus corniculatus	176
hyssop, fennel giant	27	khat	79	lovage	170
hyssop, hedge	140	kidney vetch	47	love-in-idleness	307
hyssop, wrinkled giant	28	kif	74	love-in-the-mist	203
Hyssopus officinalis	155	Knautia arvensis	162	love-lies-bleeding	41
		knitbone	280	lucerne	183
Ilex aquifolium	156	knot grass	236	lungwort	241
Indian cress	295	kümmel	78	Lycopus europaeus	176
Indian physic	137			Lysimachia nummularia	177
Indian tobacco	174	lace bark	151	Lysimachia vulgaris	177
Indian turnip	50	ladanum	87	Lythrum salicaria	178
indigo	63	lady's hen	95		
indigo, wild	62	lady's mantle	32,33	mace	196
Indigofera gerardiana	157	lady's mantle, alpine	31	Macleaya cordata	179
Indigofera gerardiana	157	Lamiastrum galeobdolon	163	Madagascar periwinkle	80
Indigofera heterantha 'Gerardiana'	157	Lamiastrum galeobdolon	163	madder	252
indigoweed	63	Lamium album	163	madonna lily	171
infusion	10	Lamium maculatum	163	Mahonia aquifolium	179
infusion	11	Lantana camara	164	maiden pink	106
Inula helenium	156	lapathum	253	maidenhair tree	138
Ipomoea rubrocaerulea	157	lappa	49	Malabar lily	139
Ipomoea tricolor 'Heavenly Blue'	157	larkspur, field	93	malaria	27
Iris florentina	158	Laurus angustifolia	165	mallow, blue	180
Iris germanica	158	Laurus camphora	86	mallow, common	180
Iris germanica 'Florentina'	158	Laurus nobilis	164	mallow, dwarf	180
Iris pseudoacorus	159	Lavandula angustifolia 'Munstead'	166	mallow, high	180
Iris pseudoacorus 'Variegata'	159	lavender	166	mallow, musk	180
		lavender, common	165	Malus domestica	181
		lavender, English	166	Malva moschata	180
		lavender, French	167	Malva neglecta	180
		lavender, spike	166	Malva sylvestris	180
		lavender-cotton	264	Malva sylvestris 'Primley Blue'	181
		Lavendula angustifolia 'Hidcote'	166	Malva verticillata 'Crispa'	181
		Lavendula dentata	166	marajuana	74
		Lavendula latifolia	166	marguerite	169
		Lavendula officinalis	165	marguerite, golden	45
		Lavendula spica	165	Maria thistle	273
		Lavendula stoechas	167	marigold	72
		Lavendula stoechas var. leucantha	168	marigold, corn	85
		Lavendula vera	165	marigold, field	71
		Lavendula x intermedia	166	marigold, French	283
		leek	36	marihuana	74
		lemon	87	marjoram	210–211
		lemon balm	185	marjoram golden wild	212-213
		lemon verbena	40	marjoram, knotted	210
		lentise	231	marjoram, sweet	210
		Leonurus cardiaca	168	marjoram, white wild	211-213
		leopard's bane	51, 112	marjoram, wild	211-214
		Lepidium sativum	168	Marrubium vulgare	182
		Leptandra virginica	305	marsh mallow	40
		Leucanthemum vulgare	169	marsh trefoil	192
		Levisticum officinale	170	Martha Washington	124
		life everlasting	45	mastic tree	231
		Ligustrum licidum	170	Matricaria chamomilla	182
		Ligustrum vulgare	171	Matricaria parthenium	284
		Lilium candidum	171	Matricaria recutita	182
		Lilium martagon	172	may	97

Arum italicum, *arum*

may apple	234	mullein, orange	301	oil of camphor	86
meadow saffron	92	mustard, black	67	Olea europaea	207
meadow-rue, French	288	mustard, hedge	274	oleander	201
meadow-rue, yellow	288	Myosotis arvensis	194	olive	207
meadowsweet	125	Myrica gale	195	onion	34
Medicago sativa ssp. sativa	183	Myricaria germanica	195	onion, Egyptian tree	35
Medicinal herbs	7	Myristica fragrans	196	onion, spring	35
medlar, Japanese	117	Myrrhis odorata	195	Ononis spinosa	208
melilot, ribbed	184	myrtle	197	Onopordum acanthium	209
melilot, yellow	184	myrtle flag	23	Onopordum nervosum	209
Melilotus arvensis	184	Myrtus communis	197	opium	219
Melilotus officinalis	184			Opuntia	103
melissa	185	naked ladies	92	orache, red	60
Melissa officinalis	185	Narcissus 'Alois Alzheimer'	198	oregano	211
Melissa officinalis 'Aurea'	185	Narcissus 'Thalia'	198	Oregon grape	179
Melittis melissophyllum	185	Narcissus poeticus	198	Origanum 'Rosenkuppel'	211
Mentha aquatica	186	narcissus, poet's	198	Origanum creticum	213
Mentha arvensis	186	Narthecium ossifragum	198	Origanum laevigatum 'Herrenhausen'	210
Mentha cardiaca	186	Nasturtium microphyllum	199	Origanum majorana	210
Mentha crispa	190	Nasturtium microphyllum	199	Origanum vulgare	211
Mentha hirsata	186	Nasturtium officinale	198	Origanum vulgare 'Album'	212
Mentha incana	187	native hops	112	Origanum vulgare 'Aureum'	212
Mentha insularis	191	Nelumbium speciosum	199	Origanum vulgare 'Charlie Gold'	213
Mentha longifolia	187	Nelumbo nucifera	199	Origanum vulgare 'Compactum'	213
Mentha longifolia 'Buddleja'	187	Nepeta cataria	200	Origanum vulgare 'Hortense'	213
Mentha macrostachya	191	Nepeta cataria 'Citriodora'	201	Origanum vulgare 'Thumble's Variety'	214
Mentha nigricans	188	Nepeta glechoma	139	Origanum vulgare creticum	213
Mentha pulegium	189	Nepeta hederacea	139	Origanum vulgare var. samotrake	215
Mentha spicata	190	Nerium oleander	201	Ornithogalum caudatum	215
Mentha spicata 'Crispa'	190	Nerium oleander 'Angiola Pucci'	201	Ornithogalum caudatum	215
Mentha spicata 'Moroccan'	190	Nerium oleander 'Papa Gambetta'	201	Ornithogalum longibracteatum	215
Mentha spicata 'Moroccan'	190	nettle, common	297	orpine	270
Mentha spicata 'Nana'	190	nettle, small	297	orpine, stone	270
Mentha suaveolens	191	nettle, stinging	297	orris	158
Mentha suaveolens 'Variegata'	191	Nicotiana rustica	201	orris root	158
Mentha sylvestris	187	Nicotiana tabacum	202	Oryza sativa	215
Mentha viridis	190	nicotine	201–202	Oryza sativa ssp. indica	215
Mentha x gentilis	186	Nigella damascena	203	Oryza sativa ssp. japonica	215
Mentha x gentilis	186	Nigella sativa	204	Osmunda regalis	215
Mentha x gentilis 'Variegata'	186	nutmeg	196	Oswego tea	193
Mentha x niliaca	187	nutmeg flower	204	oxlip	238
Mentha x piperata	188	Nymphaea alba	204		
Mentha x piperata 'Crispa'	188			padma	199
Mentha x villosa	192	oak	243	Paeonia albiflora	217
Menyanthes trifoliata	192	oak, English	243	Paeonia japonica	217
mescaline	175	oak, pedunculate	243	Paeonia lactiflora	217
Mexican tea	84	oat	61	Paeonia moutan	217
mezereum	103	Ocimum basilicum	205	Paeonia officinalis	217
milkweed	57	Ocimum basilicum 'Anise'	206	Paeonia suffruticosa	217
mint, Bowles'	192	Ocimum basilicum 'Citriodorum'	206	pansy, wild	307
mint, buddleja	187	Ocimum basilicum 'HORAPHA'	206	Papaver rhoeas	218
mint, Egyptian	187	Ocimum basilicum 'Licorice'	206	Papaver somniferum	219
mint, ginger	186	Ocimum citriodorum	206	papaya	77
mint, Korean	28	Ocimum citriodorum	206	paprika	76
mint, Moroccan	190	Oenothera biennis	206	Parietaria diffusa	220
mint, pineapple	191				
mint, water	186				
mint, woolly	191				
mistletoe	308				
Monarda didyama	193				
Monarda didyama 'Croftway Pink'	193				
monk's rhubarb	253				
monkshood	23				
morning glory	157				
morphine	219				
Morus alba	194				
Morus alba 'Pendula'	194				
Morus nigra	194				
moth balls	86				
motherwort	168				
mountain ash	277				
mountain daisy	52				
mountain tobacco	51				
mouse-ear hawkweed	150				
moutan peony	217				
Mozambique lily	139				
mugwort	55				
mulberry, black	194				
mulberry, white	194				
mullein, dark	301				
mullein, great	303				
mullein, Hungarian	303				

Herb garden

Parietaria judaica	220	
Parietaria judaica	221	
Parietaria officinalis	220	
Paris quadrifolia	221	
parsley	226	
parsley, curly-leaved	226	
parsley, flat-leaved	226	
parsnip, wild	221	
pasque flower	242	
Passiflora 'Incense'	222	
Passiflora foetida	222	
Passiflora foetida var. galapagensis	222	
Passiflora incarnata	222	
passionflower	222	
passionflower, fetid	222	
Pastinaca sativa	221	
pawpaw	77	
Pelargonium 'Rober's Lemon Rose'	224	
Pelargonium capitatum	222	
Pelargonium graveolens	223	
Pelargonium odoratissimum	224	
Pelargonium tomentosum	224	
Pelargonium tomentosum 'Chocolate'	224	

Dipsacus fullonum, *fuller's teasel*

pelargonium, apple	224	
pelargonium, peppermint	224	
pelargonium, wild	222	
pelargonium. rose	223	
pellitory-of-the-wall	220	
pennyroyal	189	
peony	217	
peony, Chinese	217	
peony, common	217	
peony, tree	217	
peppermint	188	
peppers	76	
perfume	9	
Perilla frutescens	224	
Perilla frutescens 'Atropurpurea'	224	
Perilla frutescens var. nankinensis	224	
periwinkle, greater	306	
periwinkle, lesser	306	
Persicaria bistorta	225	
persimmon, Chinese	110	
persimmon, Japanese	110	
Petasites hybridus	225	
Petroselinum crispum	226	
Petroselinum crispum var. tuberosum	226	
Peucadeneum officinale	221	
Peucadeneum sativum	221	
Peucedanum graveolens	43	

peyote	175	
Phyllitis scolopendrium	59	
Physalis alkekengi	227	
Physalis franchetti	227	
Physalis vulgaris	227	
Phytolacca americana	228	
Phytolacca decandra	228	
Phytolacca decandra	228	
Picea abies	229	
pick-pocket	75	
Pilosella officinarum	150	
pimento	76	
Pimpinella anisum	229	
Pimpinella major	229	
Pimpinella saxifraga	229	
pine, mountain	230	
pine, Scot's	230	
pineapple	42	
Pinus mugo	230	
Pinus mugo 'Zundert'	230	
Pinus sylvestris	230	
Pistacia lenticus	231	
Pittosporum viridiflorum	231	
Plantago affra	231	
Plantago lanceolata	231	
Plantago major ssp. major	232	
Plantago media	233	
plantain, glandular	231	
plantain, greater	232	
plantain, hoary	233	
plantain, rat-tail	232	
plantain, ribwort	231	
Platycodon grandiflorum	233	
pleurisy root	58	
plume poppy	179	
Podophyllum hexandrum	234	
Podophyllum peltatum	234	
poison ivy	248	
poison parsley	93	
Polemonium caeruleum	234	
Polemonium caeruleum 'Album'	234	
Polygonatum multiflorum	235	
Polygonum aviculare	236	
Polygonum bistorta	225	
Polygonum hydropiper	236	
Polygonum persicaria	236	
Polypodium vulgare	237	
polypody	237	
pomegranate	243	
poor man's weatherglass	42	
poppy, corn	218	
poppy, field	218	
poppy, opium	219	
poppy, yellow horned	138	
Porteranthus trifoliata	137	
potato	276	
Potentilla anserina	237	
Potentilla erecta	237	
Potentilla reptans	238	
Poterium officinalis	263	
pot-pourri	9	
prickly pear cactus	103	
primrose	239	
Primula elatior	238	
Primula vulgaris	239	
privet, Chinese	170	
privet, common	171	
privet, glossy	170	
Prunella vulgaris	239	
Prunus dulcis	240	
Prunus spinosa	241	
pukeweed	174	
Pulicaria dysenterica	241	
Pulmonaria officinalis	241	
pulque	29	
Pulsillata vulgaris	242	
Pulsillata vulgaris 'Alba'	242	
pumpkin	98	
Punica granatum	243	
quartan fever	27	
Queen Anne's lace	46	

queen of the meadow	120	
Quercus robur	243	
quick	97	
quickset	97	
quickthorn	97	
quince	100	
quinine	27	
radish 245		
radish, black	245	
ragwort	272	
ramsons	39	
Raphanus sativus	245	
Raphanus sativus ssp. niger	245	
rattleweed	63	
red mountain spinach	60	
red rose of Lancaster	250	
red-ink plant	228	
Reseda lutea	245	
Reseda luteola	245	
Rhamnus frangula	246	
Rheum palmatum	246	
Rhododendron ferrugineum	247	
rhubarb, wild	147	
Rhus radicans	248	
rice	215	
Ricunus communis	248	
rock rose	86	
rock samphire	97	
rocket	117	
Rorippa nasturtium-aquaticum	198-199	
Rosa canina	249	
Rosa damascena	249	
Rosa eglanteria	250-251	
Rosa gallica	250	
Rosa gallica var. officinalis	250	
Rosa rubiginosa	250	
rose, apothecary's	250	
rosemary	251	
Rosmarinus officinalis	251	
rosy periwinkle	80	
Round-leaved sundew	112	
rowan	277	
royal fern	215	
Rubus fruticosus	252	
Rubus tinctorium	252	
rue	254	
Rumex acetosa	254	
Rumex acetosa ssp. ambiguus	254	
Rumex alpinus	253	
Rumex obtusifolius	253	
Rumex pseudoalpinus	253	
Rumex rugosus	254	
rupturewort	148	
Ruta graveolens	254	
sacred lotus	199	
safflower	78	
saffron thistle	78	
sage "muscatel oil"	260	
sage, clary	260	
sage, common	258	
sage, muscatel	260	
sage, white	55	
sage, wood	287	
Salix alba	257	
salsify	293	
salve	11	
Salvia officinalis	258	
Salvia pratensis	260	
Salvia sclarea	260	
Sambucus ebulus	261	
Sambucus nigra	262	
Sanguisorba officinalis	263	
sanicle	264	
Sanicula europaea	264	
Santolina chamaecyparissus	264	
Saponaria officinalis	265	
Sarothamnus scoparius	102	
Satureja hortensis	265	
Satureja montana	266	
Satureja nepeta	70	

Chives surround a stone container

savin	162
saw wort	272
Scabiosa arvensis	162
Scabiosa arvensis	162
scabious, field	162
scabwort	156
scallions	35
scarlet pimpernel	42
scented mayweed	182
schisandra	66
Schisandra chinensis	266
Scolopendrium vulgare	59
scopalia	267
Scopalia anomala	267
Scopalia atropoides	267
Scopalia carniolica	267
scorzonera	268
Scorzonera hispanica	268
scotch broom	102
Scrophularia nodosa	268
scurvy grass, common	90
scurvy grass, small	89
Scutellaria baicalensis	269
Scutellaria galericulata	268
Scutellaria lateriflora	269
sea buckthorn	150
sea fennel	97
Sedum acre	269
Sedum reflexum	270
Sedum rupestre	270
Sedum telephium	270
Sedum telephium ssp. maximum	271
seed aril	196
selfheal	239
Sempervivum tectorum	271
Senecio jacobaea	272
Serrulata tinctoria	272
seven barks	153
Sharon fruit	110
shepherd's purse	75
signatures, doctrine of	225
signet marigold	283
silkweed	57-58
Silphium perfoliatum	272
silverweed	237
Silybum marianum	273
sisho	224
Sisymbrium officinale	274
Sium sisarum	274
skirret	274
skullcap	268
sloe	241
smallage	47
snakeweed	225
sneezewort	21

soapwort	265
soil-less flowering	92
Solanum dulcamara	275
Solanum melongena	275
Solanum tuberosum	276
soldier's woundwort	20
soldiers and sailors	241
Solidago canadensis	276
Solidago virgaurea	277
Solomon's-seal	235
Sorbus aucuparia	277
sorrel, common	254
sorrel, garden	254
southernwood	53
sowbread	100
spearmint	190
spearmint, curly	190
speedwell, common	305
speedwell, heath	305
spinach	60
spindle tree	119
Spirea ulmaria	125
spotted lady's thumb	236
spring onion	35
spring restharrow	208
spruce, common	229
spruce, Norway	229
spurge	121
spurge , wood	121
spurge, caper	122
spurge, cypress	121
squirting cucumber	114
St Barbara's herb	63
St John's wort	154
St John's wort, perforate	154
St. Gerald's herb	26
Stachys betonica	278
Stachys officinalis	278
Stachys palustris	278
Stachys sylvatica	278
stickhop bush	112
sticklewort	29
sticky willie	131
stinking hogweed	146
stonecrop, biting	269
stonecrop, common	269
stonecrop, reflexed	270
strawberry, wild	127
Succisa pratensis	279
succory	85
sugar root	274
summer savory	265
sun rose	86,97
sunflower	144
swallow wort	83

sweet almond	240
sweet Annie	54
sweet basil	205
sweet bay	164
sweet briar	250
sweet chervil	196
sweet cicely	196
sweet gale	195
sweet pepper	76
sweet rocket	149
sweet wormwood	54
Symphytum asperum	280
Symphytum officinale	280
Symphytum peregrinum	280
Symphytum x uplandicum	280
synthetic anethole	229
syrup	11
Syzygium aromaticum	281
Tagetes erecta	283
Tagetes minuta	283
Tagetes patula	283
Tagetes tenuifolia	283
tamarisk, German	195
Tanecetum balsamita	283
Tanecetum parthenium	284
Tanecetum vulgare	284
tansy	284
tansy ragwort	272
Taraxacum officinale	285
tarragon	55
tarragon vinegar	55
tarragon, French	55
tarragon, Russian	55
tarweed	141
tassel flower	41
Taxus baccata	285
Taxus brevifolia	286
tea	74
tea, black	74
tea, green	74
teaberry	133
tetterwort	83
Teucrium chamaedrys	286
Teucrium scorodonia	287
Teucrium x lucidrys	287
Thalictrum aquilegifolium	288
Thalictrum flavum ssp. flavum	288
Thalictrum flavum ssp. glaucum	288
Thalictrum speciosissimum	288
Theobroma cacao	289
thistle, cotton	209
thistle, Scottish	209
Thlaspi bursa-pastoris	75
thorn apple	104
Thuja occidentalis	290
thyme, common	292

thyme, creeping 290, 291
thyme, garden 292
thyme, Large 291
thyme, lemon-scented 290
thyme, mother of 291
thyme, wild 290, 291
Thymus praecox 290
Thymus praecox ssp. arcticus 290
Thymus praecox ssp. praecox 290
Thymus pulegioides 291
Thymus serpyllum 291
Thymus vulgaris 292
Thymus x citriodorus 290
Thymus x citriodorus 'Aureus' 290
Thymus x citriodorus 'Silver Queen' 290
Tiarella cordifolia 'Oakleaf' 292
Tilia cordata 292
Tilia platyphyllos 292
Tilia x europaea 292
tincture 11
toadflax, common 172
tobacco 202
tobacco, wild 201
tormentil 237
tormentil, creeping 238
Tragopogon porrifolius 293
Tragopogon pratensis 294
traveller's ease 237
traveller's joy 89
traveller's joy 237
Trifolium pratense 294
Trifolium repens 294
Trigonella foenicum-graecum 295
Tropaeolum majus 295
turkscap lily, common 172
Tussilago farfara 225
Urtica dioica 297
Urtica urens 297
Vaccinium myrtillus 298
Vaccinium vitis-idaea 298
valerian, common 299

valerian, Greek 234
valerian, red 81
Valeriana officinalis 299
vanilla 299
Vanilla planifolia 299
Veratrum album 299
Veratrum nigrum 301
Veratrum viride 300
Verbascum densiflorum 303
Verbascum nigrum 301
Verbascum phlomoides 301
Verbascum speciosum 303
Verbascum thapsus 303
Verbena hastata 304
Verbena officinalis 304
vermouth 53
Veronica officinalis 305
Veronica virginica 305
Veronicastrum virginicum 305
vervain 304
vervain, blue 304
Viburnum opulus 306
Vinca major 306
Vinca minor 306
Vinca rosea 80
Vincetoxicum hirundinaria 307
Vincetoxicum nigrum 307
Viola tricolor 307
Viola tricolor 'Hortensis' 307
viper's bugloss 115
Virginian pokeweed 228
Viscum album 308
Vitis vinifera 309
wall pepper 269
walnut 161
water hemlock 93
water lily, white 204
watercress 198
water-pepper 236
wax dolls 128
weed (Cannabis) 74

weld 246
Welsh onion 35
western mugwort 55
wet compress 11
wild bleeding heart 106
wild lemon 234
wild mignonette 245
willow, white 257
winter savory 266
winter squash 98
winter's bark 112
wintergreen 133
witches' pouches 75
witchhazel 143
witchhazel, Virginian 143
woad 160
wolf's bane 22,23
woodruff, dyer's 59
woodruff, sweet 132
woody nightshade 278
wormseed 84
wormwood 53
woundwort, hedge 278
woundwort, marsh 278
yarrow 20
yew, common 285
zedoary 100
Zingiber officinale 309
zinnia 310
Zinnia angustifolia 310
Zinnia elegans 310
Zinnia haageana 310
Zinnia mexicana 310
zinnia, Mexican 310

Acknowledgements

Author and publisher thank the following persons and organisations for their co-operation,
which made this publication possible.

Ad van't Hoff, Bioharma, Elburg, NL
Els & Jan de Boer, Warffum, NL
Fausto Naddeo, Oudenhoorn, NL
Frank Linschoten & Pieter Baak, Eext, NL
Henk Jongsma, The Kruidhof, Buitenpost, NL
Jan de Koning & Carla Teune, Hortus Botanicus, University of Leiden, NL
Klaas van Nierop, Domies Toen, Pieterburen, NL
Mrs van Hoorn & Mrs de Boer, Borg Verhildersum, Leens, NL
The Dutch Open Air Museum, Arnhem, NL
Rob & Ansje Leopold
Roger & Linda Bastin, Brunssum, NL
Ronald Medema & Marjo Többen, Zevenhuizen, NL
Tom Tressel, Eenrum, NL